Say 'I do' to feminism

Thanks

The Adventures and Discoveries of a Feminist Bride

What No One Tells You Before You Say "I Do"

Katrina Majkut

Katrina Majkut

BLACK ROSE writing

The final approval for this literary material is granted by the author.

First printing

The author has tried to recreate events, locales and conversations from his/her memories. In order to maintain anonymity in some instances, the author may have changed the names of individuals and places. The author may have changed some identifying characteristics and details such as physical properties, occupations and places of residence.

ISBN: 978-1-68433-011-9
PUBLISHED BY BLACK ROSE WRITING
www.blackrosewriting.com

Printed in the United States of America
Suggested Retail Price (SRP) $18.95

The Adventures and Discoveries of a Feminist Bride is printed in Minion Pro
Cover Photo courtesy of Raymond Adams Photography

To Wendy and Tom for all your love, feminism, and support.

The Adventures and Discoveries of a Feminist Bride

What No One Tells You Before You Say "I Do"

Contents

Introduction

Weddings should be easy, considering that everything anyone needs to know about them is spelled out, well, everywhere. Miss Manners-type books say it's proper to fork over a small paycheck to attend someone else's party and we should accept such financial pillaging with selfless grace and a sincere smile. Wedding reality TV shows gleefully inform that it's acceptable to say snarky things behind a bride's back or to throw a tantrum if the florist sends over carnations instead of roses. Rom-com movies with women leads strongly imply that finding a man is more important than working on ourselves. And Jezebel-type articles declare it's a single wedding guest's job, nay duty, to seek out the single groomsman (or bridesmaid) and sleep with him or her. If it's not on the internet, generations of family and friends provide unsolicited instruction on how to distribute coveted plus-one invites while excluding pertinent family members from the wedding. And there's always that person who slips in some type of uncomfortable bit of advice about wedding night sex or making babies. Wedding planning has so many guardrails and guidelines, it's almost impossible for anyone to mess up.

But mess up, I did. Horribly. Painfully. Mysteriously. Hilariously.

After multiple injuries, one wedding party expulsion, peeing on myself, breaking into my own apartment naked, too many bridal showers, not enough bachelorette parties, getting too drunk after a ceremony while marooned on atop a Michigan ski mountain, and losing friendships (but adding one spouse later), I needed to figure out what the hell I was doing wrong.

Weddings should not be this hard—especially ones with open bars.

As a smart, well educated, a little too sharp at times, lover of period films starring a strong female lead (Netflix's assessment, not mine), reluctant jogger, and superpower feminist, I wanted to understand my incessant wedding failures. Like any good nerd, I hit the books and pulled up the sordid origins of Western marital customs and traditions. Unfortunately, I discovered not all traditions are good ones. This is a scary truth. Most important, I learned that all these wedding traditions don't align with people's modern lifestyles. This is often the cause for my wedding woes and others' too. As it turned out, I was not the only one feeling drowned in a sea of tulle or suffocating via Spanx, trying to fight off narcissistic Bridezillas or obsolete gender roles. Others were also wondering why the hell women don't propose, why they need their parents' permission to marry, and what is with all the penis tiaras?

No wedding experts, sources, or unsolicited opinions explained why we should fulfill any of these traditions. Then I put the greatest gift anyone can put on a wedding registry: feminism. It is the tool that helped bail me out of my wedding purgatory. Feminism opened my eyes to traditions that didn't wholly support me as a person or as my partner's equal. Even more, it started to become apparent that these exclusively and structurally heterosexual traditions hurt women's equality, same-sex marriage, and even (gasp!) men's equality. In my ballsy bridal investigations, intersectional feminism[1] reminded me that while Western wedding culture can appear ubiquitously hetero and white, not all fiancés are.

This book focuses primarily on where the most deep-seated sexism prevails in mainstream Western weddings and marriage. It just happens to be that such intrinsic problems originate with the traditions of the stereotypically hetero, privileged pale ones. So, please, don't be alarmed or annoyed that this might superficially appear as yet another white wedding book paired with white feminism. I did my best to be intersectional, but there's certainly more that could be unveiled and modernized. So I encourage other feminist brides to share their own wedding discoveries and adventures. Only then through sharing, highlighting, creating calls to action will wedding and marriage traditions come closer to true equality. I hope this book offers a starting point and a space for constructive conversation.

---

[1] *Kimberlé Crenshaw coined intersectional feminism in 1989. It's a response to "white feminism" or the type of feminism that has historically been taken up by middle class, cis, hetero, Caucasian feminists and has not always included the needs of other women as they relate to race, class, education, sexuality, etc. Intersectional feminism focuses on diverse inclusiveness and the experiences and needs of unique individuals.*

My goal is to make wedding traditions more egalitarian, accessible, and respectful toward everyone. Feminism is, after all, the pursuit of social, political, economic, professional, and academic equality for both women and men of any age, sexual orientation, gender identity, race, religion, and class. With feminism, I could now see that for men to not wear an engagement ring is a double standard, how the wage gap determines who pays for the wedding, and how the wedding cake is a superstitious dessert aiming to knock women up. Feminism emboldened me to call B.S. (i.e., bullshit *and* benevolent sexism) on a lot of traditions. It helped me stand up to them, but most important, it showed me how I could improve and modernize them and still enjoy a wedding celebration.

It's my hope that my historical and social discoveries blow open the sexism in wedding culture and that readers gather the intellectual ammo to overcome and correct them. It is my wish that my wedding follies and misfortunes give those out there a cathartic source of entertainment and a little ego boost at the same time. And it is my desire that my defiant nature, preventing me to just go with the traditional and familial flow, will empower readers to strike their own paths in the spirit of intersectionality (even if they disagree with my ideas). Because then those readers will understand that love isn't just doing what's right for themselves, but acting selflessly for the benefit of everyone else's equality too. Becoming a feminist bride was the best thing I ever did; it helped me discover my happily ever after because, as it turns out, the perfect wedding includes perfect equality.

Chapter 1
The Engagement Ring:
The One Ring to Rule Her

The wedding. It all starts with the smallest of trinkets: the diamond engagement ring. And yet this tiny metallic thingamabob wields a powerhouse of symbolism and capitalism unseen since Monopoly's Top Hat. Well before I even had someone to spend my life with, I, like many women, ferociously lusted after the diamond engagement ring. My unfulfilled desire made Gollum from *The Lord of the Rings* seem like a regular chap with a reasonable, if oddly singular, hoarding fetish. "We wants it, we needs it. Must have the 'Precious.'" Luckily, feminism pulled an intervention, and the mesmerizing allure of the diamond engagement ring was broken, but not before I found myself wearing one. For me it was too late. However, I realized I could help break the spell on other women by revealing why the diamond engagement ring is the One Ring to rule her, and in its sexist darkness, bind her.

It's best to start with when and how this unspoken desire came about. I can personally trace it back to my mullet-sporting glory days of the 1980s. All the Disney princesses were getting a ring, and dammit, I wanted to be just like them: underage, married, and with a diamond to show for it. Ring Pop candies abetted this fantasy. I would prance and preen showing off my raspberry blue flavored crystal as I practiced for the fateful day when the plastic disc setting would be replaced by a platinum one.

My predilection for a diamond engagement ring didn't stop after puberty; in fact, it only increased as media and my friends pushed it like a drug. Unfortunately, there was no Nancy Reagan to teach you how to "say no" to it in the '90s. Now I had teen magazines and rom-coms to spur my bling cravings. Sixteen years old and on a Julia Roberts movie binge, a friend and I ripped and pasted pictures of our dream diamond into a scrapbook. As each other's best friend, our mission was to store away the booklet and, when the time was right, reveal it to each other's spouse-to-be. Theoretically, we'd get the ring we wanted without having to drop hints. It was a stealthy, premeditative move, but at sixteen, we should have been playing in the sun and running through the woods. Instead we were worrying about receiving an unattractive ring.

A decade later when the booklet was needed, my inherently messy friend couldn't find it. While the story was fun to recall, the fact that we exerted so much energy on such a trivial object from adolescence to adulthood is just, well, depressing to me now. While we grew up understanding that we could be anything we wanted from president to working CEO and mom, from a young age we were also taught that "diamonds are a girl's best friend" and frankly, who doesn't want friends?

Despite my youthful obsession, I didn't grow up to be a jewelry-person. Moments before my engagement proposal, I felt carefree walking clothed along the boardwalk of the nude beach in Barcelona, Spain. And apparently so did my soon-to-be fiancé, who seemed to think a nude beach was a good place to propose. None of that mattered the moment I became engaged, though. Suddenly I was that hip-popping, six-year-old nose-picker again. Once the overwhelming joy of the moment subsided and reality set back in (the nude people walking by also brought me back down to earth), the rock attached to my finger started to feel very heavy and I very anxious.

I knew without a doubt that I wanted to spend the rest of my life with this person, but this small traditional bauble of affection didn't fit right. It's a strange phenomenon, the engagement ring. It holds so much symbolic and financial power over an individual, whether male or female, and over a relationship. I spent most of my life bowing to the One Ring, but now that it was in my possession, I was suspicious of its power and meaning and, naturally, I sought answers.

The road to understanding why this ring held so much power over me didn't lead me to Mount Doom in the land of Mordor, but it did lead me to ancient Rome in Italy. It's said that all roads lead to Rome; this is the case for the majority of wedding traditions too. Before becoming a multiple-billion-dollar industry and sparking at least one war (the Sierra Leone War), the engagement ring humbly began in ancient Rome when a man or his family sought a wife through a matchmaker. After his match was selected, the man presented his betrothed with a ring, making the engagement binding. Their neighbors to the southeast, the Egyptians, believed a vein on the left hand's fourth finger went straight to the heart. The Romans adopted this idea as the perfect place to rest a wedding band even if love was not part of the marriage bargain. A ring came to epitomize the commitment of marriage because it has no end or beginning; it is eternal. Aside from the fact the woman wearing this engagement ring probably had little to no say regarding who she married, the ring itself started with beautiful symbolism. Surely, knowing this would lighten the weight of my own engagement ring? Unfortunately, that wasn't the case. The more I learned about the evolution of the engagement ring, my enthusiasm for it started to die like the great empire of Rome.

Unlike the simple bands in ancient Roman times, my contemporary ring sported diamonds, and I had to wonder whether it was the stone that drew me to it. The first recorded diamond engagement ring took place in Austria in the year 1477 with Archduke Maximillian's engagement to Mary of Burgundy. Upper class people started adding gems, like pearls and sapphires for fidelity and rubies for passion, to the traditional wedding band and created the gemmed engagement ring known today. Starting as early 1761 in England by King George III and Queen Charlotte, the simple metallic wedding band was reduced to a "buffer ring" to protect the more expensive jeweled engagement ring. However, it took another hundred years for diamond engagement rings to become a must-have.

In 1867, the De Beers brothers found massive diamond reserves on their farm in Africa. Cecil Rhodes bought the farm and established De Beers Consolidated Mines. Now in majority control of this mineral's world supply and demand, Rhodes, like a Bond villain, manipulated the markets and singlehandedly drove diamond prices up to private consumers. His actions were not enough to create diamond-thirsty people like me though; it took the company another seventy years to turn diamonds into a girl's best friend.[2]

De Beers left Africa and reached out to N.W. Ayer Advertising in New

---

[2] *75 percent of brides in the United States wear an engagement ring (Source: Works Cited 1).*

York. "Sell this overpriced stone to lovesick puppies," they said (or something like that). And N.W. Ayer Advertising was like, "You got it. World domination through the Wedding Industrial Complex.[3] Muhahaha." Just kidding, but the marketing strategy devised by the agency worked out that way by being genius and simple. They convinced men that buying a diamond ring for their bride-to-be was a masculine sign of leadership and a testament to their financial success, and they convinced women that the bigger the rock the greater the love. The strategy worked too well. What Americans often interpret as meaningful tradition is nothing more than cleverly implemented marketing strategy aimed to increase company profits. It never occurred to me that my desire for a diamond engagement ring wasn't born from a pure sense of love and commitment, but from the advertising genius of the Mad Men on Madison Avenue in the 1930s and '40s. And when I learned that, I felt like a sucker. This is when I started to feel that buyer's remorse; or more so, wearer's remorse, just like when I buy skinny jeans.

N.W. Ayer Advertising's impact on ring culture is significantly bigger than Beyoncé's push for lovers to "put a ring on it." And while you can't blame Becky with the good hair on this mess, a finger can be pointed at Frances Gerety. Gerety, a woman and copywriter just like *Mad Men's* Peggy Olsen, penned the fateful phrase in 1947: "A diamond is forever." (Ironically, she never married.) Those four words encapsulated a diamond ring's value and the lovers' hope for the future. It was so successful it was deemed the greatest advertising slogan of the 20th century. When I discovered this, I didn't feel as warm and fuzzy about this symbolism like when I learned about the Roman meaning because De Beers created it to make a profit off of my romantic gullibility.

I wasn't alone; N.W. Ayer Advertising's was extremely successful in driving diamond demand among couples. Even during World War II while everyone was making sacrifices in the home or on the field, Ayer managed to

---

[3] *This is as good a time as any to introduce the Wedding Industrial Complex because it will come up repeatedly throughout the book. It is the concept that intangible, emotional moments can be represented and fulfilled through capitalist and consumerist means. From a feminist perspective, the Wedding Industrial Complex is problematic because it reinforces and manipulates, for example, stereotypically binary gender roles and body confidence. It also financially preys on those susceptible to such influences.*

convince wartime couples that buying a diamond engagement ring was their civic duty. De Beers alleged that buying one kept mining costs low for industrial diamonds used in war manufacturing. I have no doubt that my fiancé presented my engagement ring with good, loving intentions, but there were hidden flaws in my engagement ring of which neither of us had bargained.

While I was very concerned with the engagement ring's power over me, I hadn't stopped to consider how it affected my boyfriend. Finding the right ring, purchasing it, and then being expected to present it in a heart-stopping manner places a lot of financial and social pressure and responsibility on one person. This all fell on my boyfriend's shoulders because of Ayer's doing, but also because of the gender wage gap and benevolent sexism (a.k.a. chivalry).

This is a perfect moment to explain benevolent sexism (B.S.) since it will pop up repeatedly. Chivalry is defined as benevolent sexism in social psychology. B.S. is the act that reinforces unequal gender roles through acts of kindness, and for this reason it is terribly deceiving. It offers protection, adoration, and affection to women who only fulfill traditional, subordinate, feminine gender roles, which puts them in the position of the weaker sex. For men, it gives them a sense of value in protecting, pampering, and worshipping women. It also conveniently puts men in the position of power and leadership over women with its, "let me take care of you," philosophy. A good example is the tradition of a man paying on a date. Chivalry is beguiling because its structure is interpreted as positive, but it is actually restricting to women.

Still not convinced it's bad? Well, what happens if a woman doesn't fit into this traditional gender role or doesn't want her door opened for her? It incites hostile sexism (benevolent and hostile sexism fall under the umbrella term "ambivalent sexism"). She's then seen as trying to usurp men's power because she's choosing to assume a "man's" role or nullify it. The negative response toward her doing so proves chivalry is about unequal power dynamics that favor men. If women, who accept and embrace chivalry, are positively regarded, then as a function of chivalry, women, who don't, are not. Think about how so many women are slut-shamed or rape-blamed for speaking out against the patriarchal establishment. Benevolent sexism is an extremely subtle form of prejudice because it is not obvious. The acts are perceived as kindnesses, and the adverse, long-term personal and social impacts on women are huge. First, it can perpetuate abusive relationships because it's an easy form of self-preservation and gives false apologies. Second, women who embrace and accept chivalry are statistically shown to have less ambitious careers and lower earning potential than men. They gradually relinquish their own independence as they become more dependent on men. A woman's acceptance of chivalry predisposes her to a self-fulfilling prophecy where she, herself, may unknowingly choose in favor of her own subordination. Most wedding traditions embrace some form of B.S.

And my fiancé and I embraced these chivalrous wedding traditions. We were taught to show respect by following time-honored traditions without question. So when the advertising agency made sure the prevailing practice was for a man to shop, buy, and present a ring to his would-be bride because he had the greater disposable income, my boyfriend obliged. And since the bride's job was to just wait on her pedestal for him to get down on one knee (i.e., benevolent sexism/B.S.), I obliged. In retrospect, it doesn't seem fair that my boyfriend should bear so much more responsibility than me in our first shared gesture as fiancés, but we were told this was the way engagements were properly performed.

N.W. Ayer Advertising also created stringent rules on how men should buy a diamond ring with the "Four C's: Cut, Color, Clarity and Carats" and the "two-months salary." It even implied that if a man couldn't turn a proposal into a Super Bowl halftime show, then he should just go home to his mom's basement where he can live out his days alone. These rules made it easy for consumers to judge a man's ability to be a good provider for his bride (i.e., more B.S.). A fat carat ring publically proved he was no scrub and had professional promise. Even the Jared Jewelers commercials coining the phrase, "He went to Jared!" asserts this idea that going to Jared is how a man gets a proposal done right. That's a lot of unfair stress.

Through the grapevine, I've heard more than a few stories of men caving into the pressure to give a ring that's a cut above the rest. In one case, a guy felt so pressured to buy a brand name ring that he bought a Tiffany's box off eBay and put a non-Tiffany's ring inside it. A friend secretly revealed that his wife's ring was a cubic zirconia, but he couldn't bring himself to admit the lie to her. Another friend took out $30,000 in debt for his fiancé's engagement ring. Now she gets her dream diamond engagement ring and her half share of the debt after they're married. (Word to the wise: no one likes to pay for their own gifts or start an engagement on a white lie.)

And I needed to ask what put this unfair pressure on them, and how can couples fix it? Lingering, archaic gender roles, N.W Ayer Advertising and B.S. are to blame along with those damn Ring Pops, but the gender wage gap is culpable too. Historically when women married, they still didn't have the individual financial means to start a life with their beau or buy the trappings to start it. The custom of men buying engagement rings remains commonplace today for the same reasons a man paying on a date continues as well: men earn more. It's no coincidence that my boyfriend and I followed this gendered tradition; we were *both* victims of gendered wage discrepancies. Feminism is often accused of stealing power away from men, but ring culture is not a zero sum game. Today there's no reason partners can't share the financial burden of the engagement ring as a first act of togetherness,[4] but to do so, both partners need to start advocating for wage equality.[5] Perhaps if men expected women to contribute equally in social customs like the engagement ring or even on dates, men would be more concerned with achieving wage parity? Not to mention, it would alleviate the sexist monetary pressure the tradition singularly places on them. This is just one of many examples why men need feminism too. Sadly, there are plenty of other traditions where feminism needs to swoop in and rescue everyone from wedding culture's inherent sexism.

Sitting together on the nude Barcelona beach bench, it occurred to me that I would be the only one marked by our new, mutual promise during *our* engagement. It felt like a double standard and a lack of team unity in what should be a moment of complete togetherness. I know in our relationship we don't need to share everything, but this seemed like an obvious one to split. By receiving an engagement ring, I, as a woman, was socially expected to

---

[4] *It's unknown whether N.W. Ayer Advertising was aware of the larger social role it was giving diamonds. Engagement ring culture was created in a time when ambivalent sexism was an everyday occurrence, wage inequality defensible and "more doctors smoked Camels than any other cigarette," (Source: Works Cited 2).*

[5] *The Paycheck Fairness Act (2013 to 2014) was designed to reduce wage inequality in the United States. Unfortunately, Senate Republicans repeatedly rejected the act (Source: Works Cited 3).*

publicize that I was betrothed and "belonged" to someone else; yet my fiancé, a man, on the other hand (sorry for the pun), was not. Until our wedding day, my fiancé would look as available to single people as water to a fish despite fishing season being closed at sea and in his personal life. Symbolically and physically branding myself with an engagement ring sent a strong message about who I was. Just like the seventy-year-old nude dude we saw at the beach, who had tattooed an elephant face on his crotch (true story).

While my fiancé and I trust each other, the idea that I would now need my ring to fend off single people (and he didn't) seemed too ludicrous and codependent for me. I managed thwarting attention well as a girlfriend without a ring; I was confident I could handle myself as a fiancé with a ring or without one too. My friends would often refuse to leave the house without an emergency tampon and their engagement ring, but only one would protect their crotch.[6] If cheating or being approached by a romantic prospector is a real concern, I always wondered why my friends weren't worried about their fiancé's complete lack of jewelry. Single women can't differentiate between an engaged man and a single one. How is that not a hypocritical double standard?

In 1956, one man recognized the imbalance between the sexes in ring culture so he created "Acceptance Rings." After a woman accepted a proposal, she would then present an acceptance ring to the man. The idea never caught on because diamonds, the hardest substance in the world, were considered too feminine. Go figure. Had N.W. Ayer Advertising been inclined to increase the diamond engagement ring market for De Beers, it would have found a way to popularize men's diamond engagement rings too. To this day though, Western American men typically do everything surrounding engagement rings except wear one of their own.

I'm not concerned with the gold standard of the ring, but rather the gendered double standard the consumer tradition reinforces. Men are raised to be lone wolves or self-ruling leaders; attaching oneself to another via an

---

[6] *This is also a fool's errand. Apparently, there is a wedding band subculture where people wear bands or engagement rings to attract a one-night stand. I guess the argument is that such a ring might imply that someone is interested in a very discreet, no-strings-attached one-nighter. Carrie in* Homeland *(Season 1, 2011) and George in* Seinfeld *(Season 2, 1991) used this tactic.*

object would go against men's identity norm.[7][8] Women don't flock to the bathroom together for nothing. We're raised to be cognitive team players and stake our identity on it. Western culture places men's value on their individuality, but habitually places a woman's value on her relationship status. The dynamics in engagement ring tradition is representative of those statuses. It's as erroneous as insisting that my mint condition Beanie Babies with their original tags are valuable and therefore give me intrinsic worth. This is why I worry the engagement ring is the One Ring to rule women *and* men, and in this sexist and consumerist darkness, bind them.

As I learned more about the history and meaning of engagement rings, the heavier the ring felt, and it was doing a great job of making my independent self seem invisible. The weight wasn't limited to the meaning of its power, but how one's "Precious" changed its wearer and those around them. I'm not opposed to public displays of affection, but I can't stomach gross public displays of wealth and luxury, which is one thing Miss Manners and I can agree on. Take for instance, how brides or wives typically pile all their relationship jewelry onto one finger to catch a passer's eye. I say, why leave nine other fingers naked?

I became painfully aware that not all objects are considered equal even if their function is the same when I rolled into my freshman year of college in my fourteen-year-old Mazda 626 rust-bucket and parked among all the new Mercedeses, Beamers, and Porsches.[9] I was not one of the Joneses. Wedding rings can highlight differences in class and wealth too, which explains the length I've seen some men go to in order to buy an impressive one and the different reactions I've seen between small and big diamonds. Small diamonds get cute, precious, and sentimental responses. Large diamonds get responses like wowza, damn, and good job Johnny. Once I witnessed a girlfriend stick another newly engaged girl's hand in her own boyfriend's face and told him, "See this? This is what a man buys." How important and

---

[7] *"Male identities are formed by themes of differentiation, separation and autonomy, whereas female identities are structured by themes of identification, connectedness, and forming relationships" (Source: Works Cited 4).*

[8] *This also relates to name-change culture, which is covered in Chapter 14 and 15.*

[9] *Admittedly, I attended a college with tons of wealthy students. While I get that even having a car is a privilege, don't be impressed, the car only survived another three months before it died.*

meaningful can a ring be if it's judged by its size[10] and places unfair stress on men alone?

When my new fiancé and I returned to the states, everyone wanted to see The Ring before anyone offered us congratulations; it felt unnatural and too boastful. It also seemed like this pay-it-forward game, where if one person oohed and aahed over my ring it made me obliged to return the flattery. I'm all for giving compliments, but I shirk when someone is fishing for one or I'm forced to out of vain propriety pretense, which is why I'm terrible at bridal showers. Dishtowels and utensils just don't do it for me. It's the same when someone announces their engagement by sticking a ring in my face or Facebook feed. What are they trying to say or prove by sharing an image of the ring rather than of a picture of their relationship?

In all honesty, I suspect this fawning over jewelry isn't 100 percent sincere. First, like an ugly baby, no one is going to admit a ring is microscopic or a gaudy eyesore out of politeness. Second, its novelty is confined to the wearer. I'm willing to bet most have seen an engagement ring before. It's no unicorn. And third, as I mentioned earlier, I find people often secretly covet, criticize, or compare on a scale far harsher than any reality TV judge panel. I'm totally guilty too. I could never get behind my girlfriends' belly piercings. Mostly because they refused to let me make a wish on their tummy like I would on a Troll Doll. Jewelry only surprises me when it's in a spot that never sees the sun.

Others, like my sixteen-year-old self, love their "Precious." With the help of N.W. Ayer Advertising, it's considered a financial sacrifice done in the name of love. It is bankable proof of someone's willingness to commit; and without this evidence, some people treat engagements as conditional or unofficial. That's the travesty of the Wedding Industrial Complex which influences people to believe that an engagement ring is required to prove a relationship's value. While I put no stock in anything the Kardashians do, I caught an episode when one of the sisters refused to acknowledge the other

---

[10] *In social psychology, this is called symbolic interactionism. Basically, it allows us to understand how the structure of social life is defined and influenced by attaching meaning to an object, which is social categorization. Social categorization asserts social positions to people based on the symbolic meaning people place in objects and their relationship to them. These positions are seldom equitable (Source: Works Cited 5).*

sister's engagement until there was a ring. Maybe by denying the sister, she thought she was protecting the other from false hope, but talk about mean and unsupportive. She finally received a ring and the family's approval and now…many of the Kardashians are divorced.

It's not just the belief that the ring is required, but also this sense of entitlement around holding out until the ring meets personal standards (like my sixteen-year-old self expected). In *Sex and the City*, Carrie Bradshaw avoided Aidan's proposal because the pear-shaped diamond was not to her liking.[I] She only accepted after she received a ring that fit her taste. If I were Aidan, I'd feel hurt and like Carrie was being a little ungrateful. I worry that engagement ring culture is becoming too based on indulgence and personal entitlement and not enough on gratitude and heartfelt thoughtfulness.

For me, the feminist issue is the Wedding Industrial Complex's disproportionate influence on women that has turned a ring into a tool of manipulation like a caveat or ultimatum. I can't tell you how many times I've heard women say, "Not until a ring is on my finger," or on the other end of the spectrum, "Why won't he propose already?" The worst part is that I played into that game. With eight cumulative years of dating, cohabitating, jointly owning a condo, co-parenting a sassy bunny, and moving across the country together, I was not so subtly pressing the question of "So when are we getting engaged? Don't you think it's time?" I was expecting a proposal during our Spain trip, but after countless wonderful opportunities to propose, nothing had happened. In front of Diego Velázquez's painting of *Las Meninas*, without a ring, I found myself mentally preparing for a serious "where-is-this-going?" stateside talk. I loved this person, and our life together was progressing nicely, but this insidious culture made me think I should throw it all away because it wasn't proclaimed with a ring.

Note to self: that's insane.

Here's what I should have been thinking about: throwing away N.W. Ayer Advertising's gendered consumer culture, embracing feminism, and taking charge of my own destiny. The gender wage gap may have prevented women from buying an engagement ring before, but women today, despite still earning less than men,[III] can conceivably pull off this splurge too.[11] I could

---

[11] *That is, if they even want to splurge. The important part—deciding to get married—is free.*

have bought an engagement ring for him. Men get all the praise for deciding to settle down, for financially committing with an engagement ring, and for facing potential rejection.[III] Did I want the same type of credit? Nope, but in retrospect, matching my fiancé's emotional and financial commitments for our joint future would have given me a sense of contribution and togetherness.

I wished having an engagement ring limited itself to representations of mutual love and commitment, but the more I researched "My Precious," the less I discovered this to be true. As a traditional bride accepting an engagement ring and proposal, I was just playing a supporting role in the movie of my life. Everything was dependent on him. What's worse is that while I was obsessed with what it meant to have one, I barely considered what it meant to *not* have one.

Tradition is a powerful tool. It helps people formulate how they see the world, how they think it should function, and it identifies who is important within it. Before the U.S. Supreme Court's 2015 ruling enforcing statewide marriage equality, rings also accentuated who had the privilege to marry and who did not. What if wedding rings, historically limited to couples of the opposite sex, helped delay the social and civil acceptance of same-sex marriage? In my feminist bride musings, I discovered the engagement ring is set with more insidious issues than the diamond itself.

Discovering feminism as I walked down the aisle was helpful in fighting against all these unfortunate discoveries and the Wedding Industrial Complex, which manipulated my purchasing habits based on my gender. Unfortunately, it never dawned on me to buy my fiancé an engagement ring. I did think to buy my own wedding band as I thought it would give the wage gap, B.S. and the sexist Wedding Industrial Complex a nice middle finger. It felt wonderful to go into a jewelry shop and buy my wedding band. I finally invested in my relationship myself and took charge of something important. It was one of the few times I felt happy giving away large sums of my hard-earned money.

Feminism became a litmus test for healthy wedding traditions. When I identified one plagued with sexism or bias, like the engagement ring, I discovered ways to treat and improve the tradition. It also made me more cognitive of existing healthy ones, and I was happy to find my bridal place within them. I was greatly moved one day when I noticed my grandmother still wearing her wedding band years and years after my grandfather had passed away. It was a simple metal gold band, tarnished and dull after decades of use.

Married young in a war-torn Europe, my Ukrainian grandparents' history was seldom spoken about because of its deep-seated pain and suffering. Two-generations removed, I held the impression that their union had experienced more struggle for survival in World War II and then as poor, uneducated immigrants in America than sweet moments. For that reason their relationship was severely bittersweet. After my grandfather's death, all pictures of their complicated past disappeared, but she continued to wear her wedding band. I found my grandmother's quiet moment of sentiment and commitment as a widow, despite everything, utterly moving. Her battered metal wedding band put shimmering diamond engagement rings into perspective for me. Diamond rings can brightly shine under similar lifetime promises, but those rings and promises can burn out just as fast. My grandmother's humble ring proved that a trinket without the fanfare of expensive jewels could tie someone to a promise, a person, and a feeling as strongly as any fancy ring. It's because of this sentiment and how a wedding band's original Roman symbolism was not totally ruined by capitalistic boardroom greed that, like my grandmother, I wear, with utter heartfelt devotion, a simple, metal wedding band.[12]

I've wondered how I would feel about my ring if I were ever widowed too. It's true I bought it for my first marriage; however, by purchasing it myself, my wedding band is not limited to that one betrothal. Instead, like a Claddagh ring,[13] it symbolizes my willingness to promise to love, honor, and commit to whomever I chose. I get a warm and fuzzy feeling knowing this ring could represent the love I'm capable of giving throughout my lifetime. No one gets a new heart just because they find someone else to love; they find more room in it to share. Why can't my wedding band do the same?

---

[12] *I do have an engagement ring (more on that later). With the exception of fancy social occasions, I keep it hidden away like Frodo and Bilbo Baggins.*
[13] *A Claddagh ring is a traditional Irish ring, handed down from mother to daughter to symbolize love, loyalty, and friendship. In more modern history, how and where one wears it symbolizes a woman's relationship status.*

The other beautiful piece of symbolism discovered in buying my own ring is avoiding the superstition that, if love sours or is lost, the ring becomes worthless. People are so convinced of its emotional value that after one marriage the ring becomes unlucky and/or unwearable for the next. But no one has ever blamed a ring's bad juju on a marriage ending. While it might be hard for some to unlink the ties between jewelry and a lost marriage, make no mistake that the diamond industry had a hand this. It's in their fiscal interest to make people believe they need a new ring for a new union. The diamond ring is a big cog in the Wedding Industrial Complex wheel that managed to convince the Emperor (and Empress) that he (she) can see his (her) new clothes.

One of the difficulties of becoming a feminist bride was resolving my desire to experience traditional wedding customs (because that was the culture I grew up in and was taught to want to participate in). I started with the engagement ring, but I hadn't expected the feminist learning curve during this discovery period. In all honesty, I often failed to put my best feminist foot forward. At first, I made small rules like "must purchase a conflict-free diamond," but it wasn't enough to balance all that was bad in engagement ring culture. The pursuit of wedding tradition equality is never perfect. My own ideas regarding what equality meant or where it was most needed constantly evolved, and sometimes my discoveries came too late in my wedding planning. Reflecting on my failures, I hope I can at least give others a better chance to achieve more wedding equality, so here are a few feminist alternatives I should have considered.

My fiancé and I could have pulled a coup d'état over the throne of Queen B and declared, "If you like it, you *don't* have to put a ring on it." Opting to skip the engagement ring tradition holds a lot of potential. The beauty is that we'd save money (or accrue less debt) and help save the environment. Plus, this way my sixteen-year-old self might have performed better on the SATs instead of learning the difference between a princess and a marquise cut. Not to mention, this option also removes the double standard of only one partner wearing a ring.

We also could have shared the engagement ring responsibility by each wearing one. This option follows the Indian engagement tradition where both sexes wear engagement rings. In Indian culture, gold rings are exchanged in a ring ceremony called the Sagai. In retrospect, it would have been sweet to shop together or separately for our rings. While there's still the Wedding Industrial Complex to consider, this option is still an upgrade as it at least eliminates the bogus impression that ring buying is the man's job.

The third option we could have followed (which I wish we did) begins an engagement with the presentation of the official wedding bands to each other. We could have stored the rings away until our wedding day or worn them on the right hand's fourth finger during our engagement period. After we exchanged wedding vows, then we'd either switch ring hands or wear the wedding bands for the first time. It's a sweet mutual promise, and there's no double standard at play either if both partners split the cost.

While I fondly remember my Ring Pop engagements, now I wonder if all the history and meaning surrounding the engagement ring is really so sweet. I totally get my younger self's obsession with diamond engagement rings. When you're younger you just want to feel loved, wanted, and to have something special of your own. That, and because everyone is making a big deal about them, it makes teenage-you want one too.

Now that I've broken the diamond's spell on me, I wish I had known there were other wonderful, egalitarian, less bank-breaking alternatives out there. And I wish I hadn't exerted so much energy coveting the One Ring. I wonder what I could have accomplished if had I refocused that energy on other endeavors. World peace? First U.S. woman president? CEO of a top Fortune 500 company? I'll never know.

Chapter 2

The Romance, Respect, and Ridiculousness of Getting Your Parents' Permission to Marry as an Adult

Growing up, I had more freedom outside the house than inside it. I think my parents trusted my street smarts more than they trusted me with their fine china. Regardless, I asked my parents' permission to sneak out of the house when I was sixteen. I knew this activity might push the limits of my unquestioned Huckleberry Finn wanderings, but I was a relatively good kid. I argued my honor roll status warranted a classic wild teenage experience. I offered the very responsible conditions that when I committed the irresponsible act, I would leave a note indicating where I was going and with whom. They accepted.

When I picked my fateful night, I pretended to hit the hay early. I even made sure they saw me brushing my teeth in my pajamas. Then I made my bed, laid out my pajamas flat on top of the sheets and put my note on the pillow. It was the perfect cover up of a crime that wasn't a crime. To this day, I have no clue if my parents know I followed through on our agreement, but if they do know, I appreciate them letting me have this fantasy that I successfully snuck out of the house.

Asking my parents' permission to sneak out is an absurd and contradictory notion. I skipped the point of it, which is assuming potential risk, disapproval, and feeding off the adrenaline rush. Nonetheless, I did it out of respect, not wanting them to worry, and knowing that if I was caught doing something against their wishes, I'd never see the light of day again. It's sort of the same reason a couple makes sure they get the woman's parents' permission to marry.

As an adult, I never need my parents' permission to do anything. I'll consult them or share with them, but they are not barriers to how I live my life. Parental supervision went out of style as soon as my old retainers did. So it struck me as odd that I can buy a gun without their help, but tradition dictated that I needed their approval to get married. So my feminist bride self wondered, after years of independence, why would I honor a tradition that made me relive my pimpled days of seeking parental approval so I could to marry?[IV]

A Western woman's ability to choose her partner in life is a relative novelty in the scope of human history, especially considering lesbians couldn't marry *anyone* they wanted until 2014 in the U.K. and 2015 in the U.S. (they needed their government's permission first). Non-Western women's autonomy abroad is much worse. UNICEF estimates that 50 million girls under the age of seventeen in developing countries were still married as child brides in 2009[V] and that number didn't even include adult women forced into marriage against their wills.

The origins of adults controlling whom a woman marries goes all the way back to ancient Rome. Even in colonial America, slaves were outright forbidden from having formal marriages (legally secular or nonsecular recognized ones). They were limited to informal marriages (permitted by the couple's own authority) within their own race, which were frequently threatened or disregarded by their owners due to the slave trade.[VI] For millennia, fathers and ruling patriarchs used daughters, and slave owners used slave or indentured women as tradable commodities. A woman's hand in marriage could bring her family (or owners) political power, wealth, business, or other beneficial opportunities. She seldom had the ability to decide her marital fate; her destiny was always in the hands of someone else.[14]

This daughter-commodity business relaxed a little in 19th century when the Industrial Revolution took hold and love-based marriages became more commonplace (although advantageous "traditional" marriages were still arranged—or pressured—into the 20th century). But such new practices didn't

---

[14] *And while men experienced arranged marriages throughout history too, they were not sexually restricted like women, before or after marriage, and had more rights and liberties than them.*

spur a free-for-all hippie love-fest. Couples still needed mom and dad to approve; otherwise there would be no wedding bells to ring. No woman left the roof of her family until the man in question proved he could provide for her. He had to have a job or trade, maybe a title, assets of the barnyard or land-kind, and some hint of moral character. He also had to be within her religion, race, and class, otherwise what would the neighbors say, and what type of future could their kids have?[15] Parents acted as the brakes to starry-eyed lovers, who would throw away the concerns and social boundaries of their time without hesitation.

The World Wars, women's academic and professional gains, the Great Depression, better birth control, and an increase in secular marriage helped loosen parents' control over their children's nuptials; but when it came to love, adults still *wanted* mom and pop's thumbs up. Plus, their endorsement prompted them to pay for the wedding. With the patriarchy controlling a woman's entrance into marriage for so long, it's not surprising that the custom of asking the parents for permission today lies strongly in the hands of dad.

Knowing the history, not wanting to feel like an item to be pawned off, and having done my own taxes since I moved out of my parents' house, you'd think I would have ditched this tradition. However, my motivations for going along with this tradition were the two R's: Respect and Romance. Asking for someone's hand in marriage emits this romantic buzz where someone loves you enough to face the lion's den and declare their undying affection. It's an *Indiana Jones* adventure, where it's unknown if one's suitor will escape alive with approval and praise. What could be more dreamy and chivalrous than the lover who returns victorious (maybe the lover who returns heartbroken yet determined to marry you anyway)? It's a process that lets the woman know she is loved, wanted, and has someone in her life willing to take risks for her. Sounds kind of nice, no?

Respect is the main force that has kept this tradition alive. Parents reared their offspring for decades through the flu, algebra homework, and their first broken hearts. Today, they just want whoever takes over their job to

---

[15] *Make no mistake: eugenics played a strong roll in influencing marriage matchups, which also explains why African Americans were denied formal marriage before imposed miscegenation laws. I'll explore this more in Chapter 10.*

unconditionally love and provide for their child in the same way. For example, 71 percent of Americans still believe a man must be able to financially support a family as a husband or partner (32 percent believe a woman should be able to do the same).[VII] Today, a man does not have to be the sole or primary provider, but money is the number one reason people divorce. Parents, knowing that love is not always enough, want to ensure a happy and successful marriage. The tradition is also revered because it also recognizes the importance of the family too. A suitor asking is a formal way to start the job transfer and connect with his future family members. With so much emotion and future prosperity on the line, it's regarded as an important step toward matrimony. That's the traditional train of thought anyway...

The tradition of respectfully asking for someone's hand in marriage is a beautiful event until the outcome is inconvenient to the couple. What if my parents told me I couldn't sneak out of the house when I was being so reasonable? The seed was planted. I would have thrown out my goody-goody Girl Scout attitude and done it anyway. The heart wants what the heart wants; and sometimes mine wants a coming-of-age experience or to watch the end of *Dirty Dancing* on loop with a bottle of wine. Unlike in ancient times when the woman had no choice but to obey her family, today there's no weight to it, no credence, no legality, and no requirement. If the parents deny the marriage request, the likely reality is the marriage will happen anyway. Therefore, the tradition is a polite formality that has no true weight.

False formality or not, I, too, was swept up in the tradition's romance. I bypassed my self-governance when I encouraged my boyfriend to ask both my parents. I wanted to embark on a future with the love of my life, but I wasn't even in the room when three other adults decided if I could do that. I recognized the typical tradition of asking my dad alone was blatantly sexist since it disregarded my mother, but I assumed including my mother was enough to bring gender balance to it. I was wrong. I hadn't considered how outrageous it was in the 21st century for a woman to need her parents' permission but a man did not need his. Plus, if the tradition today is about respect, didn't my boyfriend's parents deserve to be acknowledged too? While well intentioned, my shortsighted thinking still perpetuated centuries of keeping women in the backseat.

In retrospect, I realized there were many more ways to improve the tradition. Removing the word "permission" would have been a great start. The romantic fantasy of needing my parents' permission to marry blinded me from the fact that I was an adult who didn't need their permission, not even their approval. What I really wanted was their support. Clearly, the tradition is no longer relevant.

My boyfriend and I could have nixed this custom. No adult needs their parents' backing to have sex or eat ice cream for breakfast (or both together), so why bother getting it? The catch is figuring how to respectfully inform parents of a couple's engagement after the fact. My first recommendation is to not announce your engagement online before telling them. I hate being the asshole who congratulates the parents on their child's engagement and they have no clue what I'm talking about (true story).

My second piece of advice, depending on your parents, is to invest in some Kevlar before you share your news. Not all parents are ready to buck tradition without a heads-up. It can be precarious if the couple can't strike the right balance between independent adulthood and familial respect.

We also could have made seeking support a team sport and shared responsibility. Today, there's no reasonable argument why this tradition is a man's responsibility. I think going into the lion's den together to face rejection together and to emerge triumphant together is more romantic. That's teamwork. To the parents, it shows that a couple can work together, communicate well, and work jointly under pressure and stress. It shows parental respect while exhibiting positive evidence that a couple is ready for marriage. It would also be the first official act as an engaged couple, which to me seems like a great way to begin this journey. How sweet would it be to one day recall how scared, nervous, and excited they were, but also how confident they felt because they had each other? It's a healthy improvement that keeps the spirit of the tradition alive while removing any benevolent sexism and the symbolism of controlling women.

It also eliminates the double standard that women need their parents' approval to marry, but men do not. Another variation of this modernization is for each partner to individually ask each other's respective parents/guardians. I imagine, at first, my in-laws would be very confused about why I was seeking their endorsement, and then they'd double check to make sure this is what I really wanted. Keeping me in suspense, they'd take a moment to feed popcorn to the possums and skunks in the driveway[16] first before they conceded. For all the awkwardness and fear of getting sprayed by their outdoor pets, it would have been worth it for the future memories. The bottom line is that if it's still important to show a woman's family respect, the partner's parents deserve the same treatment.

It disheartened me to realize there were more egalitarian options to chose from. I threw away a chance to show my boyfriend and his parents how much I loved him or for us to show both sets of parents how we felt about each other. While I focused on showing respect to my parents, I did not show more toward others and myself. I put all the responsibility on my boyfriend's shoulders and bore none myself even though I was capable, and that wasn't right. The modernized options exhibit grander gestures of love, respect, and commitment than the one-sided, sexist tradition currently allows. If I could do it all over again, I would.

---

[16] *They've been doing this for years and the animals arrive at night like clockwork.*

Chapter 3
The B.S. of
the Patriarchal Proposal

Walking among the crisped butts and breasts of Barcelona's nude beach, my boyfriend suddenly needed to sit down, explaining, "I have a pebble in my shoe." Bells and whistles started to sound off in my head. My internal bullshit alarm was panicking. "He's wearing sandals. There's no such thing as a pebble-sandal problem... Wait, this is it! This is the moment; he's about to propose. Finally!"

A small internal battle struck up in my head, a little voice desperately whispered, "...but this is a nude beach. You can see that man's dick over there. This is not romantic. What will you tell your grandkids?"

A different inside voice bellowed, "You've been waiting five days wandering amid the beautiful architecture and art of Spain waiting for him to propose. Shut up about that other man's dick. Focus on the one in front of you. That's all that matters."

And when my boyfriend deftly moved from the park bench to bended knee and presented an engagement ring, all alarm bells where replaced by joyous ones. The ray of love emanating from that moment created a fortunate halo, blocking out the exposed body parts around us. He and this beautiful occasion were all that mattered. Like a dream, the details are hazy. I can't recall his exact words, but whatever he proclaimed, I knew them to be true and sincere. Without a doubt, I said, "Yes."

We kissed, we hugged, we said, "I love you forever." Then I started to tear up and shake from excitement and a little anxiety. I shouldn't have felt nervous since I was picturing everyone around me naked, but regardless, I needed a moment to collect myself and figure out how to tell those future grandkids about the nude beach.[17] Eventually, we proceeded to dinner, where we celebrated with a bottle of champagne, discussed the future, reflected on all the excitement of the day, and where everyone was completely clothed.

Somewhere between our jamón Ibérico and paella del mar, a different inside voice spoke up, a feminist one, an intrepid one, and it declared, "You could have done that." And I knew that voice was right. So why wasn't I the one to propose?

Fancying myself as one who often goes against the grain—clothed person at a nude beach, feminist trying to be a traditional bride, artist with a business degree—I realized that I had blindly followed the status quo of centuries of patriarchal proposals. Buying an engagement ring, asking permission and proposing is so ingrained as a man's job that it never occurred to me to rage against the machine. If I had, I would have upped the ante on the nude beach by hiring a nude marching band to make my proposal. Now *that* would be a proposal no one would forget...or unsee. How I got caught up in a patriarchal proposal, though, comes down to a mix of complex issues: gender wage inequality, the juice of our loins, and the desire of our hearts (i.e., hedonism, benevolent sexism, and the false perception of choice).

Adam's descendants' higher income created a slippery slope of proposal privilege. As the bigger breadwinners they became the primary purchasers of engagement rings. And with that, they got the extra perk of proposing. I shouldn't be surprised that I fell into the patriarchal proposal stereotype; income-wise, I, predictably, earned less than my boyfriend (though no one could say I was less educated or less hardworking than him). Could my own income inequality explain and corroborate Michael Webb's, author of "The Romantic's Guide to Popping the Question," estimate that only 10 percent of women propose?[18]

Women's historical inability to either earn an income or earn a fair salary set the tone for how relationship roles formed between men and women. I had always thought of wage inequality as an isolated workplace issue. It had

---

[17] *Since it all worked out well for me, my official stance on nude beach proposals is they are a great place to bare your heart and everything else.*

[18] *While I worry about the study's reliability, there aren't really any others. A 2014 Associated Press-WE TV poll lists the figure at 5 percent. It's fair to say a woman-proposal is as rare as a humble Donald Trump (Source: Works Cited 6).*

never occurred to me it was this fiend lurking in seemingly unrelated social traditions. If the right to propose is partly a result of an income advantage, then I suspect women's lack of proposing is a result of the wage gap. But even if I were a millionaire, it's still unlikely that I'd have tried bypassing the patriarchal proposal.

In the 19th century, it was considered uncouth and improper for a woman to take the lead in relationships, which might explain why my fiancé saw my pursuit of him as more annoying and cavalier than awesomely audacious. Forward women were considered salacious and of loose moral character—not marriage material, so a woman-proposal was considered as outrageous as a woman wearing trousers. Victorian etiquette prohibited a woman from being alone with a man, so a woman could forget being in charge of her relationship status. Even if I wanted to take the lead and propose, etiquette and ingrained gendered expectations still frowned on it. A 2012 University of California, Santa Clara study revealed that around two-thirds of both men and women think a man should propose.[VIII] That's why women-proposals are still considered unique and bold. They're bucking the status quo and sadly, not everyone is on board.

There's also the hedonistic romance factor that discouraged me from proposing. I literally ruined my VHS tape of *Ever After* (1998), starring Drew Barrymore, after watching it ceaselessly. As a young feminist, it had all that I could desire: a strong female lead who can sword fight, rescue herself, show compassion despite years of emotional abuse, and a prince on bended knee revealing to a lowly servant that she is his equal and the love of his life. "She is my match in every way…I kneel before you not as a prince, but as a man in love. And I would feel like a king if you, Danielle de Barbaric, would be my wife." Damnit, I wanted that romantic moment for myself.

I discovered that a man proposing on bended knee is the cinematic genius of Hollywood's Golden Age, which made it a romantic standard. There has barely been a romantic comedy since without a woman seeking love and finding it with a man pulling a Tim Tebow before the closing credits. I swooned when my boyfriend did the same; it was my Hollywood moment. I hadn't considered what the humble curtsy meant though or stopped to ask why it felt so good? It is, after all, a very odd gesture.

I discovered that the bow means two things. The first is that something

#$%$& big is about to go down; second, it means there's some irrefutable B.S. at play too.[19] The patriarchal proposal is a unique juxtaposition of masculine leadership and selfless humility. It's the perfect example of benevolent sexism. By lowering himself on one knee, he's putting himself in a submissive position at risk for rejection and public humiliation, and the woman is, literally, on benevolent sexism's pedestal. Now if women dropped to one knee as often as men, this B.S. patriarchal proposal would start to disappear because it would be an equally accessed privilege. But like a fairytale rom-com that idea is still fiction.

There's another downside to a chivalrous proposal—hostile sexism. Hostile sexism pops up when traditional gender roles are reversed and doing so is, to put this politely, unappreciated.[20] A hetero woman-proposer also faces potential rejection and financial loss, but she's assuming a higher social cost by bucking the dominant patriarchal system.[IX] Under hostile sexism, a woman proposing could be received as emasculating, unfeminine, usurping power from men, and a general system threat to the patriarchal system. In lieu of mangina jokes and other peer reprisals, a mister might also be motivated to avoid hostile sexism by maintaining the patriarchal proposal. I'd be hurt and pissed if anyone disparaged my proposal because I was a woman proposing. Why trample over something that comes from such a heartfelt place? Not cool, ever. Sadly, the potential social and emotional consequences of bucking the system were enough to deter me.

During a girls' night out, I asked some girlfriends if they would propose to a man. All agreed women should feel open to doing so, half said they would consider it, but all of them preferred to be proposed to. That's a sharp decline from lofty ideals to bum reality. When I asked why they wanted to be proposed to, they shared that, in addition to wanting to feel loved and desired, they said it gave them a sense of power. Waiting a full week to be proposed to

---

[19] *Here's the thing about benevolent sexism that future feminist fiancés need to prepare themselves for: it's like a S.B.D. (silent but deadly) fart. It stinks to high hell and it loves to sneak up and never leave. So mentally prepare yourself for discovering more examples of B.S. in places you'd never expect.*
[20] *Remember that benevolent sexism rewards fitting into traditional gender roles (i.e., chivalry), whereas hostile sexism punishes those who choose not to fit within them. They are very much connected to each other, which is why both are part of the umbrella term, ambivalent sexism.*

and then having it done in a place that would be more blurred out than a *Cops* episode did not make me feel in control or dominant by any means. Is it possible I was oblivious to a potential source of girl power?

My friends explained that the person who can accept or decline a proposal has more power over the person proposing. My '90s Cinderella movie showed some powerful class reversal; it's not every day someone who empties the bedchamber bucket each morning gets the opportunity to reject or accept a royal proposal. Even Elizabeth Bennett passed on the uninspiring initial proposal by Mr. Darcy during restrictive Victorian times. My friends were making compelling arguments; but Cinderella fairytale stories and Jane Austen books are, after all, fiction, which is what that perception of power was too.

Benevolent sexism's goal is to give women a false and temporary sense of autonomy, and I fear my friends couldn't (or didn't want to) smell the B.S. It's structured so that men treat women in a way that makes them feel appreciated (to comb over the reality of the situation) and in control (to obscure that it's actually men leading the household, relationship, or lead up to an engagement).

Are men doing this deliberately? No, not really. These are just the dynamics of raising children in a biased gender binary culture: men are raised to chivalrously love and respect a woman, and women are taught to accept such terms. In a sense, everyone is a victim of ambivalent sexism. I followed this path because it dominated the world in which I grew up. That's the catch-22 of B.S. It can seem like kindness, but it's underhanded and misguiding. I discovered there's more to my friends' power theory, though; it's not power per se, as to what fuels that sense of control, instead it's the sense of free choice.

I discovered that my friends' power theory stemmed from "choice feminism."[21] My friends believed that feminism encouraged them to choose whatever they wanted through the second wave concept of "freedom of choice" (FoC).[22] If they can chose freely, feel good about their choice, and be

---

[21] *Linda R. Hirshman coined the term.*

[22] *On the contrary, this second wave of feminism was about making educated, informed and well-reasoned decisions within the scope of reproductive freedoms. During feminism's third-wave, women modified FoC's coverage to use choice for*

in control, then no harm and no patriarchal problems, right? My friends felt that the ability to choose was hands down the most radical and autonomous gesture they could make in the name of women's equality and as feminist brides.[23] Except, believe it or not, that's not necessarily true.[24]

They're making marriage and wedding decisions within an already patriarchal system.[25] The proposer (i.e., the groom) sets the stakes; a bride merely needs to respond to the terms he has set for her. Choice feminism is beguiling. It seems like free choice, but it's decision-making within unfair limits. The proposal power my friends believed in is a mirage. What's dangerous about choice feminism is that it does not prevent or protect any woman from making sexist or suppressive decisions against herself.[26] If women keep choosing to be proposed to, that's not Woman Power, that's maintaining the patriarchal proposal standard. I've met lots of brides who disagree with this assertion regardless of the evidence. But the reality is women have never experienced a period in history when they were the

---

anything and everything they wanted.

[23] *It's important to know that the FoC isn't about idly gorging on anything you want and then justifying your gluttony with "…but I chose to do so, and that's my right." In feminism, there's an implied obligation to choose, not necessarily in favor of the matriarchy, but always towards equality for both sexes.*

[24] *And they are right that choice is a fundamental component of feminism, but its radicalism was more pronounced fifty years ago when women had fewer choices. They are also assuming that all choice is blatantly free and independent, but today we know that true choice is more nuanced.*

[25] *The problem with choice feminism, like privilege,. is that most who adhere to this methodology are also blind to the fact that they are making decisions within an already biased and limited system. One's reasoning and rationalizing is never a virgin slate. It's always preconditioned by the subjectivity of religion, education, media, class, environment, sex, family, money all the way to one's overwhelming love of cilantro and the movie,* The Goonies *(1985) (but that last part might just be me). Patriarchal systems are globally pervasive; like death, there's currently no escaping them.*

[26] *Since choice often reflects fulfilling personal desire, today's choice feminists might actually be experiencing, what economists call, declining marginal benefit. This means, for example, that choosing to eat that first slice of wedding cake is going to make you very happy, but that benefit declines by the fifth slice, because now you're in a sugar coma mumbling incoherently about how Ellen DeGeneres is your spirit animal. Initially, the choice felt right, but there is no substantial long-term gain for anyone.*

primary proposer. That absence makes all the difference when understanding the scope, availability, and reality of free choice. Choice feminism a misguided type of feminism that places importance on *how* one chooses over *what* one chooses that might otherwise help correct imbalanced, sexist systems.[27]

Choice feminism is one of those concepts that are hard to swallow if you're just learning about it. With bridezilla/bridal entitlement, it's easy to not want to believe a word of it. This is the issue most people get mad at me about. Trying to reform proposals is like sending someone to rehab. There's a lot of reluctance because people want to maintain the bridal high they are accustomed to and expect (thank you, Wedding Industrial Complex). I find that not many want to come to terms with the bitter truth that choice feminism runs rampant within wedding traditions and all areas of women's lives. Sometimes it's for the better, but in my feminist bride discoveries, it can also be for the worse. There are clearly obstacles prohibiting women-proposals, though I assume there would also be more if women could lead by example.

Imagine how spectacular my nude marching band proposal would have been had I thought to propose myself—everyone playing with their instruments and twirling their batons while engulfing us in an intimate circle formation. Unfortunately, I didn't have any real-life examples to show me how it's done.[28] In my overconsumption of TV and movies, I seldom

---

[27] *I get it...there are so many types of feminisms that it's hard to keep track of which ones are bad or good, or perhaps too often misunderstood. It might be hard to know the difference between feminisms like intersectional feminism, which is considerate of diversity and inclusive, versus poorly named types like choice feminism, which is restricted by patriarchal power, can reinforce discrimination, and warps the good intentions of healthy feminisms. Healthy feminism doesn't encourage people to make decisions based on personal, selfish whimsy. It recognizes that personal choice is amazingly important and the needs influencing those choices are always different, but it acts as more like a checks-and-balances system rather than an egotistical free for all. For example, if everyone had the freedom to choose between setting pro-life or pro-choice laws and it just happened that 90 percent wanted to be pro-life, then institutionalized choice would actually be cannibalizing real choice. It would, in effect, take itself away, so that is why making choices that are cognizant of others' needs is imperative. Good feminism is supposed to be the method that levels the playing field for everyone.*

[28] *My high school did try to bring parity to the who-should-ask divide by encouraging the girls to ask the boys (Sadie Hawkins-style) to the winter dance (boys*

witnessed a woman proposing. So I did some digging to discover if there were any famous real or fictitious women who had managed to escape the patriarchal proposal status quo.

In the past, few women could acceptably propose, but English women sovereigns are one exception. Queen Victoria asked Prince Phillip for his hand in marriage by showing him Windsor and saying, "All this can be yours..." (I mean who would say no?).[X] And Queen Elizabeth I refused to marry altogether, much to the dismay of her subjects.[29] Much to my dismay, not one Disney princess has formally proposed.

Seeing a woman-proposal on TV as a youngster might have sparked my imagination in adulthood. After all, I mimicked what I saw on TV with a force greater than the Truffle Shuffle, but the pickings were slim to say the least. In *Sex and the City* (2003), Miranda proposes to Steve casually over $3 beers. He replied, "Hell yeah!" and then questioned her proposal's sincerity. How sweet. Angela in *Who's The Boss?* (1991) proposed to Tony...but only after Tony's initial debauched proposal. In *Friends*, Monica started to propose to Chandler, but quickly recanted in her emotion saying, "There's a reason girls don't do this." (Case in point.) So Chandler proposed instead.[XI]

The movie *Leap Year* (2009) circles around the Irish tradition that a woman can propose to a man once every four years on February 29th. Amy Adams plays a strong woman determined to propose to her boyfriend but (surprise, surprise) doesn't and lets the guy do it instead. These plots are restricted to silly, romantic comedy contexts where all women characters can't be taken seriously or are bailed out in the end by a man (this might also have stoked my fear that a woman-led proposal would not be well-received). What's more painful is that the *Leap Year* woman-proposal is a real tradition. What does it say when a woman can only be in charge of her destiny one day every four years?

---

got to ask for prom). High school in the 1990s was still very much about heterosexual gender binaries though.

[29] *It's important to note why men could not propose to women sovereigns. According to the divine right, God legitimizes royalty's ruling power. Ruling sovereigns are not subject to any earthly authority. If a man proposes to a queen, he would be usurping her power mandated by God and expecting her identity and that power to be absorbed into his station, but that can't happen with a sovereign. This is yet another example of how the person* who *proposes has the real power and control.*

What's odd about the lack of women-proposals is that, despite the economic and B.S. disadvantages, modern women have enough consumer power to make them proposers. Women control the world economy by consuming $20 trillion annually and that number is expected to increase.[XII] Maybe they could use that cash to buy an engagement ring for him instead. And with women earning more college degrees and with better post-2009 recession job retention than men, they are becoming the more fiscally secure partner. Those conditions are what gave men the proposal power in the first place. This momentum should, in theory, help to level the proposal playing field. However, with woman proposals still lagging, Jennifer Golhool of *Forbes* put it best: "While women hold the largest checkbook in the world, they do not recognize their power."[XIII]

I do believe the saving grace that will influence more hetero women-proposals is actually Grace and her lesbian relationship. My own patriarchal proposal came in the summer of 2009, six years before marriage equality reached the entire United States. Back then, same-sex marriage rates were increasing but far from an everyday occurrence. The generations of single people after 2015 will be exposed to so many more ladies in love getting down on bended knee before their future bride than I ever witnessed before 2009. I hope it will inspire more hetero women to abandon the chivalry of traditional guy-proposals, to rise to the proposal occasion, and to find their own version of a spectacular nude marching band proposal. I've been searching for examples of women-proposals all over, and I think marriage equality will be the first to create a true model of romantic, woman leadership.

Realizing my real lack of power and all that prevented me from proposing didn't ruin the romance of my own proposal, but I'll admit there's this lingering regret that I wasn't more involved. I loved my stark-naked proposal; looking back it's hilariously unique to both of us.[30] The crazy part about me waiting for my boyfriend to propose is that we both agreed that we should get married beforehand. The proposal was not an unexpected curve ball. Following tradition, we ridiculously pretended like it was unplanned. Had we stuck to reality and bucked the pretentious patriarchal proposal, we could have mutually proposed to each other.

---

[30] *To be fair to my spouse, he didn't deliberately choose a nude beach. It just happened to be a nude beach.*

How sweet it would have been for us to mutually pick an occasion to make it official. How romantic it would have been for us to ask each other in our own sweet words, "Will you marry me?" just as an officiant asks newlyweds to simultaneously share their vows at a wedding ceremony. We also could have separately planned our own surprise proposals and our engagement would not have been complete until each party proposed in her or his own fashion.[31] Then again, since I was the one pushing for marriage in the first place, I should have seized the opportunity to propose on my own.

Until men and women grow up in a culture that treats marriage proposals as an equal opportunity event for both sexes, proposing will always be considered a man's job. Out of all the great adventures one can have in life, why shouldn't proposing be one enjoyed by women too? While I hope to never be in a position where a new proposal for a new marriage is on the table, I do think, if given a second chance, I will jump at the opportunity to propose—nude marching band and all.

---

[31] *My proposal fashion being terrorizing my boyfriend with a medley of false alarms, red herrings, and proposal pranks.*

Chapter 4
The Herstory, Price, and Sex Politics of Wedding Planning

Once my engagement was in full swing, it was time to plan a wedding. The last time I planned a formal party for myself was my thirteenth birthday. My grand vision of how I wanted to celebrate leaving behind *Sesame Street* and being old enough to watch *90210* somehow translated to me and my friends consuming massive amounts of sugar, wearing my gift wrapping as clothing, singing to a cassette tape of the Beach Boys (yes, a cassette tape; and yes, the Beach Boys) and going to the theatre to see a movie about drag queens. It was the perfect coming-of-age event; I went from a *Nancy-Drew*-loving twelve-year-old and became a retro-Millennial, fashion disaster on a sugar high overnight.[32]

Now at twenty-seven, I had never planned a wedding, but that wasn't going to stop an assortment of people from contributing to an unrestricted five-figure budget for me to spend on a party that would last one day. What could go wrong? If past party-planning results are a predictor of future performance, I expected this wedding to be a great success.

I don't know about other women, but throughout my life, it was nearly impossible for me to avoid learning about wedding planning. This pervasive, domestic training made me feel like a professional athlete and my wedding the marital equivalent of the Olympics. I knew what went into a wedding from an unnecessarily early age. I was prepared to design decorations, walk down the aisle, pee in a massive dress, mush cake in my spouse's face and dance the night away. I blame magazines, media, and oral traditions, but I

---

[32] *The movie was* To Wong Foo Thanks for Everything! Julie Newmar *(1995) starring Wesley Snipes, John Leguizamo and the late, great Patrick Swayze.*

needed to point my finger at who started this mess too. And I rudely aimed my American finger at the British.

The British can be thanked for many things: American accents, America's love of coffee, Helen Mirren, the pay toilet, and gravity, just to name a few things. However, they have never received credit for creating the wedding industry. Yes, it's true. While their neighbors to the south, the French, invented love, the French kiss, and lingerie (I don't know if this is true, but it seems appropriate), the English inadvertently invented the wedding industry.[33]

The English monarchy with its aristocratic pomp and circumstance liked to throw a party or two. Take, for instance, Henry VIII, who had eight wives and probably had eight celebrations between the annulments, divorces, and beheadings. They celebrated tradition with such flair and consistency in such an immensely public way that all us commoners watched, envied, and aimed to imitate them. The world has followed their escapades in bed and down the aisle for centuries, and as a result, their wedding culture became the gold standard. British royal weddings are more than just celebrations; they are cultural powerhouses that accidentally created a for-profit industry.

If prostitution is the oldest industry in human history going back thousands of years, the wedding industry is a baby by comparison at a mere two centuries old. Its main contributor, Queen Victoria married in 1840. She was the celebrity du jour of the time and her influence on the public was immense. If anyone should thank Queen Victoria for her contributions to wedding culture, it's Vera Wang and David's Bridal because she set the white wedding dress trend. Her fashion influence also coincided with the birth of the Industrial Revolution and department stores (a real French invention), which inspired an era of change from do-it-yourself homemade weddings to commercialized, prepackaged, affordable, mass-produced, machine-made trinkets. Everyday folks could suddenly afford to look like Queen Victoria without robbing the Tower of London.

The moment engaged couples said goodbye to homemade weddings, they

---

[33] *To clarify, the English aren't the inventors of marriage, they're just highly influential party planners.*

gave birth to the Wedding Industrial Complex,[34] creating an industry that was estimated to be around $72 billion in 2016.[XIV] A wedding's feeling of happiness, belonging, perfection, and grandeur were experiences that money could now buy. Westerners can also thank Queen Victoria for popularizing lace, silk, satin and the obscenely sized wedding cake (hers was said to be three yards in circumference). While capitalist America took the Wedding Industrial Complex and supersized it, Queen Victoria's influence still reigns supreme two-hundred years later.

For example, Victoria also solidified photography (a new jazzy invention) as a wedding must-have. It's not that I don't want to thank her for photo booths being the new wedding staple, but its importance lies more in how photography helped cement the English monarchy's influence. Photography made the exclusive royal wedding accessible to the masses through print media, then the advent of television made England's 20th century marriages even more accessible. King George VI and Queen Elizabeth The Queen Mother's wedding on April 26, 1923, was the first to be captured with the moving image. Few other weddings (even other monarchies') were important enough to be broadcasted, which increased a royal English wedding's trend-setting power.

On July 29, 1981, the English were ready to throw the "wedding of the century" to the tune of $30 million to $40 million, reminding the world...that they *are* the wedding Joneses.[XV] 750 million[XVI] other uninvited guests vicariously watched the nuptials of the ill-fated Prince Charles and Lady Diana.[XVII] She embodied a real-life Cinderella (minus the poverty) with her 25-foot train, diamond tiara, glass coach, red carpet, and prince, which further raised the Wedding Industrial Complex bar. Lady Diana became a beloved style icon overnight, forcing the rest of us to endure a decade of gross, puffy sleeves and princess complexes (sometimes the impacts are not always good). The English monarchy firmly established what a princess wedding looks like.

Thirty years later on April 29, 2011, their son, Prince William, walked down the aisle with commoner Kate Middleton. His parents' wedding came

---

[34] *The Wedding Industrial Complex is an important term, but it's not the primary focus of this book, just an underlying theme. I encourage readers to keep it in the back of their minds when they reflect on how consumerism affects power and gender.*

before the internet, but now with the help of the it and social media, two *billion* people (including myself) around the world watched, shared, and commented on his big day from the comfort of their living rooms. This technological change alone marks a huge cultural shift in how we share and experience weddings and other relationship mile markers (for example, wedding hashtags).

Overnight, Ms. Middleton escalated to the iconic level of her mother-in-law. I wonder if Kate's commoner status reignited the princess dream in little girls. If she can come from a family that once supported itself on the salaries of a flight attendant and flight dispatcher, to one day become Queen Catherine, little girls will think, "Why can't I?" Although, as the first potential queen to have a college degree, have dated her beau long-term, and (gasp!) lived in sin, maybe her feminist bride qualities will seep into mainstream wedding culture just like her great-great-great-great mother-in-law's choices did.

English monarchs' weddings embody what it means to have a fairytale wedding, but fairytale weddings seldom include images of fairy godmothers and pumpkin carriages anymore. A fairytale wedding implies more of an unlimited budget to purchase all the equipment necessary to have the wedding of one's childhood dreams. Imagine how much better my birthday party would have been with the actual Beach Boys singing *Kokomo* instead of flipping to the cassette tape's B-side. What I could afford to buy for my own wedding very much reflected the taste of royal British brides, lace gown and all. Of course, a royal wedding is easy to attain when you have a menagerie of etiquette experts, wedding planners, servants and footmen (that used be talking mice) at your disposal and a ridiculously rich family to pay for it all. Other people don't have it so easy.

Tradition at Brides' Expense

When I began making my career transition from asset management to the art and literary world, the most common response from family, friends and coworkers was, "Hope you marry rich!" If I had a dollar for how many times I heard that, I'd *be* rich. Nonetheless, I had no illusions. I was switching from a lucrative career to careers associated with dying poor and tragically. I found the comment demeaning to me, to artists, and to women. It was dismaying to hear that most people expected me to fail, but also that, I, a woman, could only succeed with the financial help a marriage (to a man) would theoretically provide (benevolent sexism). The whole exchange irked me. While my new careers came with their own financial stereotypes, I was additionally dealing with the wedding planning tradition that says a bride is/should be financially dependent on her parents and fiancé in order to host a wedding.

It's a shame that wedding culture decided to make wedding customs dependent on bank accounts, and it's horrible that such practices came at women's literal expense. Love is not cheap; in fact, declaring one's love at a U.S. wedding cost an average of $35,329 in 2016 (not including the honeymoon).[XVIII] I didn't want the wedding planning process to be a series of monetary transactions that occurred with higher frequency than exchanges of love. However, when facing a one-day party that will, on average, cost more than a college semester or a car, it's easy to lock up access to your own bank account and embrace the tradition that says it's the bride's parents' job to pay for the wedding.

The who-pays-for-the-wedding tradition comes from nothing more than the days when brides were prevented from holding a career (and the education that would support one too). For most of human history, brides have gone straight from their parents' houses to their husbands'. Historically, the bride's family threw a wedding party as thanks to the groom and his family for taking on their financially draining daughter for the rest of her life. And because so few wanted to take on a dependent woman, they also sent her over with a dowry to help subsidize the cost of her living.[35] In return, as a sign of trust, class, and cordiality, the groom's side paid for the rehearsal dinner. Rather than empower women professionally and therefore fiscally, dowries and financially biased wedding traditions were created.

Since most modern Western women work these days, dowries can seem like the nasty practice of a bygone era. Sadly, they still exist. They continue to exist every time the bride's parents fork over the majority of wedding funds, which still happens a lot. My feminist concern with this is that how can

---

[35] *Lower status brides had smaller dowries because they could work as laborers. If parents couldn't afford to pay a dowry or were carelessly frugal, they sometimes sent their daughters to a convent to lead the life of a nun instead.*

society ever close the gender wage gap if culturally it maintains social practices that treat women as financial dependents? If fiancés didn't expect parents to subsidize the cost of the wedding, I hope people would take women's earning and saving potential more seriously. Wouldn't modernizing this tradition at least help in some incremental way?

Dowry traditions are practiced around the world. The impact of dowries on Western brides pales in comparison to the impact on their sisters in developing nations, often within conservative religious communities (though not exclusive to them). Abroad dowries and bride prices traditions are a cause for major human rights violations. To clarify, a bride price (a reverse dowry) is the cost a groom's family will pay for a bride (the United Nations has equated this with trafficking).[XIX] These issues seldom receive adequate media coverage and the effects are so devastating and horrific it's hard to believe that some countries don't even outlaw or monitor them. Because I know we are all strong, intersectional feminist fiancés with crazy amounts of empathy, I know you won't mind if I take a serious moment to address it.

The marriage arrangements these traditions inspire are particularly dangerous because the exchange is centered a woman's virginity and lack of earning potential. Because these wedding traditions hedge against the effects of women's financial dependence and communities believe marriage will protect girls from premarital sexual violence; they are often tied to child marriage, another human rights issue. To ensure a woman's purity and to protect her family financially, brides tend to get betrothed at alarmingly young ages—like single digits—sometimes to vastly older men. 15 million girls are married every year before they turn eighteen; that is roughly one in every three girls in developing countries. In 2016, the areas with the highest rates are South Asia (45 percent), sub-Saharan Africa (39 percent), Latin America and the Caribbean (23 percent) and in the Middle East and North Africa (18 percent).[XX] After the marriage or betrothal, the bride will stay with her parents until a more "appropriate" age.[36]

---

[36] *In the U.S., every five in one thousand minors aged fifteen to seventeen will get married each year (statistics change per states and regions). Child marriage is illegal in every state except under special considerations. For example, if the girl has become pregnant or has permission from at least one guardian or a judge, she can marry (Source: Works Cited 7).*

At that "appropriate" time, if it's discovered she is not a virgin or if the husband's family feels they have been shamed by the size of a bride's dowry or bride price, they will enact dowry-related violence. The United Nations Division for the Advancement of Women describes it as "any act of violence or harassment associated with the giving or receiving of dowry at any time before, during, or after the marriage."[XXI] It's very similar to domestic violence, except the perpetrator might be multiple people in addition to the husband. Dowry-related violence is most prevalent in South Asia, India, Pakistan, Sri Lanka, and Bangladesh. It includes punishments such as marital rape, false imprisonment, starvation, and honor killings, which include stoning, bride burning, and acid throwing.[37] In some cases, families will force the bride into prostitution and drug dealing in order to recover lost monies or to pay for her keep. And in the worst cases, a bride will use these as a suicide method to escape her life. The cost of dowries and raising dependent women can be so burdensome that some people will commit female infanticide (killing a newborn girl right after birth) or female feticide (a gender-selected abortion).

Dowry-related violence, wage disparities, and their influence on child marriage is proof that wedding traditions can have a profound impact on women's rights. It's a stark reminder why educating women in general and educating everyone else on the discriminatory impact of wedding traditions is so imperative. It's my hope that by eliminating the wage-gap-inspired wedding traditions, feminist fiancés can create healthier traditions. And those new and improved traditions will permeate cultures globally (not in a neo-colonialism way, but in a "it's not cool to kill women because they weren't virgins or because they can't earn an income" way).

Luckily, there are a handful of agencies that help provide sanctuary and medical support to these embattled women in need, but there's still a huge need for institutional, civil, and social help to stop honor killings and dowry traditions.[38] It can seem like Western brides' lives and those of their sisters in these strict cultures are worlds apart, but what they share in common is a

---

[37] *In regards to the latter two, some brides are just permanently disfigured and then cast out of their in-laws.*
[38] *Chapter 5 covers how fiancés can use their wedding registry to economically empower these women.*

dowry, using their parents' financial support to marry, and not believing or supporting the true potential of women.

When I learned how globally entrenched and problematic money and matrimony traditions are, I couldn't in good conscience stand by them. I was already perturbed knowing that who pays for a wedding (like a date or engagement ring) was a function of people not letting women work or respecting their labor so they could aspire to be more than wives or mothers (if they wanted). I didn't want to carry on the tradition of a bride's family paying for the entire shindig if an ounce of it meant I'd be keeping the idea of the dowry even remotely alive.

However, from the dress to caterer to the honeymoon, somebody would have to pony up for these priceless moments. As I was developing a better sense of what I needed to do to be a better feminist bride, I knew I had to break away from my parents' paying the lion's share. I needed to start balancing my own checkbook for this unprecedented dent I was about to put into it and my fiancé needed to similarly prepare.[39] As a traditional guy, this was not an element he had bargained for, but he came to accept it was his wedding too.

My vision was to split the wedding three ways: between our two sets of parents and ourselves. I thought by including the groom's side it would mitigate the whole dowry element and make my parents' contribution more of a wedding gift than a she's-your-problem-now dowry payment. I had good intentions, but I underestimated the finesse it would take to make sure everyone contributed evenly. The three-way split idea is good in theory, but when it's not a widespread or accepted tradition, it runs the risk of counting his family's money, not taking into consideration their limitations or catching them off guard because they never anticipated such costs the moment they had a son.

What we shoulda/coulda done is foot the entire bill ourselves. We are, after all, independent adults throwing a party in our own honor. A contributing bride's vested interest makes her more income conscious and independent (and kinda awesome if you ask me) than the brides before her

---

[39] *For the record, no couple should ever go into debt in order to host a wedding. If you can't afford the magician, the lawn swans, or the skywriter, you don't need them.*

who might have cared less about their earning potential because they didn't have to pay the catering bill. What's great about making the groom chip in equally is that it also eliminates the idea that wedding planning is limited to women. Now, he wants to know what his hard-earned money is paying for (and now he can insist on having a Journey cover band). Modernizing outmoded traditions founded on gendered economics is a great way to eliminate money arguments and help streamline wedding planning. Equal personal investment by both fiancés is a massive win-win for everyone.

Wedding Planning as Women's Work

I had no plans to reprise the embarrassing particulars of my thirteenth birthday party, so it was time to up the ante for my wedding. I'm talking ice luges, '80's cover bands, pink stretch Hummer limousines, and fireworks. And while logic talked me out of my Billy Idol themed white wedding, a guest did smuggle in some illegal fireworks during our reception.[40] To start wedding planning, there was this insidious feeling that it was my job to get the ball rolling.

That's when it dawned on me that wedding planning was yet another wedding tradition divvied up between the sexes. Men, like the bride's dad, wrote checks for the wedding, and women got to decide how the funds were spent. Unlike Queen Victoria, Victorian women's only sovereignty was the domesticity of the home, and since men apparently had more cliché masculine things to do like shoot things, cavort in saloons, and show up for work the next day, planning a wedding was traditionally designated as a women's chore. The frilly and lacy domain of wedding planning helped set up barriers to what constituted masculinity and femininity.

What cemented wedding planning as Eve's other burden was also the fact that its traditions were typically handed down from mother to daughter. Then bridal media emerged with magazines like *Godey's Lady's Book* (1830–1878), which told women and brides what to do. Even today, men's magazines don't elaborate on how to plan an impressive wedding or what bouquet flowers are popular. On a day that was supposed to represent both my fiancé and myself,

---

[40] *Luckily, the fire marshal, who subsequently showed up much to his displeasure, did not fine anyone.*

I started to resent the consumerist and feminine culture and media that unfairly placed wedding planning on my shoulders just because of my uterus.

Roping my fiancé into organizing wasn't easy, though. His monosyllabic responses indicated he had zero excitement or opinion whatsoever over centerpieces, decor, color schemes, or if we should hire a cocktail hour magician to perform gynecological exams. I quickly became irritated because it was apparent he had not dream-boarded his own wedding since childhood like I had, and because it was clear he was not listening when he agreed to the magician.

It was a painful experience trying to elicit an opinion over peonies versus roses, but for the open bar debate of Jack Daniels or Maker's Mark, I got an immediate, "Duh, both." As a result, I accidentally defaulted to giving him typically "masculine" jobs: the bar, transportation, etc. (He also was in charge of music, but that's because he is a band geek.) In my futile attempt to get him to give two hoots about wedding planning, I erroneously played into gender stereotypes, which in the long run still wouldn't bring parity to planning. Mea culpa.

The laissez faire attitude started to perturb me, but it wasn't his fault and neither was my hyper-attention to detail mine. Some men's lack of interest, inability or unwillingness to contribute creatively to a wedding is largely influenced by their lack of consumer and peer education in the area, whereas weddings are pushed on women the moment someone hands them a princess story (not to say all men feel this way, but I'm willing to bet my signed Mia Hamm soccer ball that it's pretty damn common). There are no men's magazines explaining that the magician should perform testicular cancer screenings because it's the groom's day too. And my future father-in-law was not giving him advice on how to find The Tux, nor were my fiancé's friends encouraging his participation when they asked, "Isn't that the bride's job?" Since the inception of the bridal industry, women have been the primary targets of all major ad campaigns. With the bride's side typically funding the wedding, there was little incentive to target men. Not to mention, wedding help books often unjustly portray men as incorrigible incompetents and make women believe they are the solution to it.

It's no wonder wedding planning goes awry more often than Republicans' attempts to reform U.S. healthcare. It should be a 50/50 team effort, but instead it's divided up into his and her jobs and each comes with a conflicting attitude. Exposing men to more wedding culture is definitely a solution. Influencers could also stop pushing wedding planning exclusively on women as well. Wedding planning will be filled with drama if it remains in the exclusive realm of "women's work," which is why it was totally worth getting my fiancé to realize the magician was a terrible idea.

A modernization against wedding planning conventions is the do-it-yourself (DIY) wedding. Hippies and feminists of the 1960s and '70s embraced the humble backyard, non-consumerist wedding, but DIY weddings evaporated with the plasticity of the '80s and the tech bubble of the '90s. But it was the early 2000s downturn that made DIY fashionable again. Overnight, organic, handmade, local crafts became all the rage. Etsy.com brought recycled material centerpieces, forgotten vintage wedding dresses and hand-pressed invitations by some crafter in say Portland, Oregon, to posh hipster weddings across the country. DIY culture inspired economically strapped brides to grab their glue guns and use gross amounts of glitter. Many praise this DIY wedding trend as powerfully feminist because it fights back against the ugly Wedding Industrial Complex; as a serious crafter myself, I'm a little dubious.

Sewing (via samplers) was originally a tool for young women to show off their domestic skills to prospective husbands who sought a wife with the right skills to establish a household. Nowadays, the role of craft has changed. Both men and women now sew by choice, which means craft's function, purpose, and opportunities are no longer theoretically bound to domestic stereotypes. With the invention of e-commerce craft stores, crafting does not create a domesticated wife, but an income-earning entrepreneur and artist. In just a few years since its inception in 2005, Etsy.com became a multi-million-dollar business, and its DIY culture encourages a reawakening of self-sufficiency. Women no longer need to ask for help when using power tools; they'll show you how to use theirs. Artisanal skill sets make women less dependent and more autonomous, which is great. It's reasonable to see how a DIY wedding seems feminist when it generates such a sense of creativity, skill, independence, and personal accomplishment.

Except, a DIY wedding is not necessarily an egalitarian one. Sure, DIY brides are sticking it to the Wedding Industrial Complex, but it still made her want something that was marketed to her based on her gender. She just found a different way to get it. Sure, men can pick up a needle too, but obsolete ideas of anti-craft masculinity still reign. How feminist is a DIY wedding if it's just the bride designing tissue puff decoration balls and leading the DIY charge and not the groom? Victorian brides technically had DIY weddings too. How are their DIY weddings any different than the modern bride's if its still just crafts done by women? It might even reinforce the stereotype that design and craft are women's work since a DIY wedding is not always a gender-free entrepreneurial pursuit.

I'm inclined to say DIY weddings are not feminist, especially if the ribbon supplies are purchased from Hobby Lobby, which insisted that a for-profit company can have religious beliefs and those beliefs trump the reproductive medical and health needs of the real-life women in the company's employ.[XXII] Taking down the Wedding Industrial Complex is important while supporting (hopefully) more sustainable and environmentally friendly wedding accouterments, like not throwing rice in case a bird ingests it and its stomach explodes.[41] Yet again, a DIY wedding's feminism comes down to how it contributes to more equality and not necessarily making wedding favors from scratch. If men partake in DIY projects, it can also help to remove the gender bias that lace is only for the ladies. I'd be happy to learn the art of calligraphy with my fiancé. And if he passes out from boredom due to pushed wedding gender biases, I will be compelled to write "poop" in Edwardian script on his forehead. While the politics of wedding planning may seem a little bleak right now, I have hope the party won't be ruined. A DIY wedding can be feminist so long as people participate equally, like making out together in all that glitter. Isn't that a nice win for everyone?

The Bedroom Politics of the Wedding Guest List

Kristen Wiig's character in *Bridesmaids* (2011) and I both excel at being unwary, beleaguered bridesmaids. I, too, found myself in a wedding that, I'm pretty sure, no one wanted me in anymore, and I was facing the

---

[41] *This is a myth, but that did not stop a Connecticut legislator from proposing a bill in 1985 titled, "An Act Prohibiting The Use Of Uncooked Rice At Nuptial Affairs" that would make it illegal to throw rice at weddings (Source: Works Cited 8).*

uncomfortable reality that I would have to attend it alone since my boyfriend was out of town (Chapter 7 explains why). I politely begged the bride to let me bring a mutual friend as my date to her wedding. She took pity on me and obliged, knowing I was desperate for some company. My replacement date knew this wedding was stressing me out, too, and bless him, he promised me all the weed and unlimited HBO back at his place so long as we did not wake up his doctor girlfriend sleeping in their bedroom. After the wedding (which I successfully attended without incident), I passed out on my date's couch in my bridesmaid dress, clutching a bong and my bouquet, knowing the nightmare was behind me. Best plus-one date ever.

Not everyone is so lucky as to bring a plus-one to a wedding, though. A popular plus-one prevention strategy is the "no ring, no bring" policy. It's widely used, but violates intersectional feminism. It discriminates against lifestyle singles, those in long-term relationships who willingly forego the hoopla of marriage and, once upon a time, LGBTQs who couldn't marry. It's a wedding guest list policy that places marriage on a preferential pedestal and disregards the quality or nature of other lifestyles or relationships. Regarding the sex politics of the guest list, this might be the most corrupted political maneuver out there.

I like curating the guest list via a "know thy neighbors" strategy, which gives quality and quantity control without exclusion based on marital status or sexuality. It limits the list to familiar faces. For example, if the newlyweds have not met a friend's significant other, then the beau is not invited. (Although, I made exceptions to this rule, like when the aforementioned bride, who let me bring a plus-one, wanted to bring a date to my wedding after her recent divorce.) No guest policy is foolproof, but this one does not judge the quality of a relationship, just a couple's familiarity with it. If this were standard practice, people might be more motivated to work on their friendships more, which is a good thing. I also like it because it prevents the newlyweds from being surrounded by strangers at their own wedding.

Even with a chosen plus-one policy, it's hard to solve the plus-one conundrum. People can fail to understand why the card was addressed only to them and not their beloved children, significant other, or hell, their chihuahua. Unfortunately, no guest selection strategy works perfectly. Site capacity and budget restraints dominate how a guest list is created, but since communicating money constraints is less preferred than the sordid task of grading friendships and the guests' relationship status, ugly methods prevail. Hopefully fiancés find ways to invite guests without judging them on their sexual relationships, but unfortunately, when inviting guests from a fiancé's sexual past, the same rules may not apply.

A past sexual relationship turned platonic is not always tolerated on a wedding guest list. People scoffed at Prince William and Kate Middleton when they invited their exes to their wedding. Despite being 21st century wedding trendsetters, many refused to jump on board with this one, which tells me there are one too many unrepaired, broken hearts out there. To be fair, not all exes are post-relationship-friend material. Some unhealthy relationships and people should stay where they are—out of sight and out of mind. When Kelsey Grammar invited his ex-wife and former *Real Housewife of Beverly Hills* Camille to his wedding with the woman he abruptly left her for, I'm willing to agree that his invitation might have been too much, too soon. And when it was reported that Princess Diana scoured the pews for Camilla Parker as she walked down the aisle at her own wedding; the problem wasn't having an ex at the wedding, it was that Prince Charles and Diana shouldn't have been getting married to each other.

According to a 2011 article by Lois Smith Brady in *The New York Times*, peace agreements or friendships with exes are an upper class thing.[XXIII] I assume she means us "lower class folks" ain't got the sophistimacation to do the same. The article further affirmed that it is acceptable for a current relationship to feel socially awkward in the presence of a past one that had an emotional or physical history. It implied having a "hot ex" around is a smack in the face to the current beau. But what if this post-lover etiquette perpetuates unhealthy sexual standards?

Most people come with a history of romantic predecessors. To treat it with a "don't ask, don't tell" policy preserves the misconception that previous relationships are something to be ashamed of, kept secret, or feared. I believe that breeds jealousy and distrust. Most of my boyfriends treated my amorous past by plugging their fingers into their ears and singing la-la-la; and they declined to share theirs. Choosing to deny, ignore, or silence one's personal history is just another form of slut shaming and virginity worshiping. Imagine how much healthier a couple could be if they learned about and accepted what came before them.

It's important to remember that not all relationships are meant to be romantic, and sometimes it takes a breakup to realize this. A lack of chemistry in the bedroom doesn't negate a different connection two people may share. It takes maturity to stay friends post-coitus, just as it takes maturity to recognize the value a past-beau/now-friend brings to an existing relationship. I love telling people that my senior prom date came to our wedding (he even dated one of my bridesmaids at some point) and we're all still friends. He and my spouse are now friends, and I love that.

I've been on the uninvited-ex list too. I was deeply hurt by it considering I brought the couple together and remained very close friends with my ex years after our breakup. He refused to invite me on the grounds that my presence would make his fiancé feel insecure despite how long ago our relationship expired (and the fact she was the one standing beside him wearing white). In retrospect, I think my ostracism was not a function of our history, but more a deep-seated issue between the other parties involved. After my blacklisting, he lost me as a friend. Coincidentally, a year later he ended up divorced. I was just collateral damage. From the experience, I learned how important it is for a relationship to accept all types of friendships.

As a traditional bride, I realized that relationships are hard to maintain if people choose to treat them with obsolete sex and gender rules. Feminism taught me empathy, consideration, and respect for amorous pasts. This gift raised my emotional intelligence. I learned how to treat people better and created stronger friendships as a result. I hope others can learn the same lessons; that way when an ex makes a wedding toast, everyone will know it's sincere.

Chapter 5

Exchanging Sexism in the Wedding Registry and Shower

Wedding Registries: Bed, Bath and Beyond Logic

In the late 1980s and early '90s, *Nickelodeon* aired a TV segment called the *Super Toy Run*. One lucky kid got a shopping cart and five minutes to haul ass through a toy store collecting as many toys as possible. The unbridled consumerism and lack of adult supervision made it every kid's first wet dream. I watched with insurmountable envy and fervent mania, knowing that this must be how adults feel when they overreact during Sunday football. I never got to be one of those kids, but I got a feel for what they might have experienced when the wedding registry consultant put a scan gun in my hand and said, "Have at it."

"You mean I just scan the bar code and that item is added to my wedding registry?"

"Yes."

"And whoever I give this list to will just buy it for me, no questions asked?"

"Yes."

"And I can put whatever I want on it? Those are the rules?"

"There are no rules."

And with that, I finally understood what "Beyond" stood for in Bed, Bath and Beyond.

Wedding registries are like heroin to an already insatiable, preexisting consumerist habit. It wasn't always a free-for-all among shopaholics, though. In the DIY days of the 19th century, brides collected and made items to be placed into a collection called a trousseau, which is sort of like a combination of a dowry and the modern wedding registry. A trousseau is an assortment of linens, household items, and clothing collected during the engagement period. One staple that has lasted until today is the classic white negligee for the wedding night. The trousseau is made complete through contributions from friends and family, which is now accomplished with the help of wedding showers and registries.

When DIY Victorian weddings went out of fashion, registries popped up as early as 1901. Back then they were called bridal registries since wives were the domestic goddesses. In 1926, the National Bridal Service figured out jewelers and other retailers could make boatloads more money if they became a one-stop shop for weddings. In the '30s, it was *Brides* magazine collusion with Lenox China that cemented bridal registries as tradition. Lenox wanted to sell more china, and *Brides* magazine subscribers wanted to be told what products would construct the perfect house and make them the perfect bride. Brides didn't go to Tiffany's for breakfast; they went there to get crystal and silverware on which *to eat* breakfast. What is perceived as bridal tradition is no more than business-to-business deals encouraging extraneous consumerism.

Newlyweds once required a laundry list of domestic products to create a household because they went straight from their parents' homes to their married one, and had little to their name. This doesn't represent today's relationship trends, though. Despite HBO's *Girls* representing Millennials as dependent brats, most adults (including Millennials) hold an income-earning job and live independently before marriage. In today's age of IKEA, the Salvation Army, Walmart, Craigslist, and Amazon, most people either have everything they already need or affordable access to whatever they might want. (I know I'm not the only one who isn't above picking up free stuff off the sidewalk either.) Maybe adults today don't have a $500 KitchenAid mixer, but elbow grease is free, green, and will never break down. Not to mention, folks marry older and older these days and are more likely to live independently and/or cohabitate before it, which means they probably own the essentials.

Despite all the consumerist, environmental, and greedy logic for skipping the registry, like a hardcore second amendment supporter, I refused to relinquish the scan gun. In order to attain the chicken-shaped kitchen timer that clucks and poops chocolate eggs (despite my oven, microwave, cell phone, watch, cable box and wall clock also keeping time), I was willing to embrace the title of "registry hypocrite." Not that this was the right thing to do. What I needed to ask myself was, "How does feminism fit within the issue of the rampant consumerism of the wedding registry?"

Here's the thing. At its core, intersectional feminism is about altruism by fighting against and fixing things like the Wedding Industrial Complex and sexism. I believe in supporting people in their time of need. However, I'm not sure getting married constitutes a "need" these days, and I'm definitely suspicious of whether the wedding registry is designed to create and support a healthy, egalitarian marriage.

Home goods are not realistic barriers to entering matrimony because establishing a home and eventually filling it with kids is not the main point of modern marriage anymore. (It can be and still is a goal for some, but companionship over family is the leading motivator for getting married these days.) "We would get married…but we don't own two pillows," said no one in modern history, ever. To marry, all a couple needs to afford is the marriage license and the officiant's fee.[42]

Despite the registry's irrelevance, it still remains a staple in wedding traditions. That is why I worry the wedding registry feels less like healthy generosity and more like giving into Willy Wonka and the Chocolate Factory's Veruca Salt who wants her golden goose. It's taken a tawdry turn, and it's hard to ignore the smell of greed, vanity, and sexist consumerism. But I suppose one could just register for Chanel No. 5 to cover up the stench.

All is not lost, though. The altruism and selflessness of feminism can turn this boat around. I came across a wedding-registry-first that showed hope for an old tradition gone astray. My dear friends asked that if their guests felt compelled to provide a wedding gift that they make a donation to a microfinance nonprofit in their name. It's a wonderful opportunity to support economic opportunities to those living in poverty. For example, women at risk of dowry-related violence benefit significantly from such investments.

---

[42] *I paid $40 for mine in Brookline, Massachusetts, in 2010. Our officiant was a friend. For him to gain the legal authority to marry us in Massachusetts, he had to pay a fee of $25 and submit a written recommendation from his friend. It's insane to think our wedding could have cost a mere $65.*

Women who can bring in an income are also more likely to send their daughters to school, which kicks off a healthy economic cycle for the family and their community. My friends may not be popping Cristal with celebrities, but they are hardworking individuals capable of supporting themselves without shiny new kitchen appliances or wedding money. And they can continue to reinvest the microfinance loan funds until they need the money. If a registry is a must, put it to good use so that it benefits someone who needs it. What better way to get good marital karma than to help others first?

It's incredibly hard to break the registry habit. My spouse and I appreciated the gifts given to us, but we're also guilty of participating in this "give me" culture. We didn't responsibly reflect on needs versus wants, the environment over wasteful surplus, or useful wedding gifts in lieu of stereotypical domestic ones. A wedding gift should legitimately build upon a new life. And that might be accomplished with a deposit into an IRA, a reduction in student debt or asking for a hammer to fix the front door, not a cupcake tin. Or sometimes, a good gift is reveling with the couple's family and friends by saying, "Please no gifts. On our wedding day your presence is all that is requested." We may have been sucked into the Wedding Industrial Complex vortex that is the wedding registry, but we managed to escape our own wedding shower. However, that wasn't enough to save me from the party's stench of consumerist sexism…

Curing My Bridal Shower Blues

I was about nineteen years old when I attended my first bridal shower. I was thrilled to be important enough to be invited to such a social milestone. It was held in a massive hall with another sixty important women. We ate for half an hour and then it was time to open the presents. An hour into present opening with no end in sight, I turned to my mother and whispered with a bored desperation, "Is this it?"

"Yes."

I replied with an incredulous, whispered roar, "Are you fucking kidding me?"

My retort didn't go over well with her, but in my first-timer experience, neither did the party.

I was twenty-four when I attended my next bridal shower, now as a bridesmaid, so I assumed my enthusiasm and support this time would not falter. I was wrong. As the bride opened gift after gift, I felt the same wave of disappointment and horror rush over me. The bride was earning her Ph.D., and there she was oohing and aahing over a butter dish shaped like a cow. I thought, well it is cute, maybe I should lighten up. Then she got to the salad spinner. She swooned over it with a fervor greater than anything Martha Stewart could muster. *A salad spinner.* I couldn't help but feel this domestic reverie was a disservice to a bright woman on her way to great accomplishments. This was not how I wanted her to be honored. I also couldn't help but feel like she was faking it. Gift or not, it is, after all, a salad spinner. There is an economy to how much applause such an appliance deserves. Not to mention, she picked out these gifts herself ahead of the party. Why was she so surprised?

I asked myself, why couldn't I enjoy the party like everyone else? Or if my instincts weren't wrong, fake it like them? The bride noticed and asked if I was okay. I said I was just tired. Was there something about bridal showers that I was missing? It is a party with heartfelt intentions, yet I found myself scowling in the corner sipping my mimosa with guarded suspicion. It is a happy occasion for friends, families, and neighbors to generously support the bride. Even its origin story reads like the sweetest of *Lifetime* movies.

A Dutch woman fell in love with a poor man below her station, but the father forbade their marriage on the grounds that the man could not provide for his beautiful daughter. Upon hearing the father's wedding denial, the villagers gathered and gifted household items to fill the bride's trousseau until the father acquiesced to the marriage. It worked and the couple lived happily ever after with a completely stocked kitchen.

This supposedly true story would mark the inception of the bridal shower tradition. It's a party format that has survived pretty much unchanged for three-hundred years. Surely such a time-tested event proves *I'm* the one with the spoon stuck up my disposal.

It's not just a shower's mass consumerism that rubs me the wrong way. It's also the symbol of my friend, the soon-to-be doctor, receiving that damn salad spinner. A bride at her shower receives countless domestic gifts: utensils, bowls, glassware, etc. The scene looks indiscernible from a 1950s

Redbook magazine. It's not a personal vendetta against kitchen appliances that propels my argument (I love me a coffee machine and garlic press), but by the third gift of cookware or extravagant stainless steel utensils, I start to see the inescapable makings of a domestic princess in her Williams Sonoma palace.[43] The women I know want to master Microsoft Excel, not an eggbeater. They think marinating is a process through which you take time to ponder an idea, and I love them for that. Regardless, I watch in a dumbfounded stupor as countless brides transform into a textbook housewife.

A few friends have argued this isn't true; they are just playing their part in the occasion and showing appreciation for their new arsenal of pantry items. This attitude gives me the urge to smash some Mikasa plates. First, no one should be insincerely "playing a part." Second, I fervently insist that showers perpetuate the stereotype that a wife's responsibility is in the kitchen, and the husband's, being that he is typically absent from the bridal shower affair, is not. Even if the groom shows up, he's likely playing a very passive role of putter-of-things-in-the-car and one who watches the bride open "their" gifts. There are also no other men celebrating this domestic reverie. Women are no longer the exclusive queens of the kitchen either, so shower gifts need to stop reflecting like they are. Not all brides want to serve a martini to their breadwinner husband when he comes home from work, so why treat them across the board as if they do? Why practice something this old-fashioned if it misrepresents the modern woman and perpetuates old stereotypes?

My friends can look the other way from the piles of gifted sexism and consumerism, but that doesn't mean my concerns disappear. If a woman receives nothing but say, hunting gear and chainsaws, I'd say guests are blatantly pressuring her to become either a self-sufficient lumberjack or the next General Zaroff from *The Most Dangerous Game*. Uniform gifts send messages. Reverse the gender roles. Imagine the symbolism of only men giving men kitchenware or linens. It would be unusual and misplaced due to gender stereotypes, just like Ted Cruz at a pro-abortion rally. Women were

---

[43] *And beware the recipe collection game played at bridal showers. This is when all the women bring in a recipe for the bride. I assume so she can start cooking good meals for her husband when he comes home with the bacon. Not too spoil this game too, but this only reinforces the stereotype that wives belong in the kitchen. Instead, everyone should bring in a visual cue card of a Kama Sutra position to keep in the box next to the bed.*

liberated from the kitchen forty-plus years ago; women need to stop exclusively giving brides frying pans.

It's not enough to say, "It's the thought that counts." Gifts can be well intentioned and still fall short of what's healthy for the receiver and for all the women who will one day practice this tradition. I believe in being generous (I insist, I do), but I think true generosity is a curated act keeping in mind the modern needs of the receiver. This is why I love the partygoer who gives the basket of lingerie, oils, and edible underwear. That person understands domestic pots and pans won't ensure a successful marriage, but good sex can.

And speaking of sex, what about the other outdated goal of the wedding party—to get the bride barefoot and pregnant? There is a little superstition at the bridal shower that for every gift-wrap ribbon that is broken, a baby will be born to the newlyweds. Whether the bride breaks every single ribbon in fertile hopes or defies those pushing for grandchildren by breaking none, the issue lies in the idea that, yet again, women are reminded or coerced into thinking that with marriage should come babies. The game discretely places a faux pas on those who have children outside of marriage and unfairly puts parenthood on women's shoulders since men do not play this game.

Maybe once upon a time a woman's sole purpose was to have this full package, but The Pill changed all that. Nowadays, one in five American women choose not have kids compared to one in ten in the 1970s.[XXIV] And 41 percent of adults no longer think kids are a requirement of marriage[XXV] so why practice a superstition that suggests it is?

There's a simple solution to modernize this tradition: for every ribbon broken, an orgasm on the wedding night. Who in their right mind is going to argue with that?

And it's not what we give, but who we choose to honor that ruffles my feminist feathers. I've already recounted how men are excluded from these celebratory parties, but Carrie Bradshaw in *Sex and the City* poignantly observed that single people are excluded in a way too. These traditional parties exclusively reward those in married relationships. There are no similar traditions of generosity that celebrate a lifetime single person. A friend scolded me over this once. I used to say, "When you get married, I'll give you a painting of mine." She countered to the effect of, "Why can't you just celebrate me as I am? Why is marriage the only way to justify such generosity and a reason to celebrate my life (birthdays aside because everyone has them)?" She was totally right and put me in my place. I sent her a painting immediately to celebrate her fabulousness and friendship.

At some point, the term "bridal shower" was given the boot for being too gendered, and it was rebranded as a "wedding shower" to imply the party is for everyone and not just women. The new, more politically correct name is just a smokescreen, though. I may be seeking solace near the sorbet and champagne punchbowl, but don't think for one second that I didn't notice the party is still a boob fest. I've begged brides to let me bring my spouse since they were closer friends, but I still get the invite and he gets to stay home. If wedding showers were the epitome of a good party, men would insist on an invite. There's a reason they don't…because no one in their right mind enjoys wedding gift bingo. There, I said it. At the very least, if I am suffering at these parties, I believe the men should be too. Bringing men into these rituals neutralizes the party scene where stereotyped gender roles run amok.

Jack and Jill to the Rescue

As a party-lover, I want to arrive with the best of intentions and spirits. That's why I'm thankful for the greatest feminist invention since The Pill—the Jack and Jill party.[44] A Jack and Jill party is a joint, unisex celebration where both fiancés and their anatomically dissimilar friends show up. Hosting a Jack and Jill shower levels the playing field and eliminates all the yucky stuff. It's inclusive and free from the sexist traditions rampant in the bridal shower.

My first Jack and Jill was a joint bachelor and bachelorette party. I had a great time bar-hopping and hanging out with everyone. It meant a lot because as a friend of the groom, I wouldn't have been able to celebrate with him if he had a segregated party. I also would not have been able to invite my boyfriend (who I eventually married) so both could meet. I wouldn't have had the chance to relish watching my friend projectile vomit across the bar floor, nor send my boyfriend into the bathroom with him to make sure he was okay.

---

[44] *I'll admit the name itself is problematic because it is limited to a gender binary. There is no equivalent for same-sex couples, aside from altering it to "Jack and Joe" or "Joanne and Jill." Naming issue aside, the point of this style of party is to celebrate inclusivity.*

And without a pan-gender invitation, my boyfriend wouldn't have exited the bathroom exclaiming, "I tore a poster off the wall, rolled it up, and stirred his vomit down the drain. I think that means we are friends forever." And, you know what? They are.

I think the best, most generous, and most fun celebrations are the ones that are wholly inclusive. If a wedding shower is to support the new life of the couple, then it should include the couple and all their contrasting-crotched friends. So please, for the love of Geraldine Ferraro, invite the men too. If the host can't make that change, at the very least, then I'm going to chain myself to the nearest man à la *O Brother, Where Art Thou?* (2000). We can either politely golf clap over accidental duplicate toasters or *Shawshank* our way out together with the bride's new spoons. There are plenty of reason to modernize the bridal shower and no reasons not to.

Until it is, though, I'll be in my corner sipping my mimosa waiting for my unorthodox gift to shock and horrify those who cling to misogynistic wedding shower ideas—that's if anyone wants to invite me anymore.

Chapter 6
Stripping Bare the Bachelorette Party

I unabashedly approve of one type of engagement period party and that's the last call, the final mile, the last hurrah—the bachelorette party. While the wedding shower will inspire me to escape like a Looney Tunes character through a brick wall, if I remotely know you and I find out you or someone you know is having a bachelorette party—beware, I *will* invite myself to the party. There's a lot of fascinating feminist empowerment in the bachelorette party, but there are a few unsexy kinks to work out.

I am pro-bachelorette party because the mere ability for a woman to go on such a party is a sign of women's parity and progress. Yes, the bachelorette party, with its penis straws, feather boas and princess tiaras, are a major advancement in women's sexual freedom. With the "bride-to-be" sashes, hooting and hollering about their right to party on par with a bachelor party, the small swarm of bachelorette partygoers marching down the street to the next bar is my generation's version of the suffragist march. Sometimes they even travel by old-fashioned trolley like Susan B. Anthony; it's just decked out in neon, strobe lights, and a stripper pole now.

Here's why it's so avant-garde and important: bachelorette parties have been around for about twenty to thirty years, but the sexual escapades of men and their bachelor parties go back two millennia. That's two-thousand fucking years. Men have been partying for a hundred times longer than women, who just earned the social approval to host such parties. If that's not a double standard, I don't know what is.

Are you outraged? You should be. Do as I did and take it out on the party piñata.

The ancient Spartans started the bachelor party by hosting a dinner in the groom's honor. Given Sparta's reputation, it was probably riddled with machismo and fist pumping. Over time, bachelor parties turned into more of the familiar festivities we see today—cue naked ladies, sumptuous amounts of alcohol, pranks, and hijinks, maybe something outdoorsy. Wait...looking more closely, I bet they are exactly the same. The bachelor party historically and stereotypically allowed men one last chance of sexual freedom before the reigns of marriage (not that this always stopped them, but it has been often lauded as a get-out-of-jail free card event). The party that gave men the green light to be freely sexual remained theirs for most of written human history.

Women, however, never enjoyed equivalent parties prior to the late 20th century. Baby boomers or older most likely had a bridal shower or luncheon. Before then, modeling a ladies night after a bachelor party would have been considered lewd and lascivious. Women were expected to embrace the confines of marriage; men were allowed to approach it with reluctance and use the bachelor party as a chance to escape the idea of sleeping with one person for the rest of their lives.

In the movie *Sideways* (2004), Miles (Paul Giamatti) hosts a bachelor party excursion for his friend, Jack (Thomas Haden Church) to California's wine country. Jack uses the party as an opportunity to "sow his wild oats." His reasoning was that monogamy was a burdensome concept for him. For the record, there is no such thing as a sexual "last hurrah." Couples said goodbye to singlehood the moment they stepped into a monogamous relationship. There are still people who side with Jack, such as my former male colleague, who declared, "If you don't cheat at your bachelor party, you're a pussy!"

Before I could respond, his best friend got fired up and challenged the comment, "I didn't cheat during my bachelor party. Does that make me a pussy?"[45]

The oat-sower, who happened to be engaged at the time, showed remorse to his friend. "No, of course not, you're cool." He then blatantly turned his back to his friend and reiterated to me, "...but as I said, you'd [anyone] be a pussy if you didn't."

I don't quite remember whether I schooled him about his overly enthusiastic and misplaced use of the word "pussy" or explained that cheating only made someone an asshole. I definitely asked him if his fiancé was aware of his belief and morality system, to which he just walked away mumbling

---

[45] *Kudos to our friend who stood up to him.*

about pussies. This man teaches children now.

To some, this fear of b-party cheating is real, and it's warranted if they're engaged to people like my former colleague or Jack. What constitutes cheating is totally subjective: some might view air-rubbing the guest of honor's face into a dancer's crotch as cheating; others might view it as a Reiki massage realigning someone's sexual chakra. For the record though, parties don't make people cheat. People chose to cheat.

Regardless, I've seen lots of fearful couples try to control and censor their partner's party behavior through abstinence/boycott manipulation. For example, if a b-party is considering visiting a strip club, I've witnessed both men and women negotiate that if he or she abstains from seeing a stripper then their partner should too. I've even seen negotiations around alcohol consumption. I'm all for supporting someone by matching their behavior in the short-term to help them quit smoking or join them in a therapeutic *Harry Potter* marathon, but I draw the line when they try to manipulate my behavior to ease their own insecurities. That's not relationship equality; that's not even healthy. My feminist bride spidey-sense tingles when someone manipulates another's behavior rather than relying on mutual trust.

Brides' late arrival to the bachelorette party and the former sexual restraint on their parties is why women are less likely to adopt the "get-out-of-sexual-jail" card that bachelors have enjoyed for too long. Today, a bachelorette party is more about camaraderie between friends, to laugh, to relax, and for me to karaoke to Michael Bolton's *How Can We Be Lovers*. But for many bachelorettes, it's an opportunity to express their sexuality. Women may spend the day volunteering, dispersing a wad of one dollar bills into someone's jockstrap, camping in the woods, or hosting a sex toy party, but it's women's ability to choose from a list of unlimited activities that marks a major milestone in our social and sexual rights.[46] It's a freedom that is a direct result of the women's sexual revolution in the 1970s. And while bachelorettes have more options, that unfortunately doesn't stop even the most open-

---

[46] *How is this not choice feminism you ask? Well, I'm examining this from the perspective that b-parties are now equal opportunity events (assuming people come from a community where this is true). The decision to have a bachelorette party is not socially restricted (a tenet of choice feminism) as it once was, and inarguably, the party relates directly to sex and sexuality, which are part of the FoC tenet.*

minded bachelorettes from being influenced by outdated ideas of "appropriate" women's sexual decorum.

The casualness with which some brides wanted to treat this festive opportunity depressed me. They forbid alcohol, scantily clad men, penis pops, disastrous costumes suitable for Halloween parties, and Michael Bolton karaoke. It's not that I'm opposed to a reading day on the beach, but their motivation seemed biasedly corrupt. One bride explained to me that the typical bachelorette brouhaha was unbecoming, classless, and inappropriate for a wife-to-be. "Those days are over for me. If I'm going to be someone's wife, I should act like it." A sunny day at the beach is a fine idea so long as it doesn't mean getting burned by misguided gendered attitudes.

I couldn't help suspecting this self-censorship was a result of obsolete gender roles. This attitude seems no different than the Victorian brides who were expected to be complacent and obedient wives. Becoming a wife doesn't require demure behavior, either (which sounds like B.S. anyway). If someone wants to embrace being either a horny Blanche Devereaux or a naïve Rose Nylund, they should do it to please themselves and no one else. Besides, how fun can a bachelorette party be if it its controlled by old-fashioned behavioral stereotypes?

I've been on plenty of crazy, successful non-penis-paraphernalia bachelorette parties. I organized a Wild West themed party for my best friend; we drove cattle on horseback, white-water rafted, and attended a beer festival. It was great because we were able to be ourselves, and we weren't bothered by any restrictions of stereotypical femininity, gendered behavior, or class.[47] But sometimes, in my experience, honesty and the freedom to party are not always respected by others. Nothing ruins a party more than experiencing slut shaming, street harassment, and body objectification when all you want to do is celebrate with friends.

Nothing ruins a party more than experiencing slut shaming, street harassment, and body objectification when all you want to do is celebrate with friends.

---

[47] *I was, however, bothered by the massive White Russian cocktail pitcher my friend ordered during the bar's last call. Holding trophies I had acquired but not earned. I announced like Will Ferrell's* Anchorman, *"Milk was a bad choice!" and demanded someone take me home.*

At a bachelorette party in Newport, Rhode Island, my friends and I encountered a group of guys who thought it would be funny to talk about penetrating our panties as we walked down the street in front of them. Lots of people enjoy a good pickle tickle, but when it's so aggressively one-sided, it's just sexual street harassment. We crossed to the other side of the street to feel safe because we had no clue if the harassment would stop at just those words. They booed us for running away and ruining their fun (i.e., male entitlement/hostile sexism). When their sober friend approached us and apologized, I laid into him…but in the politest way possible because, despite my feminism, I still fear men's retaliation when their sense of entitlement and idea of "fun" is challenged.

And I will not disclose what we were wearing because that does not matter. Nothing in the world justifies such treatment. Bachelorette parties often include outlandish clothing like sparkly sashes and a penis tiara. There seems to be a prevalent culture where people (men) see these types of parties and feel entitled or justified to harass partygoers and then slut-shame them for their appearance and revelry afterwards. For the record, a b-party is never a public solicitation for surrounding dicks to join the party and then act like one.

Helping people understand how to engage with a b-party is crucial so everyone feels respected, safe, and celebratory. Bachelorette parties are seen as gregarious, with their interactive games like Suck for a Buck[48] or scavenger hunts with bawdy themes. This, for the record, is *not* an open invitation to engage in unwelcome or offensive ways, or, frankly, in *any* way without the party's consent. When the bachelorette gets up on stage to dance or do buttery nipple shots off a volunteer's belly button, she's absolutely engaging an audience but one she *chose.*[49] In these situations, she is the boss. Her consent must be given before anyone engages with her and the b-party. And that consent must be asked for and received first.

Even mild harassment is a real problem. For example, at bachelorette parties, it's common to hear a random guy yell at the bride, "Don't do it!" as

---

[48] *It's a fundraiser game where bachelorettes sell $1 lollipops to strangers, primarily men. It's a sexual game because men use just their mouths to grab the lollipop.*
[49] *I'll argue this choice falls under the freedom of choice and not choice feminism because it relates to physical bodily autonomy and consent.*

in don't get married. Forget the passive aggressiveness of the jeer; on a comedic level, it's terrible. Jeff Foxworthy wouldn't even use it. What are they expecting—that she'll realize the folly of her choice, throw her engagement ring into her tiki drink, and gallop into sunset with him? Oftentimes, brides politely smile or ignore them (there's that fear of reprisal/high road/better-to-absorb-than-to-engage response). One poignantly lamented, "Why can't they just wish me well? Is that so hard?" I worry about this subsection of guy culture that puts male entitlement and sexual hostility before respecting and positively celebrating the bride, her fiancé, and this celebratory right of passage. There's a range of negative reactions that bachelorette parties receive from straight up sexual harassment to passive aggressiveness. Unsupportive catcalls to emotional abuse to full out physical assault all fall within the spectrum of harassment.

One infamous story I heard from friends was a bachelor party that started the day with golfing and breaking the golf cart but ended with the drunk tank. One insanely drunk partygoer saw a woman he liked and thought it would be fun to pull up her skirt outside a bar. She didn't like it, and neither did her Green Beret boyfriend who reacted by punching and kicking him on the ground until the cops came. The EMTs placed the unconscious sexual assaulter into a neck brace, but by the powers of alcohol he popped up alive and unharmed, much to everyone's surprise. He told the officers not to press charges on the Green Beret and proceeded to declare to the cops the most bullshit excuse for sexual assault and physical violence ever: "These are the things that happen at da' clubs."

The Green Beret was let go and the sexual assaulter went into the drunk tank. Awake and sober the next morning, the assailant marched out before a judge on a chain gang filled with other drunks and brawlers.[50] He was subsequently let go. The sexual assaulter saw the celebration as an excuse to treat a woman as an object. I'm baffled at how some see the b-party as an opportunity to act like molesters.

A short skirt and/or a b-party are in no way an invitation invade a

---

[50] *And to his surprise, his friend Bobby. Bobby flirtatiously winked hello to the sexual assaulter from down the line. Bobby's infraction involved dancing barefoot and singing Cory Hart's Sunglasses at Night in front of a cop who was...drumroll please...wearing his sunglasses at night.*

woman's privacy or take away her right to control her body. Unfortunately, those ugly, hidden kinks in b-party culture touch on tough topics like rape culture and male entitlement. It's hard to know exactly how to stop it. Avoidance doesn't teach people how to behave correctly, but sadly, it may be the only safe option. Confrontation is certainly important but no easy task. If yelling doesn't work, throwing a drink in his face like a *Real Housewife* can only escalate the problem (it's also assault and therefore a big no-no). Instead, inform the bartender, bouncer, or nearby authority of the situation.

I believe strongly in the power of story sharing and conversation as an effective way to raise empathy and awareness. It's important to teach people how to respectfully celebrate with others; and not let a culture that would rather threaten, harass, and tear down others persist. I'm honestly flabbergasted: why would not just men but anyone want to celebrate during a friend's party in that way or treat strangers who are similarly celebrating?

While I sign up faster for a bachelorette party than a college kid at a sperm bank giving away Bud Light, it's no wonder that others are less enthusiastic. To be fair, these are just worst case stories. There are men who conduct themselves appropriately and with kindness. At my Vegas bachelorette party, for instance, we bumped into several guys who were incredibly nice. One of them worked for a California major league baseball team, which was enough for me to decide, in my beer-goggled state, that this young man and one of my baseball-loving b-party attendees were soul mates. They didn't fall in love, but for one night they almost hit a homerun in Vegas. We all had a fun, crazy time together; no one needed to pull up skirts in order to feel like they were maximizing their party potential or getting the attention they thought they deserved. Those who were available to "get some" got some in the best most beautiful way—consensually. They didn't have to pay for it, treat the other like dirt or objectify them.

There are ways for b-parties to engage in wild, story-worthy behavior and have everyone walk away with their self-decency intact. I've received my fair share of disastrous b-party phone calls weeping, "…I lost my license (can you FedEx my passport?)/all my money/cell phone/suitcase/I got kicked out of the hotel/I have third degree sun burns because I passed out by the pool/…but don't worry *I* wasn't the one who got put in the drunk tank." I've learned that, regardless of the tomfooleries, most partiers return home in roughly one piece wanting nothing more then a comforting hug and a lot of aspirin.

Sexual harassment is clearly one of those party kinks that can be kicked to the curb, but does that mean all sex-related activities need to get the boot too? Sex is a quintessential theme in b-parties, and I wonder if there is a healthy way, in the words of Justin Timberlake, "to get your sexy on?" I admit nothing stops a party in its tracks like questioning whether it's moral to stick a dollar bill in a thong, but everyone needs to ask it. How can anyone be sure patronizing a strip club or hiring a stripper isn't contributing to a dancer's underlying body image, substance abuse, or childhood trauma issues? Does the question unfairly generalize and stereotype a dancer's personal motivation for taking the job too? There's a lot of talk about the sex industry exploiting disenfranchised minorities, the poor, the young, and the uneducated. Are patrons just as guilty of this exploitation if they attend a cabaret? As a feminist, I'm stuck between my desire to make sure a bachelorette party enjoys the same festivities that bachelor parties enjoy and my feminist moral compass to stop the [male] gaze.[51] Is there a happy medium to this conflict? I realized it was dangerous to assume getting a stripper is part of the innocent fun, games, and tradition of a b-party. Not everything is as transparent as a dancer's Lucite heels.

Wanting to have a little element of the classic erotica for my own bachelorette, half of my b-party attended Las Vegas's *Thunder From Down Under* (think Channing Tatum and *Magic Mike* but Australian); the other half wanted a different type of stud and went to go see Jon Stewart (to each their own hottie I guess). Neither the *Thunder* nor Stewart offered any full-frontal entertainment, but the Abercrombie & Fitch-looking hunks (sorry, I'm not talking about you, Stewart) offered a chance to sit on their laps and take a $20 photo to send back home.

With the popularity of the *Magic Mike* movies, this type of entertainment has become wildly popular and a lot more mainstream. My best description of the crowd's reaction to the *Thunder* is when Roger Rabbit sees Jessica Rabbit for the first time: cue jaw hitting the floor, tongue rolling out, panting,

---

[51] *"The gaze" is both a feminist and art term, whereby the viewer (normally a man, though anyone can do it) uses their position of privilege and power to subvert the autonomy of the subject (normally a nude woman), which reduces them to an object and eliminates their sense of power and personhood.*

drooling, howling, and other Technicolor nonsense. It's easy to defend this behavior—everybody is doing it, so it must be okay. However, should I be worried that these men are someone's sons or fiancés?

I often feel like Roxanne Gay of *Bad Feminist,* who too often finds herself complicit with unhealthy social systems or cultures or does not always know where to draw the line regarding her participation in them. With such paradoxes and with polarizing feminist opinions (which is no help), I'm still stuck between lusting over flexed, Vaselined biceps and trying to comprehend that these Adonises might just want to talk about their feelings or the refugee crisis in Syria without someone shrieking, "Take it off!" For all I know, there might be one performer on stage who believes they are doing precisely what God put them on this earth for and love it. Despite my feminist brain grappling with how healthy this type of performance is—full confession—I admit there's something cathartic about throwing women's restrictive sexual decorum to the wind and cheering on a dancing dick-in-the-box to an overly choreographed dance paired to the music of ABBA. But am I as guilty as men who go to a strip club? Are the performances comparable in their adverse exploitative effects, or is there an important difference in women stripping compared to men? I haven't dug into all the research into the sex industry, so I can't say for sure. But for all my misgivings, I believe a silver lining in sexual entertainment exists.

I needed to explore other risqué forms of sexual entertainment to find out. Another bachelorette and I visited a famous Boston bar called Jacque's Cabaret, where drag queens dance and sing on stage. It's a lot of fun as the performers at Jacque's are great entertainers, but Jacque's patrons snuck gropes without permission, which is sexual harassment. Patrons were crossing the line of consent. Why? I can only guess it stems from a sense of entitlement and power, where people feel at liberty to take advantage of and objectify others they see as having no power or personhood. As much as I love the artistry of drag, as a non-drag-queen and with none in the audience, it started to become apparent that I was a tourist in their culture. I would be happier enjoying drag performances if the audience acted with more respect. I realized that the venue, style of entertainment, and behavior of the crowd helps determine how healthy a setting and performance is. On the other hand, the Broadway show *Kinky Boots* does a great job of humanizing and respecting drag queens while honoring the artistry and pizzazz that comes with size thirteen go-go boots. Drag performances are empowering and important.

Not wanting to cancel any b-parties, I needed to find a safe space for women (and men) to express their sexuality, to enjoy sexual performances, and in the process, not objectify or exploit anyone. I still had hope I'd find my silver lining. Turns out it was hidden behind a sequined thong and waiting eagerly to be revealed.

I believe a b-party's healthiest sex-tertainment lies in burlesque. Burlesque performances and personas are personally created and choreographed, not manufactured by silicon or stripper tropes, which is why it is considered an art form over traditional sex-tertainment. These elements give the performers a sense of sexual autonomy over their own bodies despite all the onlookers. Its all-body-types philosophy extends to men too, and since the audience is pan-gender, an all-inclusive burlesque show is one of the healthiest and positive sex-tertainment options for a b-party.[XXVI]

For my bachelorette, we also attended *Zumanity*, which is Cirque du Soleil's sexy, acrobatic, burlesque show. *Zumanity* embraces the body in all forms: cis, trans, drag, large, small, so on, and so on. We gazed upon a very diverse cast where I rooted for their beautiful stunts and artistry, unlike where in the *Thunder* we hooted at one male body type and/or part. At *Zumanity*, it was the first time I learned how truly athletic and gravity-defying pole dancing could be, as in…it should be an Olympic sport. And sure, there was a woman dressed as a Catholic schoolgirl, but the trite costume became a moot feature when you watched her perform. It wasn't about her breasts or butt, it was about figuring out how in the hell she managed to twirl suspended hundred feet in the air using only her neck and jaw. *Zumanity* brought sexual equality to the party and showed how sex-tertainment can avoid sexual objectification despite using many of the same tools.

My concern over the party politics is rooted in the idea that celebrations should be, not Martha Stewart party flawless, but parity flawless. Hosting a great party and being an even better host is not just about cake pops, signature drinks or goodie bags (unless Martha is baking a batch of chocolate dick pops or vajayjays, *then* she has my attention). It's about making sure everyone is treated with the dignity they deserve. There should be no sexism, harassment, gross consumerism, or exploitation sneaking in the back door like unwanted guests.

Do I have hope that women can wear whatever they want without harassment at a bachelorette party? You betcha. Do I have hope that I can find a way to watch and enjoy a sprayed-tanned body dancing to Ginuwine's *Pony* in a fireman hat twirling a hose? Absolutely. I just need to make sure that there's balance in the audience, on stage, and in the artistic nature of the performance. Do I have hope that I won't have to look for escape routes at these parties in case they turn out to be unhealthy ones? No, because realistically, ninjas could attack at any time.

Wedding-related parties tend to be more discriminating than a bouncer's guest list, but I don't want to be a party pooper, I swear. I want to lower the limbo bar while raising the equality bar. I don't want to show up to the dance and see the gym divided between girls and guys. Everyone should be dancing to Whitney with equal abandon. I want everyone to mix and feel free to be themselves without judgment, restrictive gender norms, or concerns over gluten allergies. The sign of a good host is making sure sexist party politics don't weigh down the celebratory atmosphere and making sure there are extra batteries on hand in case the penis tiara lights blow out. That's basic common courtesy and human kindness. When b-parties—bachelor *and* bachelorette—manage to honor everyone without sexist agenda and with respect, then I will be first to the party and last to leave.

Chapter 7
The Beleaguering of Bridesmaids

The first time I was a bridesmaid, I was sixteen and I didn't even know I was one. I thought I was showing up to become someone's godmother. As the ceremony droned on and the baby incessantly cried in my arms, actual adults thought it best to take the baby away from me. After a two-hour ceremony in a foreign language I didn't understand, everyone was in a bad mood. I thought it was my fault for failing to show the nurturing required of a godmother. Apparently, the parents failed to mention that the ceremony would double as a wedding too. It didn't resemble a classic white, Western wedding. I had no clue I was filling the role of bridesmaid too, which is kind of the one thing you need to know to be a successful one. It was technically the first time I failed at being a bridesmaid, and it would not be the last.

The responsibilities of the bridesmaid were established around the Middle Ages. The sorority has stood for centuries to safeguard the welfare of innocent virgin brides. Bridesmaids originally protected the bride from demons seeking to ruin the wedding. To deflect the bad juju, bridesmaids wore identical bridal garments to confuse the demons as a diversion.[52] Pippa Middleton, who dressed in white for her sister's wedding to Prince William, is a modern example of how this tradition works. Instead of letting audiences critique or sexualize her sister, she and her derrière stole the show and absorbed the blatant objectification instead.[53] Nothing says loyalty like when a

---

[52] *Flower girls and ring bearers dressed as miniature brides and grooms are fertility symbols. The use of small children in a wedding represents future children. The flower girl showering pedals is like a botanical, get-pregnant-now blessing. The [boy] ring bearer represents the patriarchal control over the consummation of the marriage by delivering the ring, the binding element of the marriage. (Seems less "cute" now, doesn't it?)*

[53] *For the most part, the twin look and superstition is out of fashion.*

bridesmaid is willing to create a diversion when you need to leave someone at the altar, cover up a nip slip during the bouquet toss or to not let the bride feel like a piece of meat for the [male] gaze. As a feminist, I love this sense of camaraderie and devotion bridesmaids exhibit. It's something I have loved and coveted years...that is, until I became one myself the second and third time around.

I'm twenty-four and a bridesmaid again. Now older, wiser, and no longer playing with my American Dolls, I had a better sense of my bridesmaid duties: buy a dress, organize a bachelorette party, and incorporate penis paraphernalia, give gifts, be in some pictures, stuff some potpourri into little gifts while drinking wine, and wish the newlyweds well.[54] Except no one had ever explained to me the subtle nuances of being a bridesmaid. No matter my intentions or effort, I never did anything well. I don't think my incompetence was only to blame, though. It might have been my subconscious feminist bride fighting against the old-fashioned gender roles bridesmaids are expected to fill.

Bridesmaids are expected to show up to everything: the bridal gown fitting sessions, the engagement party, rehearsal dinner, bachelorette party, and wedding shower. Then they're expected to pay for their own uniform[55] and beautification, be on call 24/7 in case of a mental breakdown, then cure said mental breakdown and keep their own to themselves (cuz nobody wants to add to the bride's stress level), and of course, be available for non-wedding-related events because the bride needs a break from it all. The list goes on forever. Is it all part of sisterly camaraderie and I'm incapable of being a team player?

Consider that groomsmen's responsibilities are much shorter than a bridesmaid's. They just need to pick up their tuxedos or suits (which are *rented*—no fair), throw an epic bachelor party with a stripper that doesn't look like the groom's mom, and show up for the wedding. Simple! Groomsmen aren't burdened with the expenses or emotional expectations that bridesmaids are, making it hard for groomsmen to disappoint a groom.

---

[54] *To put it into perspective, in 2016 it will cost $743 to be a wedding party member, but $893 if you are a Millennial (Source: Works Cited 9).*
[55] *Henry David Thoreau rightly stated, "Beware of all enterprises that require new clothes."*

Isn't that a double standard for two jobs that are held in equal esteem? My best theory to this gender divide is the idea that a wedding is "women's work," not for just the bride but for all her bosom buddies too.

In the beginning of my second bridesmaid tour of duty, I unintentionally committed small indiscretions. At the bridal shower while discussing world events, another bridesmaid scolded me saying I should be polite and pay more attention to the bride. When the bride ordered shoes on our behalf without consulting us, she yelled at me for letting her order the wrong color.[56] Apparently, this was my responsibility because I was the "artistic one." There was the time when I was at work unable to answer my phone. The bride panicked, calling twelve times in an hour about my bridesmaid dress. In hysterics now, she called her mother crying about my aloofness and disregard. Her mother decided the best course of action was to call my mother (who knew nothing of my whereabouts or this wedding) and scream about (and I'm paraphrasing here) how I was acting like a complete fuck-up for her daughter's wedding. Pretty fed up now, I called the bride to stand up for myself, but she laughed it all off saying it was an irrational bridezilla moment and "no big deal."

I support team bride (seriously, I do), but I worry respect in this sense is a one-way street. The current role of bridesmaids doesn't permit brides to account for modern women's lifestyles. Women have business meetings to attend, paychecks to cash, sports to play, and casual, guilt-free sex to have. They can't always lick invitation envelopes for the bride. Feminism granted women the freedom from domestic chores, so why do brides continue to expect bridesmaids to do them as a sign of friendship? And why are women's long-term friendships held to such unreasonable, short-term standards and rules, begging the post-wedding question, "...are you still friends with her?"

In what is still a painful omission, during my third run as a bridesmaid I got kicked out without warning. Right now, you are probably thinking, "She must have done something to get thrown out." Did I hit on or sleep with the groom? Barely met the guy. Did I sabotage her dress by releasing a litter of

---

[56] *When I asked if I could wear my own dress shoes to save money (which would be invisible under the long bridesmaid dress), the bride defensively replied, "Yeah...why is it a problem if we all wear the same shoes?" as if by asking, I was creating one.*

kittens and locking the door behind me? If I did, I would have stayed and watched and then shared that adorable video on YouTube. Or maybe, I disrespected her behind her back? No, but a few other people did and I got blamed for it (I make it a life policy that whatever I say about someone, I will always be okay saying it to his or her face). Without having violated the most obvious transgressions, I was a little shocked, a little ashamed, but mostly stunned by this unexpected, harsh verdict. I asked why and she replied, after fifteen years of friendship, "I don't have to justify my decision."

And that's when I lost my fucking shit.

Looking back, there were sequences of small and petty infractions: not being able to make it to any parties (I was living on the other side of the country, and I *was* budgeting to fly back for the actual event); forgetting she was waiting for me in a bar for a non-wedding-related group activity (a complete accident that I spent months apologizing for); being concerned she went from an emotionally abusive relationship straight into an engagement with a new beau six months later (many were apprehensive, but I openly questioned the speed of her romance out of concern); or accidentally giving away some expired museum tickets in a bridal shower raffle (which I didn't replace before she kicked me out, and I regret it to this day). I would not describe it as a lack of trying or purposeful disruption, but more a result of my burdensome talent of being the perfectly imperfect bridesmaid. Apparently, she ignored my initial disclaimer that I am horrible at weddings.

In retrospect though, without knowing her real reasons, I think it came down to her needing to feel important and validated in her decision to get married, and I was not fulfilling that need. I just wasn't aware that whether I bought custom satin shoes within her set timeframe would reflect on the quality of our friendship or send the message that I didn't care about her as a person. My inability to read minds or assess the situation in real time has hurt me significantly as a bridesmaid. I can't elaborate on how many times I got in trouble because I heard "optional service" like make up and hair; no one bothered to tell me optional meant "just do it."

It's true that feminism's core is about support, empathy, and teamwork, but I worry that there's something insidious in bridesmaid culture that nullifies this unifying aspect. Solidarity and devotion through consumerist practices or yes-man attitudes cannot be the degree to which women should judge the value, sincerity, and importance of friendship. Had the bride verbally expressed her *true* needs and given me a straightforward warning to shape up or ship out, I would have heeded it because even if I didn't care for the orange dress she selected, I still care about her and her future happiness. No friendship should face the guillotine without any communication and attempt at understanding first. Had the bride and I behaved and communicated better, we might have salvaged our friendship, if not ended it amicably. Though, I'll argue the culture of unreasonable expectations placed on bridesmaids, sense of bridal entitlement, and our ignorance of that culture at the time, prevented that.

I bet you're wondering how hurt feelings, attention needs, and failed expectations of friendships relate to feminism. Women were once limited to the domestic role of wife and mother. These roles expected them to help others before themselves. I'll argue that the current expectation of a bridesmaid is the same—bride before self. Except that feminism has modernized the role of wife and mother. Each can now go out and become part of the labor force without judgment, and any judgment for putting career first or balancing one with a family is now considered sexist. That's not the case within this strange world of bridesmaid culture. There was always resentment when work or a higher priority prevented me from showing up to a bridal event or being available at a moment's notice.

Small infractions can seem like a moot issue when looking at things objectively, but there's an undercurrent of ambivalent sexism at work here.[57] Being a bridesmaid is considered a position of high honor and emotional importance, so when a bridesmaid goes along with the role, she is emotionally rewarded by the bride (benevolent sexism); but when she fails to meet those unspoken expectations because of her own busy lifestyle, she is emotionally punished (hostile sexism). While I'm willing to own my mistakes (and there were many), it's clear that, even though I was just living my life and being myself, I was failing at being a bridesmaid because of ambivalent sexism.

Yes, it is possible to be sexist against your own sex. Let's call this concept intragroup sexism, and a woman who believes and acts with bias toward other

---

[57] *Quick reminder: ambivalent sexism is an umbrella term for benevolent and hostile sexism. It helps to frame the dichotomies and spectrums where sexism occurs.*

women is a misorolist.[58] Women are absolutely capable of holding their own gendered prejudice toward their own sex. And I bet most of these attitudes or belief systems are subconsciously ingrained, normalized, or aren't interpreted as bad if the woman committing intragroup sexism is comfortable treating herself with those same values. I believe this is an important realization to have if women want to be treated as equals. Equality is not just something to be earned between the different sexes; it also needs to be achieved internally among peers too.

As you can imagine, if I could reform this age-old appointment, I would completely abolish it. I'd throw it out along with products painted pink to appeal to women. I'd at least severely cut down the number of bridesmaids to one or two, with one position going to a beloved pet. Doing so would help dismantle the Wedding Industrial Complex more and intragroup ambivalent sexism...plus I'd probably have a few more friends. At the very least, I would break the ties of the wedding as women's work so bridesmaids weren't held to the outdated expectations of their gender that conflict with their modern lifestyles. If the groomsmen can get out of baking cakes for the shower or writing out name cards, why can't the bridesmaids? If the fiancés can't manage the synchronized kiss and dove release or the customized centerpieces, then it's time to scale back or hire a wedding coordinator. Bridesmaids, like groomsmen, are there for mental and emotional support. Their role is ceremonial and celebratory; bridesmaids are not obligated to bag candy-covered pretzels for someone else's shower because it's sentimental to the bride. They can do that out of courtesy and kindness, but not because of roles bestowed upon them on account of their gender.

And if you're not convinced of any of this, here is my gratuitous story from my second bridesmaid stint. It's proof that bridesmaids are held to unreasonable standards, which forces them to do insane shit.

It's midnight and I'm returning home from the bride's rehearsal dinner. The end of my misery is in sight; my remaining duties for tomorrow include arriving at the mother of the bride's house at 10 a.m. with my bridesmaid

---

[58] Mis *is Greek for hate and a prefix meaning badly or wrongly (think* misogynist: *men who hate women;* misandrist: *women who hate men; and* misrepresent). Sororal *is relating to or like a sister(s) (think* sorority). *Pronounced: "mis-sor-rol-ist" (Source: Works Cited 10).*

dress and a good attitude. My boyfriend's car, which I'd borrowed, starts lurching and stalling. It agonizes its way into my underground garage parking spot and hisses as it shuts off. Unbeknownst to me, the car is the least of my problems.

Trying to enter my condo building, I realize my house keys have fallen off my key chain and all spares happen to be with people who are on vacation. This is a huge problem because my bridesmaid dress is locked inside my condo. At this point, a rational person might call a locksmith or, say, walk a block down the street to the fire station, but oh no, I'm thinking like a totally exhausted and totally stressed person, who accidentally peed on herself earlier in the day (you'll read about this later). Failure, I decide, is not an option.

I must find a way in. I must retrieve the dress.

I walk over to the patio, praying a window is open or the back door unlocked. Nothing. Panic now starts to replace my dread. Then I notice it—a window cracked open about two inches. The problem is this window is four feet off the patio rail with a twenty-foot drop below it onto asphalt. I manage to rip the window screen off and it crashes onto the pavement.

I retrieve a broom from the shed and use it to pry the window open using both scientific lever methods and caveman smashing. It opens to about a foot and a half. To get into the window, there's a small, square, tin light right below it that needs to support all 148 pounds of me. I am also wearing a small cocktail dress. The dress is so tight and inflexible that in order to acrobatically reach the flimsy light box, I have to pull the dress above my waist. And it so happens that underneath, I'm wearing a thong. If I fall, the best case scenario is a broken ankle, worst case scenario is that tomorrow's newspaper headline will read, "Pantsless Perpetrator Falls to Naked Death." Any outcome, I decide, is worth proving to the bride that I am not a horrible bridesmaid.

I pull myself onto my patio railing Humpty-Dumpty style, bum cheeks glistening in the moonlight for all of my city neighbors to see. The plan is to reach the tin box with my foot closest to the wall, grab the nearest window frame with my opposite hand, and pivot myself into the opening swiftly. In my thong underwear, I straddle the side of the building and, in one fluid motion, pirouette into the window Spider Man-style.

Waking up at dawn, I grab my bridesmaid dress and take the car (which decided to take pity on me and come back to life) back to the rehearsal dinner restaurant an hour away. There in the parking lot, glittering in the sun, are my house keys.

I arrive at the mother of the bride's house by 10 a.m., as I had been told to do, only to be nonchalantly told, "Oh, you didn't have to come so early. Feel free to go home and kill some time." I respectfully decline without explaining the miracle it took to get me to her house. I refuse to leave and politely sit in the corner painting my nails waiting until everyone else arrived.

I went into this wedding and my bridesmaid duties optimistic, but I ended up desperate, pantsless, urine-soaked, and disenchanted instead. I learned the art of wedding survival, discovered intragroup sexism, and realized I will go out on a limb, literally, to not be a terrible bridesmaid. However, even these important life lessons weren't enough to fix this sisterhood.

When I examined the etymology and root structure of the word itself, I discovered even more sex discrimination. Most people think the difference between a *bridesmaid* and *matron of honor* is marriage, but the difference is based on sexual activity. A *maid* of the domestic, renaissance fair, or fairytale kind is presumably a virgin because she is unmarried. Whereas a *matron* is not because she is married and historical and social convention dictates that sex should only happen within marriage. Most people these days aren't the big "V" past the age of eighteen, so calling someone *maid* is a huge misnomer.

Linguistically, *bridesmaid* is an inaccurate mess and sexist double standard that should drive grammar nerds and feminist fiancés equally batty. Wedding party labels are another example of how a woman's identity and value is defined by her sexual status and a man's is not. The coveted title of *bridesmaid* implies significance and friendship, but creating distinctions that are contingent on a woman's sexual experience hurts women's equality in the long run. It's a dangerous precedent because most use the sexist terminology freely without a second thought. Over time, people become desensitized to the impact of its meaning, but they aren't immune to its sexist content. That's how I know I'm on team sisterhood; I don't want anyone within it to be treated unjustly. I think women deserve to be treated better and with more respect.

Comparatively, the label of *groomsman*[59] has nothing to do with a man's sexual experience. The root of *groom* is German for male child. The name is devoid of a man's sexual standing. The 19th century etymology of *groomsman* is a "male servant who attends to horses."[60] The term might have originated as early as Anglo-Saxon times when the *bridegroom* may have kidnapped an eligible maiden (i.e., unmarried virgin) from the village yonder and "consummated" (i.e., raped) the marriage with the "bride" to make it binding. As this happened, the *groomsmen* tended the horses and kept a lookout. Gives new meaning to *best man*, huh?[61]

As a deep-seated tradition, it felt natural to call the women standing by my side *bridesmaids*. It never dawned on me that I was calling my wedding party by labels that were sexist and unfair. Now that I know better, I wish I showed them more respect with a better title like my "best ladies," but even that jargon is problematic.[62] People keep gender fluid and crotch-diverse friends these days. If a fiancé wants to form a wedding entourage, why not give the members titles that don't highlight their sexual status or gender and can be used ubiquitously across all parties, like wedding crew, "altar ego," or best mate.[63] [64]

There are many feminist opportunities to improve the role of an altar ego.

---

[59] *A groomsman might also be called a bridal knight, an usher, and a swordsman of the sword honor guard (in military weddings).*

[60] *And as a fun wedding horse fact, there is a Hindu wedding tradition called the Baraat where the groom travels to the wedding venue on a horse.*

[61] *This is also one theory about where the term "honeymoon" originates. The bridegroom would keep the kidnapped bride hidden for one month or one full moon.*

[62] *Scholar Robin Lakoff studied the term* lady *in 1975. She saw the use of it as problematic because it implied a specific type of feminine behavior. Behavior, I would argue, that fits within the terms of benevolent sexism. She also believed it infantilized a woman (like calling her a* girl*) despite her age, accomplishments and maturity.*

[63] *I am going to refer to a bridesmaid or groomsmen as an altar ego when used with egalitarian practices (the term also fits their original purpose, which was to deflect bad juju by looking like the bride). If the practice is still based in sexism, I will use the traditional terms.*

[64] *I would also like to point out that even the terms bride and groom are troublesome because they are for people who fit into gender binaries. I suppose non-binary, gender-fluid folks could use fiancé, newlywed or beloved, but there's no dictionary-accepted term to replace bride or groom for gender non-conforming folks.*

Unfortunately for me, I learned the hard way, but I learned an altar ego's purpose is not to make the bride look better by looking worse themselves (a theme I see way too often on WE TV's *Bridezilla*) or to blindly agree because there is such a thing as too much tulle. When I was in wedding parties that embraced more feminist expectations, being an altar ego was more rewarding, enjoyable, and less stressful. However, since many brides still embrace the traditional bridesmaid role, I will think long and hard before ever agreeing to such a position again; for my sanity's, wallet's and pride's sake; and for my neighbors who don't want to see my bare ass in the moonlight again.

Today, I aim to make an altar ego's official wedding role a supportive one. Ceremonially, the position should stand as a witness to a love united; supportively, as a supplier of tissues to catch rogue tears; sensibly, as a reality check when a bride or groom wants their altar egos to wear fluorescent green attire; and festively, as a dance coach to encourage them to dance like no one is watching even though everyone is. When the sexism and consumerism are removed from the bridesmaid job description, I will be the best altar ego ever.

Chapter 8

Vanity Affairs and
the Other Revlon Revolution

I would not describe myself as a makeup girl. My everyday look includes some cheap-ass eye shadow and mascara. For special occasions—parties, date nights, puffy post-crying days—I might go the face paint distance just short of a classy clown. Though I would never call myself makeup savvy or superficial per se, considering I learned makeup application from a Mary Kay party when I was thirteen. For my own nuptials, however, pressured by the beautiful magazine brides and the unspoken societal pressure to make the day flawless, I assumed my regular everyday practices were not good enough for such an important occasion.

To up my game, I hired a professional makeup artist from the trusty internet. I swallowed my frugal pride that I would have to pay her a $50 consultation to *maybe* hire her later for another $150 plus tip. She was a nice, Jersey Shore-ish lady with a wicked Boston accent. The application was pretty, but it wasn't for a wedding occasion. I looked like the daughter of George Hamilton and Jem from *Jem from the Holograms*.[65] I also felt uncomfortable when I didn't recognize myself in the mirror. I decided, why hand over a job I could do myself? After all, I had a masters in studio art and painting. Isn't makeup application nothing more than face painting?

Confident my cheap makeup wouldn't last the full day of tears and sweat that comes with a wedding, I found myself at my local department store for a product upgrade. There I got a free consultation with a $50 product purchase and a lesson on how to use my new swag. Seemed like a win to me. With my

---

[65] Jem *is a '80s cartoon that looked like a prostitute in the movie* Pretty Woman *with metallic hair.*

mother for moral makeup support and guidance after the 1980s cartoon debacle, the next consultant was an unmarried, early twenty-something man with blue eyeliner, a soft David Beckam faux-hawk, and gauged-ears. Sitting in a director's chair, he applied a final wisp of makeup, pointed across the large department store aisle to another counter and said, "Why don't you get up and take a look in the mirror over there?"

In the midst of getting up, my pant leg caught the footrest of the director's chair. I jumped a few times trying to catch my balance, but it was no use. In what seemed like painful slow motion, both the chair and I flew to the floor in a perfectly executed but very violent belly flop. On the floor, against all rules of physics, I somehow started penguin belly sliding across the aisle toward the L'Oreal counter. Sprawled across the aisle like a crime scene victim outline, I took a moment to collect myself on the floor before getting up. My instincts told me to start laughing, to play the whole thing off, but when I got to my feet the look of horror and pity from both the emo-punk salesperson and my mother immediately negated my preplanned brush off. Both just stood and stared wide-eyed in silence not knowing how to respond.

Despite feeling severely humbled with a considerable bloody gash on my shin from the chair, my makeup looked flawless. If it could survive one of my worst public embarrassments, it was good enough for the big day. I ended up buying about $180 worth of makeup, $130 past my required purchase. I paid way past anything I had budgeted for or ever spent on makeup in my lifetime. Maybe it was my inner glam goddess saying, "You definitely deserve something nice now," or maybe I was compensating for one of my worst public embarrassments. Maybe it was as simple as me joining the centuries of women before me who also played into others' ridiculous beauty standards. But as a feminist, I wondered where my true makeup motivations truly came from.

From Cleopatra with her luring eyes to Marilyn Monroe with her come hither look, women have always sought ways to embody the perfect image of a woman based on the subjectivity of the time in which they lived. The path to perfection was a wayward one, as ladies started with burned matches to darken the eyes, squeezed red berries for lipstick, applied young boys' urine to fade their freckles and swallowed ox blood to improve their complexions. The history of makeup and its application is gruesome, not because most ancient products were laced with arsenic, but because women painted their faces for centuries just to ensnare a spouse.

Like the popularity of blue glitter eye shadow, makeup's value in society changed over time, but it always controlled and pressured women to fit specific tastes and moralities and cast out those who did not fit the standard. In the Victorian era, makeup conjured images of prostitutes and actresses, an unfit look for a prospective bride and someone's future wife. Instead, Victorians focused on other ridiculous forms of perfection, like eighteen-inch, corseted waistlines, perfectly coiffed hair, long skirts to hide lustful ankles, and a nice rump courtesy of a skirt hoop. To get that fresh and rosy look against a white complexion, ladies pinched their cheeks, and acted like a vampire by staying out of the sun.

Even beauty companies in the 1930s advertised tools that would achieve the perfect wedding look. Their ads and advice mimicked the strategies of De Beers and department store registries. Emily Post, Godey's Lady's Book, "how-to" books and other wedding media reinforced the idea that beautification practices and products would ensure happiness, love, and sweet memories at the altar. They touted that uncovered blemishes, frizzy hair, and yellowish teeth marred the day's events, memories, and the photos that would last a lifetime. The beauty bar has set moving targets throughout history.

Today's makeup promotes a new ideal: a sunkissed glow, skin that looks like it bathes daily in the fountain of youth, augmented fuller lips, Nicki Minaj's booty, or Kate Upton's cleavage. Women still try to embody what they perceive to be the ideal woman. It's not just about blinding a potential partner with a brighter-than-the-sun teeth whitening job and carrying them back to the woman cave. It's unfortunately become about meeting impossible beauty standards purported by beauty product companies that tell women they'll find bridal perfection through artificial, store-bought enhancements and not their own natural look. And this bridal beautification regime is as ingrained as that errant hair the electrolysis ad wants you to remove before the big day.

I've fallen prey to this Wedding Beauty Complex. During my second bridesmaid adventure, I found myself in the mother of the bride's bathroom hours before a wedding with a few other bridesmaids fixing our hair like it was prom 2000. From magazines and the internet, I was under the impression a proper bridal hairdo includes a massive curly up-do, except I had no clue *how* to do this with my new Dora the Explorer haircut.

Working with a curling iron that was too large for my short locks and about a half bottle of hairspray, I ended up searing my neck just hours before the ceremony. At first, the profanity I screamed seemed worse than the three-by-one-inch burn on my neck. The makeup artist (I didn't pay for) came to my rescue. Not for medical attention, but to cover it up with some foundation so it wasn't visible in the pictures. Not wanting to alert the bride, I whispered to the other bridesmaids that it f#%$@king hurt.[66] By some stroke of luck, the burn didn't rear its puss-seeping, swollen head until the next day, but I spent the next three months explaining to my coworkers and other associates that it wasn't a hickey.

The burning lesson here is not to hire a professional next time, but to say damn those industry standards that pressure me and anyone else into thinking that women have to look better than what they already do or fit into something they are not. That, and I shouldn't use so much hairspray next time.

My scars prove that women can go to great physical, financial, and time lengths to achieve what they perceive as their best self. People hire a trainer to get rid of flabby arms, dye their hair, go to the spa, get their nails done, pluck hair in unwanted places, and then add hair to all the right ones. I've known women to undergo teeth straightening, teeth whitening, and laser eye surgery just because it's their wedding. Then there are the smaller items: makeup, hair, nails. And don't forget the spray tan that created more than one Oompa Loompa bride in its time. The list of embellishments is endless.

Even expensive photographers with exceptional Photoshop skills are hired to catch and hide any lingering flaws. Unfortunate zit on your special day? No worries, we'll digitally cover that up. Is that a booger? We can edit that out too. Have a little nip slip during the cocktail hour? We'll just cut and paste it onto the bridesmaid next to you instead. That's what she's there for, right? Photographers cost a pretty penny, so you're damn right I'm also going to pose as if it's for an issue of *Vogue*.

In college, I worked as a server at a million dollar wedding (they belonged to one of the Industrial Revolution family magnates). I was the third person assigned to cater to the bride's every whim and want; the other two included a

---

[66] *Oh, there are even more disasters coming.*

hair stylist and makeup artist. Their job was to make sure she looked perfect throughout the entire day. My job was to make sure the Cristal flowed, but not to over-serve her. I was at odds as to whether this bride was being superficial by having a 24/7 beauty squad at her beck and call. Was it okay because she had the money to do so, or was she just another schmo caught in an unhealthy body image, consumerist society made worse by her Daddy Warbucks? Is she setting an unfair precedent with her unlimited resources by implying women need a team to keep them aesthetically perfect? Besides, a glamazon entourage wasn't coddling her groom.

And there's my smoking gun, err, overcooked perm job: how the different sexes treat wedding beauty. Beautification can seem like just another delightful tradition that pampers the bride and her companions on their little pedestal, but it's not legitimate wedding culture. It is consumer culture disguised behind a smoky eye look, and it's obvious that this culture has cultivated vastly unequal practices for both men and women. Wedding beauty standards are nothing more than double standards imposed only on women. Men aren't forced into this superficial box the same way women are. To look their prettiest for a wedding, most men go only as far as the three S's: shit, shower, and shave. Of course there are exceptions. Perhaps a man might try to lose some weight, get a haircut, and wax that back hair for the wedding night. The most vain comment I heard from a guy was, "Gotta get married before I go bald, you know, for the pictures."

And of course a woman can be a feminist and love makeup, but there's a distinct gender issue when a groom's beauty is not affected by or targeted by industry experts the same way a bride is. To be fair, I understand the desire to look and feel one's best for a wedding, the need to knock 'em dead walking down the aisle or melt their partner on the wedding night. I wanted to look my best too. Tina Fey makes a great point in her book *Bossypants* about industry-pushed editorial beauty versus the power of feminist-inspired photo shoots, which take "a photo as if you were caught on your best day in the best light." Isn't that the best anyone can ask for? Then why is it that the wedding industry creates this unspoken pressure on women to be better than their best self on their best day? It's ludicrous that wedding culture makes people believe their bodies aren't good enough for just one day.

Bridal beauty concerns are more than just skin deep. In fact, there's also pressure to be perfect underneath the surface (i.e., muscles and fat) too. The pressure to not be pear-shaped can come from all sides; wedding media is particularly brutal. VH1 aired a reality contest show called *Bridal Bootcamp* (2010). In a tacky summer camp setting, "overweight" girls competed to "fit into their dream dress" by exercising on obstacle courses. The girl who lost the most weight won. Now, I have two issues with this show: First, a dream dress is not size-exclusive. Second, some of the girls were not overweight. Perhaps they were out of shape, but a size 10 or 12, as they were, is not necessarily overweight. What type of message does it send to viewers when a contestant's *beginning* weight is a mere 140 and size 8?

Even worse was the E! TV show *Bridalplasty* (2010), where brides competed for plastic surgery and their dream wedding. It's similar to a former reality show called *The Swan* (2004), where "ugly ducklings" underwent the knife to become beautiful "swans" and compete in a beauty pageant. Just like in *Bridal Boot Camp,* these contestants constantly used the "p" word in relation to their wedding and selves—perfection. None of these women suffered from regretful face tattoos. They were beautiful before the surgery. The show teaches women and brides that wedding perfection is achieved with plastic surgery, not healthy eating, exercise, or an appreciation for their natural beauty, or heaven forbid, what's inside their minds or hearts.

These unhealthy messages are not limited to reality show contestants either; peers can do just as much damage. In the WE network television series *Bridezillas*, it's common to hear a bridezilla demand that her bridesmaids go on diets or even not diet (so the bride could look skinnier beside them). In a personal instance, a bridal shop accused a fellow bridesmaid of "growing" three-inches in the month between her fittings. The shop owner preferred to hurt her feelings rather then admit they wrote her measurements down wrong. If you ask me, the wedding industry needs a bridal Revlon Revolution that includes more body positivity.

With bridal shops' standard sample gown being a size 6 or 8 to 12 and the average size of U.S. women being a 16,[XXVII] I imagine trying on dresses is not everyone's cup of tea. It gets more uncomfortable with the very public presentation of it, where brides step up on the pedestal inside the 360 degree mirror and receive a range of criticism from "that doesn't look good" to "it does nothing for your figure." It's a daunting process. And most brides need help getting into and out of dresses. My poor sister had to witness my Pooh-Bear-like indignity when my head got stuck in the bodice while my ass helplessly hung out the back.

There's also tons of pressure within the wedding industry and media to fit into a wedding dress three sizes smaller than your regular size despite the fact that a wedding dress can be ordered in any size. And there are plenty of other clothing apparatuses to turn one's silhouette into your cartoon doppelganger. Not feeling voluptuous enough? Why not make the priest blush during the ceremony with chicken cutlets stuffed into a bra for chin-tapping cleavage? Got a gut? Spanx will mush it all inside. Mind you though, if you drop the wedding band during the ceremony it will be easier to just walk away from the whole thing than to pick it up. It's outrageous that wedding diets dictate eating and exercising to look pretty over being healthy, it's as ridiculous as Emily Blunt in the *Devil Wears Prada* (2006), who celebrates that she's one stomach flu away from her goal weight.

I usually hover around a size 8 or 10 and I tend to have an athletic and muscular build. My body's happy weight is 148. I generally don't obsess with the scale, but I can get moody about fitness, firmness, and cellulite. Regardless, I think it is empowering to shout out what you weigh. For me, I think telling someone helps removes the fear or stigma over scale numbers. Think about how powerful it was when Amy Schumer declared, "I'm like, 160 pounds right now and I can catch a dick...whenever I want." It's hard to find such examples of body positivity and pride in wedding media, let alone body or even demographic diversity. Most wedding trade publications feature models or newlyweds that fall within white, hetero and low body mass index (BMI) characteristics. Intersectional feminism and Roxanne Gay's *Bad Feminist* reminded me that it's important to explore other perspectives, too, to understand how we can treat our own bodies and other people's better. Maybe if fashion and health services created an environment where people felt comfortable owning their size instead of encouraging them to distance themselves from it, business and industry leaders would listen to the needs of their clientele and accommodate them better.

A few weeks before my own wedding, I booked a massage to relax and forget about wedding planning woes. The goal: feel good about myself. As I was leaving the massage parlor in my Zen zone, the masseuse unexpectedly stopped me, grabbed my shoulders, and shoved them backward, "If you want to take good wedding photos, you need to do something about your hunchback." Now not only did this unsolicited advice kill my Zen, but it also gave me a savage urge to give this masseuse the most painful wedgie he's ever experienced. I know he saw this as constructive criticism, but it loses its helpfulness when it's uninvited advice out of left field, and weeks before my wedding. No number of yoga classes would reverse my Quasimodo look in time. Now I possessed a new problem to feel self-conscious about. I understand weddings are important, but what good is cutting people down in order to reach this idea of perfection?

To prepare for my own wedding, I hit the streets to run off those "extra pounds." But I abruptly stopped running in what I describe as my Forrest-Gump-running-epiphany. I was done running. I was tired. Tired of thinking and being told that I wasn't good enough for my wedding day. I walked home, cracked a beer, and shared my revelation with my fiancé.

"So you are never going to exercise again?" he asked.

"No, no, but I'm done running for the wedding. I'll go back to running tomorrow, but this time it will be for me, my health, not some ridiculous, nonspecific, short-term idea of who I should be."

The next day, I ran faster, longer, and with more invigoration and reward. And I kept running well after my wedding day.

The relationship between brides, makeup, and exercise is about as complex as putting on those self-adhesive fake eyelashes. So can a bride find a balance between enjoying the thrills of a bikini wax and her natural, sunkissed look? My personal opinion is that it's possible, but it's not easy. I will admit having someone replicate your everyday look (if not do it better) on an anxiety-ridden day is very relaxing and one less thing to think about.[67] But I knew not to get sucked into this Wedding Beauty Complex. I needed to possess the wherewithal to either rise above it or accept pube monogramming as the next hair trend.

---

[67] *I did get my nails done with my family the day before my wedding, and that quiet moment sitting in a massage chair was heaven for my nerves. And besides, that makeup professional is just someone trying to support themselves while doing something she or he loves, and not everyone can say that about their paycheck.*

I want others to find the courage to ignore the unachievable beauty standard perpetuated by ad campaigns and wedding media that also exclude men and diverse people from their ad pages. Women can love makeup and call themselves feminist; although, beware of using choice feminism as makeup justification, as all choice is dangerously preconditioned. Overall, feminists nowadays don't discriminate against those who like to have their nails done and their hair done, but they do tend to be less understanding toward those pumped with so much Botox that they can't smile.

Most people marry for someone's internal beauty, not for a number on the scale. So I propose an alternative thought process toward physically preparing for the big day. Don't think in terms of diet and weight loss—think in terms of healthy living. Couples vow "to love in sickness and in health," but diets only fulfill short-term goals. A healthy lifestyle can reduce the chance of sickness and stress and theoretically add years to a lifespan. I want to love and live in health (and not sickness) for as long as I can. Still not convinced to skip the crash diet? Consider that true fitness will allow anyone to dance longer on the dance floor and when dancing the horizontal polka on the honeymoon.

No matter if the bride is a size 6 or a 26, people will be telling her how amazing she looks. A wedding is considered one of the best days of a couple's life because they're committing to someone they love. A diet will not achieve that natural glow like good self-esteem. Diets are temporary and weddings last a single day. Couples should live healthy in the long-term, for each other and for themselves. By the end of my wedding day none of my makeup remained on my face anyway. My eyeliner was smudged, my lipstick was smeared on a wine glass, my foundation was kissed away by my new spouse, and after all the dancing, my hair looked like I wrestled a kangaroo. None of that mattered because I was having a fabulous time at my wedding. I was beautiful because I was happy.

Chapter 9
Unveiling the Sheer Sexism of the Wedding Dress and Veil

I am not a nudist. This indisputable fact means I have to wear something down the aisle. As a connoisseur of Disney princess movies and the *Father of the Bride* movies, deciding on what to wear was a no brainer—I would wear a white wedding dress. It seemed like such an obvious choice that it never occurred to me to want to wear anything else. It didn't help that the Wedding Industry Complex had been dangling this white whale in front of me for decades. My hunger and lust for it bordered on Captain Ahab's own monomaniacal fanaticism. And what better way than to feed that irrational desire for yards of white satin and lace than by denying me the privilege and approval to wear white most of the year? Fashion, class, and gendered tradition dictated that I couldn't wear white in the cold months between Labor Day and Memorial Day, when it's raining, when my Aunt Flo is in town, and when I'm consuming copious amounts of red foods like spaghetti Bolognese, beets, or red wine (okay, this latter part is reasonable). If a small window, like getting married, opened allowing me to wear white, you're damn right I was going to seize the moment.

It almost felt like a feminist decision to wear white since so many other feminist decisions and actions are predicated on what's typically denied me due to my gender. Or could it be that I was exercising choice feminism to justify what I wanted while ignoring some nasty social politics behind all those soft layers of fabric? I wasn't sure, but like Ahab, I couldn't resist the urge to follow and capture this white whale. The question became, why in the hell was I so captivated by this colorless, overpriced, impractical, short-term outfit, and why did so many other brides feel the same? I think it comes down to the fact that the wedding dress will be the fanciest attire most of us will ever wear. Few of us will attend the Oscars, the Met Ball, or a White House Inaugural Ball,[68] so it's very tempting to go all out and indulge in this fashion tradition. Before I took aim at my white whale, I did stop to consider whether it and its accessories were tied to any unfair sexual standards, biases, or purchasing habits.

Before Queen Victoria's nuptials, brides simply wore their best, most versatile dress. Women only owned a few dresses, and in an era sans dry cleaning, white was not a practical color. Then all fashion hell broke loose when Queen Victoria wore a white gown for her wedding in 1840. She created a royal pain in the ass fairytale fantasy that has persisted to today. Overnight, white became en vogue and a symbol of wealth and class. The color white was not only a luxury that the upper class could afford or used as a fashion manipulation tool to keep out new money and social climbers from their small, intimate circle of old money though. It was symbol to promote for unfair sex and racial politics.

The white wedding gown also asserted the idea of sexual and moral decorum and cleanliness. Christianity related the color white with purity (e.g., virginity and cleansed of sin) and being close to God. It also functioned as a tool for literally Western, white colonialism. For example, Christian missionaries spread their religion and the importance of marriage to non-Caucasians. They used the white wedding gown as emotional, spiritual and class bait by associating it with values of purity (virginity), cleanliness, and morality. And then they harshly judged those who did not adhere to its edict or wore non-white for such occasions. To be cleansed and granted this white privilege with their new white friends, new recruits had to convert. It was a clever way to create desire for the privilege of wearing white during baptism, confirmation, or a non-secular wedding. As a result, non-white wedding dress colors became a fashion faux pas and were only appropriate for sullied, promiscuous heathens and the classless. Not a virgin on your wedding day? No white dress for you. Even today, repeat brides tend to opt for a non-white dress or a subdued version due to their experience in the boudoir. Take for instance, Reese Witherspoon who remarried in pink.

A bridal epigram, along with support from *Godey's Lady's Book* and other

---

[68] *I'm still waiting on my invite to all of those.*

industry experts, reinforced these biased stereotypes around wedding dress hues: *Married in white, you will have chosen all right. Married in grey, you will go far away. Married in black, you will wish yourself back. Married in red, you'll wish yourself dead. Married in blue, you will always be true. Married in pearl, you'll live in a whirl. Married in green, ashamed to be seen, Married in yellow, ashamed of the fellow. Married in brown, you'll live out of town. Married in pink, your spirits will sink.*

Today, times have changed. Most brides wear white, but most brides are also not virgins (95 percent in fact).[XXVIII] Is it possible that these white-wearing brides are just liars, or could it be possible that this wedding tradition has modernized itself? As someone who wore white, and well—stop reading this immediately, Mom and Dad, and skip to the next page—was part of that 95 percent, I (courtesy of the Wedding Industrial Complex) wanted to look and feel like a bride by wearing the classic white dress. I didn't feel like the white dress was accounting for my sexual status and, therefore, my intrinsic value, but I'm aware in some U.S. and global communities it does.[69]

I think outside observers hold the most power to modernizing the white wedding dress tradition so it doesn't judge a women's value on her sexual status. I definitely can recall moments when, long before the birth of my website *TheFeministBride.com*, I threw shade by asking what color dress the bride was wearing and responding with a snotty, "Oh, really?" I regret the unfairness and cruelty of those comments, and I regret perpetuating the double standard. No one judges a groom's sexual experience via his wedding clothing. In this day and age, it's just ridiculous that a uniform should indicate whether a bride's hymen is broken.

I'm all for dethroning the white wedding dress and increasing understanding and acceptance of different ethnic traditions too. For example, Chinese women wear a *qi pao*, which is red for good luck. Indian women wear a *lengha* that is a shade of pink, red, orange, or yellow. My Indian friend explained Indian culture comes with its own wedding color etiquette. "White is worn at funerals and a no-no for weddings. Black is basically forbidden, and darker colors such as blues and greens are frowned upon as primary colors for wedding outfits."

---

[69] *I'll admit that feeling exempt from this social context is part of my demographic privilege.*

Breaking traditional Western color threads is not so easy though. When it was time for one of my altar egos to get married, she found the white wedding dress too conventional and not to her taste. Much to her dismay, she struggled to find a suitable dress that didn't look like a prom dress. What was worse is that not everyone was on board with her idea, which worsened her shopping and wedding planning experience. Pressured by her naysayers and limited clothing racks, she compromised and bought a sheath cut blue dress covered by antique white lace and a matching blue waist ribbon. Everyone loved the dress and the naysayers were astounded at how a wedding dress didn't have to be all white to capture the moment or make a bride.

Queen of bridal couture, Vera Wang also understood the need to move past the white dress and showcased a black and nude wedding collection in the fall of 2012. Initially, pessimists equated the collection with a fancy funeral and Morticia Adams, but as the collection rolled out on the runway, concerns over the morbid dresses dissipated as the audience became enamored with their show-stopping beauty. Vera Wang proved that even if a bride walked down the aisle in black or nude, she could still steal the show. The entire collection became a pièce de résistance of traditional bridal culture, though it still arguably fit within traditional hetero wedding culture.

It was Betsey Johnson who thoughtfully modernized bridal fashion with her 2015 spring collection that included unisex wedding dresses, tuxes, and honeymoon lingerie. She redefined the image of a blushing bride (and groom), an important distinction for marriage equality. And she blurred the boundaries of masculinity and femininity within an archetype style that strictly adheres to gender binaries and distinctions. Unfortunately, too few wedding designers offer suits for brides or anything beyond the classic white dress or dark tux. With same-sex couples developing their own clothing traditions, more people identifying as non-binary, and the virginal white gown symbol dying, both Wang's and Johnson's polarizing collections chipped away at the white wedding requirements of the past. They opened up space for new, groundbreaking traditions, and for more free expression and representation. I sincerely hope that other designers follow their lead. Had others done so, maybe I would not have been so committed or narrow-sighted to think that a white wedding dress was my bridal end all, be all.

Two hundred years ago, brides were more levelheaded and dyed their white wedding dresses afterward so they could be worn again. Even as late as the 1930s, wedding dresses were once rentable. But today's big businesses know many brides feel an emotional connection with the dress and are willing to pay the price for it (ah, the Wedding Industrial Complex again). Companies understand they can require brides to buy their dresses and charge big bucks for them (they created the demand and then manipulated the supply). As a result, the average cost in 2016 for a one-time-wear wedding gown was $1,564.[XXIX] With 2.1 million marriages a year, that equates to *big* boardroom profits.[XXX] No wonder the U.S. wedding industry was estimated to be $72 billion in 2016.[XXXI] Even bridesmaids can't catch a break and are expected to buy.

On the other hand, grooms and groomsmen typically rent their suits or tuxedos. And if a groom did buy his suit for a first wedding and becomes a second-time groom, he could simply wear the same suit (if he can still fit into it). It's a sexist consumer double standard because it implies that a bride must look unique for each spouse she marries, but men, as suit and tuxedo styles rarely change, are exempt. The different fashion guidelines between the sexes are unmerited.

As religion reinforced marriage as a once-in-a-lifetime event, this pressured brides to pick a wedding gown that reflected the importance of such a singular occasion. The tradition of keeping the dress a big secret to reveal on wedding day also heightens its fanfare. Women once walked down the aisle wearing their best dress. Now, the Wedding Industrial Complex has turned the aisle into a fashion runway. Bridal consumer culture went to great lengths to raise the stakes around the dress too, just like engagement ring traditions. It claimed dresses from old marriages were "unlucky" for new ones down the road, which is a ridiculous assertion. I say burn some sage, save your money, and add some flair if necessary or dye it a different color for spouse number two, three, or four. It's all a financial conspiracy against the bride, but logic was lost on me; the myth of this elusive white whale was created, and I wanted to sink my harpoon into it.

I accepted that if I was going to buy into this culture then I should be financially responsible for my purchases; no one was going to buy my dress for me but me. Like any rational person about to buy her most expensive article of clothing in her life, I decided to start at one of the top tier luxury stores, Priscilla's of Boston. I found *the* dress right off the bat. It was $2,500 for a sample and way past my budget. Had the store given me some champagne, I might have pulled the trigger in my buzzed state. Reality set in, though, and I couldn't justify throwing out my own budget and financial morals for a one-time dress. I couldn't get past the idea that I'd pay $2,500 for a dress I'd wear for four to five hours and then never again. That's $500 to $625 an hour, money better spent reducing student debt or giving out, roughly, sixty-three to seventy-nine paperback copies of Chimamanda Ngozi Adichie's book *We Should All Be Feminists* to your wedding guests as gifts. Eventually, after what felt like an aimless quest, I found a dress. I ended up supporting a small mom-and-pop shop in a town that was severely hit by the 2009 recession. However, I still ended up paying $1,100 (after negotiating) or $220/hour to wear a dress that fashion houses, wedding businesses, and style experts say I can never wear again.

Perturbed by this wear-once gown culture, I have warned my spouse that if he ever returns home early from a trip, there's a high probability he will catch me doing something...unseemly. Like sitting alone at home in my wedding dress, eating pizza out of a box, drinking red wine, and watching *Father of the Bride*. I love my dress and want to wear it again; stains, grease and embarrassment are the risks I'm willing to take to get a little more mileage out of it.[70] I can't help but wonder if the new fad of "trash the dress," where brides jump into lakes, roll around on sand like a swimsuit model or start a mud fight with their spouse is more an outlet of rebellion against this costly tradition or a last ditch attempt to bond more with it? Maybe it's feminist rebellion against its uptight, virginal symbolism though? For me, I have no desire to ruin something that cost me $220/hour to wear. I would rather it collect dust in my closet for eternity than wear it one more hour so I can sling some mud at my new spouse, but that's just me.

There's something to be said about being a well-informed feminist bride who wears white to snuff out its erroneous sexual symbolism. As a child, I grew up understanding that a white wedding dress meant the bride was a virgin, but as an adult, that symbolism seemed removed and reformed enough to wear it. I also hoped wearing a white wedding dress would help

---

[70] *I wore it for a college lecture at Tufts University called* The Sexy and Sexist Layers of the Wedding Cake *and I wore it for the cover of this book.*

chip away at its unhealthy virginal symbolism too. However, my choice to wear white was not solely founded on a feminist desire to modernize it; it was also the dirty influence of choice feminism. Like Ahab, I fell victim to an obsessive consumerism that was repeatedly denied me. Nothing makes someone want something more than society obstructing the object of their desire. I found a white gown that I felt represented myself, but I wonder, had I not been so unknowingly restricted to this visual idea of what a bride looked like, what other possibilities I might have entertained.

The wedding fashion industry needs to be more inclusive of different aesthetic tastes and ethnic needs and not exclusively push a style that carries historical and political stains. Whether someone wants to walk down the aisle as a tie-dyed Princess Leia, wear a dress from a first marriage or in one of Betsey Johnson's gender fluid attires, people need to be supported and respected to step outside the box and the available options need to be significantly widened. It's even more imperative that fashion traditions loosen the threads that tie wedding attire to a wearer's sexual activity. Some feminist rhetoric suggests the best solution is cutting out the wedding dress altogether, and I respect those who do that, but most brides need to wear *something* down the aisle or to City Hall—unless there are, in fact, nudist feminist brides out there, to whom I can only advise some sunscreen.

Unveiling the Veil

I gave my altar egos one serious rule to abide by: no crying. I'm a lot like Kristen Bell: if I'm not emotionally between a three and a seven on a scale of ten then I'm crying.[71] If anyone turned on the waterworks during my ceremony, I would not be able to stop my own oncoming flood. On a dress-shopping excursion with an altar ego, I was perched atop a pedestal in front of a three-way mirror admiring *the* dress. The bridal consultant placed the finishing touch atop my head—the veil. It epitomized everything: I was a bride and I was getting married. I turned to my altar ego for her opinion on "veil or no veil," but the moment had overtaken her and she was a wet, crying mess. My own eyes welled up and we proceeded to blabber incoherent words

---

[71] *YouTube it. You won't be disappointed (Kristen Bell's Sloth Meltdown,* The Ellen Show, *2012).*

while finger pointing blame at each other for crying. Regaining my composure, I said, "You're fired."

The jest broke our tears and we laughed, but the wedding veil, so thin and sheer, had this unspeakable power that both my altar ego and I felt. How could such an odd piece of millinery move us so much? Surely, there must be some anti-feminist agenda that could reduce two grown, smart women to piles of mush? I needed to know if a feminist could acceptably wear a veil.

It's important to consider that veils are not limited to brides. They are a long-lasting clothing style dating back to before biblical times. Veils throughout "herstory" recall images of concubines, genies (slaves to a lamp and its owner), virginal sacrifices (they didn't volunteer themselves), mourners (think Jackie Kennedy), nuns, belly dancers, the ancient upper class, and religious women across Christianity, Judaism, and Islam. Ironically, shrouded ladies include the most sexual as well as the most prudish—yet another example of how sex is tied to women's attire.

A veil, depending on the wearer, can carry different purposes, but it always revolved around sex and gender. Its purpose was to contain sexuality, represent virginity or protect a wearer's identity, and that is used in different ways by the sexperts and the sexless. The veil separates innocent women from dangerous, outside influences. Ancient Rome's upper class used it to prevent them from seeing the lower class. The courtesans, belly dancers, and other sexual women used the veil as a sort of mysterious tease to lure patrons. And it's even thought that when marriage was limited to negotiated contracts, the bride wore a veil to shroud her lack of beauty from her husband before he could change his mind. And like brides, religious persons wore it, for example, to represent the presence of their virginity and modesty or to show their monogamy and obedience as wives to husbands or to their god.

The first Roman brides wore non-white veils called *flammeum*. The colors ranged from red to yellow depending on the countenance of the bride and how much color was needed to cover up her blushing. Other interpretations see red as a sacrificial color (bye-bye virginity, hello blood from breaking her hymen) or an indication to how strong a fire she'd keep in her new household (both in the kitchen hearth and bedroom). A yellow-red veil symbolized protection for the bride in her new, foreign household. Some bridal guides suspected the veil's purpose was to protect brides from evil spirits, as a second protective guard should her look-alike bridesmaids fail to deflect them.

Wearing the veil for religious purposes is up to the wearer (though it's important to consider the presence of choice feminism since so many religions are controlled by men and patriarchal rules). Some houses of worship require a bride to wear headgear out of respect, which is explained in the Bible in the book of Corinthians, chapter 11: "(3)But I want you to understand that the head of every man is Christ, the head of a wife is her husband, and the head of Christ is God. ... (7)For a man ought not to cover his head, since he is the image and glory of God; but woman is the glory of man." In biblical terms, the veil is a tool to show respect. It shows to whom she is considered subservient to, people she is not equal to. Veils in this scenario conflict with the feminist tenet that all people are equal.

The big question as to whether a feminist bride can wear a veil, I believe, all comes down to how it's used. In the movie *The Father of the Bride* the moment when George Banks lifts the veil away from his daughter's face exemplifies the most common way the veil is activated. It seems super endearing and sentimental right? I used to think so, but then I learned what it symbolized. The act of the father lifting the veil from the bride's face means, "Sweetie, you are your husband's now, I bequeath you to him," which is reminiscent of the days when he picked out her husband. It also means that dad is now symbolically removing the bride's chastity curtain (i.e., bye-bye hymen) and saying to the fiancé, "Please, have your way with my daughter. I approve now that you're married." I even considered if the meaning would change if I lifted the veil myself, but I realized that I don't like the idea of "giving myself away" to someone else (I'm still my own person, after all), so lifting it up myself was out of the question too. Then I asked: if the veil exists as a stagnant object on top of my head, would the property and virginity symbolism disappear? And if the answer was yes, could a feminist bride wear it?

I decided yes on all accounts. Like the white bridal gown, I think the veil is getting further and further away from being a sexual symbol especially if a secular bride, like me, wears it (although, I would argue this millinery modernization doesn't apply to everyone). I, personally, could wear it without indicating my sexual status.[72] Because of who I am, my belief system, and my decision to not activate the veil, it simply became a fashion statement that epitomized the image of a bride. It's kind of similar to the weird headgear academic graduates wear. I know without a flat square on my head, I somehow wouldn't feel as much like a graduate. I wore the veil in a way that did not sign over my autonomy to another or signal my sexual status; and that, in my book (sorry for the pun), is a massive distinction.

I received a lot of criticism for being a feminist bride then appearing as a traditional one. In my defense, I think my decision to wear white and a veil had a lot to do with the privileges of who I am (a secular, white, feminist, liberal American). I possessed the power to change how the items were used and what they meant by simply declaring it so. And I won't argue against the accusation that there might be some choice feminism at play that I haven't resolved yet. Couture is complicated, and in a way, intersectional. My resolutions and modernizations for these wearable traditions won't work for everyone, because despite fashion's superficial stereotype, it contains a lot of weighty and unresolved secular and nonsecular politics that affect others differently.

Taking a note from Betsey Johnson's unisex line, another feminist solution to these runs in the fabric is inspiring a culture where fiancés wear the same attire for a wedding, or couples can simply opt out of the traditional duds and wear their own comfortable clothing. I think the real crux of this knotty issue is that fashion's gendering will improve if women's social and civil rights improve first. Only then will the benefits of true equality permeate into the industry and its traditions.

---

[72] *And I respect other feminist brides who disagree with my assessment and think it's more progressive to skip it altogether.*

Chapter 10

The Love Shock of

Elopements and Baby Mamas

When I was seventeen, my boss at my afterschool job celebrated thirty years of marriage. She was forty-five. As a B- honors calculus student, I figured that equated to marrying at an age younger than me. While counting my register money, she recounted how she and her boyfriend wanted to get married, but because they were under sixteen they needed their parents' consent to marry—except in Maine. Instead of showing up to softball practice or detention after school, they took off to Maine and came back with a big surprise for their parents. I went home after my shift and shared the story with my parents in order to remind them what a good kid I was. They curtly thanked me for not eloping, told me I was never allowed in Maine with a boyfriend, and sent me to my room to finish my homework.

Three years later when I was in college, I was driving around with a friend. They pulled into a parking spot, turned off the car and before I could open the door my friend gravely turned to me, "Don't get out." The sternness with which my friend addressed me put me into a panic—who died? Is this my Bonnie and Clyde moment where I go from innocent bystander to unlawful accomplice by robbing The Gap and grabbing all the corduroy jeans our hearts desire? Did I make out with someone gross during the last college party on Thirsty Thursday? The driver proceeded to tell me how our mutual friend abruptly dropped out of college to elope with a person more than twice her age. My second reaction was spitting my soda á la *Saved by the Bell* all over her dashboard paired with an incredulous, "Are you fucking kidding me?"

Despite everyone's initial protests, friends reluctantly embraced the marriage, but it wasn't meant to last. They divorced a few years later. I can't explain the friend's motivation. Sometimes love is just impetuous and inexplicable. What bothered me the most was that our friend thought dropping out of school was a necessity. It's not. An education is hugely important to any women's future, married or not. Eloping may be something for the bold of heart, but it should never come at the cost of important things like an education. Such a condition is a good warning sign about the future.

And that's how I learned how complicated elopements could be. Eloping is stereotypically and traditionally reserved for social outcasts: soon-to-be unwed mothers, forbidden lovers, the lustfully longing, impatient youth, or family avoiders. But is that fair to them, or even accurate? The herstory of elopements reveals that they were done to save people from being socially unconventional. A quick marriage protected those who would otherwise be ostracized or harshly judged for bucking tradition like having premarital sex or a child out of wedlock. Marriage sanctified those actions and saved the reputation of those who might be socially or financially punished for them. (And make no mistake, this sexual morality hurt women the most.) It's pretty clear that eloping was a result of discrimination against lovers and unmarried parents, but the romantic in me wanted to know if eloping was ever used for positive purposes.

In a unique twist, I discovered that eloping could be a powerful tool to fight against these ridiculous social and sexual restrictions and conventions. Consider the four-thousand LGBTQ couples who flocked to San Francisco's City Hall between February 12 and March 11, 2004, to get marriage licenses before California's Supreme Court shut it down.[73] This unprecedented brief window[74] created an opportunity for LGBTQs who wanted to honor their love and commitment to someone else and demonstrate a need for marriage regardless of whether the couple was heterosexual. Those four-thousand

---

[73] *On August 12, 2008, the California Supreme Court voided all the LGBTQ marriages held during that period in 2004, which led to the 2008 case of* In re Marriage Cases *and Proposition 8.*

[74] *While civil unions and domestic partnerships existed in various U.S. states, Massachusetts became the first state to offer full-out equal marriage rights to same-sex couples on May 17, 2004. It would not be until 2008 when the second state, Connecticut, would do the same. Between 2004 and 2008, many states continued to constitutionally ban same-sex marriage.*

couples exemplified how eloping is used to defy convention, not just in the name of love, but also in the name of basic civil rights; and I think that is pretty damn romantic.

Or what about the story of Mildred Jeter, a black woman, and Richard Loving, a white man, who both met as children in Virginia? Once adults, they crossed state lines to Washington, D.C., where in 1958 interracial marriage (miscegenation) was legal, and married. The appropriately named Lovings returned to Virginia shortly after their nuptials and stayed with Mildred's parents in Virginia. In the middle of the night, they awoke in their marital bed to three police officers with flashlights hovering above them. They were immediately arrested for violating the state's Racial Integrity Act of 1924 and marrying in a loophole.[75] Found guilty, they faced banishment from the state for twenty-five years or imprisonment for a year, so they left Virginia and their families and went to D.C. This love and elopement story would lead to the U.S. Supreme Court landmark case of *Loving v. Virginia* that on June 12, 1967, deemed Virginia's anti-miscegenation laws unconstitutional according to the fourteenth amendment.[XXXII] "The freedom to marry has long been recognized as one of the vital personal rights essential to the orderly pursuit of happiness by free men," said Chief Justice Earl Warren.

Don't let that ruling fool you, though. South Carolina didn't officially lift its own ban until 1998 and Alabama until 2000.

While interracial marriage was frowned upon, the real perceived crime was the children that came from such marriages. The Lovings brought their case to the American Civil Liberties Union (ACLU) five years after their state exile because they missed Virginia and their family there. They also wanted

---

[75] *The historical prevention of interfaith and interracial marriage existed because of civil and social prejudice, but much like same-sex marriage, the argument against such unions rested on issues related to procreation. At the state-level retrial in 1963, Judge Bazile declared, "Almighty God created the races...and he then placed them on separate continents. And for the interference of such arrangement there would be no cause for such marriages. The fact that he separated the races shows that he did not intend for the races to mix." The law that banned the Lovings' marriage was 176 years old. It originated from a 1691 law from the Virginia Colony's House of Burgesses, which was the first elected legislation in North America. The law sought to reduce the number of mixed-race children. While interracial marriage was frowned upon, the real perceived crime was the children that came from the marriages (Source: Works Cited 11).*

their marriage recognized so they could protect their family legally (illegitimate children were not protected by the law at the time; I'll also get into that in a moment). At the Supreme Court level, their lawyer argued, "The Lovings have the right to go to sleep at night knowing that if should they not wake in the morning, their children would have the right to inherit from them. They have the right to be secure in knowing that...a survivor of them has the right to social security benefits. All of these are denied to them, and they will not be denied to them if the whole anti-miscegenistic scheme of Virginia... [is] found unconstitutional." It was an appropriate concern, Richard Loving died in 1975 after being hit by a drunk driver. Mildred survived the crash, but lost an eye. He left behind her and their three children. Mildred never remarried.

That idea of love defying all odds that has captured the heart and imagination of Hollywood and would-be elopers,[76] which is why when one thinks of eloping, little images of Las Vegas, Elvis Presley, and Britney Spears flood the mind. The ultimate single girl, Carrie Bradshaw of *Sex and the City*, couldn't find happiness after an elaborate, designer ceremony but discovered a quick trip to City Hall better honored herself as an independent woman. Maybe Carrie managed to get her happy ending, but that does not necessarily mean an elopement saves someone from stereotypical wedding woes. Just ask literature's timeless couple, Romeo and Juliet. Eloping couldn't settle an ancient grudge between two households, and the star-crossed lovers' lustful loins led to their fatal end. Elopers might gain the love of another, but once the honeymoon is over, it won't necessarily exempt a couple from the problems or motivations that drove them to elope.

If a big fat traditional wedding is too fraught with ugly consumerism and sexist customs, then an elopement seems like a nice feminist solution, right? As much as I wish elopements were a cure-all, I worry it is not the solution some feminist fiancés thinks it is. It can be just as stressful, drama-filled, and expensive. An elopement to City Hall can still include all the trims and fixings a regular wedding might have: dress, ring, and wedding cake. It doesn't necessarily save a ceremony and marriage from exhibiting obsolete and sexist traditions, either. An eloping bride might still be asked to obey or take his

---

[76] *There are two movies about the Lovings and their court case:* Loving *(2016) and* HBO's The Loving Story *(2012).*

name. The lingering, unfair stigma that it's to save unmarried, knocked-up people from shame is still a pock on what could be a nice wedding alternative. Eloping may be unconventional, but it's not always necessarily ripe with equality.

The major difference between a traditional wedding and an elopement is stealth, speed, and witness count. To become an acceptable, mainstream wedding free from its historical stereotypes, context, and approach are imperative. When my fiancé and I were filling out our own marriage license at City Hall, a young couple emerged from the judge's chamber and ecstatically embraced. They never uttered a word to each other before they left the municipal building but the smiles on the faces said it all. They had just married in the simplest and most private way imaginable, and I don't think I've ever seen such happy people before. I may not know what drove them to elope, but it seemed right for them. I've also known friends who, for work or lifestyle reasons, needed to marry in a hurry but planned on celebrating with pomp and flair when the time was right.

I've also been privy to a few scandalous elopements, like green card marriages. (I've always thought it was odd they were willing to share such illegal actions, considering it is punishable by a $250,000 fine and five years in prison.) And I've heard a number of stories from people who were cruelly told, "Why don't you just run off and elope and put all of us out of our misery?"

I, personally, never dreamed of eloping, mostly because I like a big party, but also because during my impressionable years, my peers treated elopement as a negative action done only by those who couldn't keep it in their pants or who started to multiply before marriage, which I now understand is unfair. I regret this point of view and how it made me treat others.

A friend got secretly engaged and married within a month, and when my shock wore off and I stopped swearing, my next (equally mature) response was, "Are you pregnant?"[77] I knew she wasn't but I felt compelled to put the question out there. And apparently I was not the only one to pose it to her, either. When there's a race to the altar, many want to know is if there's a bun in the oven. Reactions to elopements, like mine, show that the stigma

---

[77] *Amazingly enough, she forgave me for all my verbal diarrhea and twenty minutes into the convo I realized the appropriate response should be, "Congratulations!"*

attached to such actions runs deep in society's collective psyche. To understand benefits and downsides of elopements and not put a foot in my mouth again, I had to investigate deeper and figure out where the stigma began.

Religion is a great place to start as it created the demand for elopements when it created edicts to punish outsiders (e.g., mothers and their out-of-wedlock children). Broadly speaking, a lot of religious doctrines condemn pre-marital sex and unmarried procreation (remember the chapter about child brides and honor killings?). Religion (and the men in charge of them) used marriage to regulate women's bodies and reproductive lives by creating really harsh sexual codes. And although in the U.S. there is a separation of church and state, make no mistake that the church managed to influence civil laws, which severely limited (i.e., punished) the civil rights of those who did not agree with the lawmakers' religious views, and punished those who acted independently of religious moral codes. So being born out of wedlock historically meant coming into a lot of terrible stereotypes and names: bastard, illegitimate heir, love child, natural child (the polite title used by the upper class), or fillius nullius (the child of no one). To make matters worse, the unholy offspring of two unmarried people were not legally entitled to birthrights, titles, inheritances, and certain basic rights.

To avoid bastardization, societal and religious disapproval, and legal ramifications, people raced to the altar in what is called a shotgun wedding. The shotgun element originates from the folk myth that the father of the bride must coerce the reluctant father-to-be to marry his daughter via the end of his shotgun barrel (because, sarcasm and euphemism alert, what man would want to buy the cow when he could get the milk for free? And I'll add, buy the cheese if he didn't order it or spend nine months making and aging it?).[78] If the groom tried to make a break for it, then pops would pull the trigger and kablooey![79] The quick marriage is meant to reconcile and restore

---

[78] *If I were a man, I'd be enraged that the male stereotype of pre-marital fatherhood is that men would rather be delinquent fathers than step up and be part of the family. And while I don't doubt there is some historical truth to men who skirted their fatherly duties, I can't help but wonder if such a stereotype created self-fulfilling prophecies and actually made the situation worse.*

[79] *This threat of death is ridiculous because it's suggesting a dead father is better than a negligent one. How moral are these family values if murder is OK but an*

the parents' perceived moral, spiritual, and social reputation, along with that of their unborn child. Though it should be noted that couples, in the past, often had about a year to make reparations within Christian faiths by marrying and then baptizing their children (if they could).

This last-minute fix benefited mostly white people throughout the majority of Western history. If readers recall in Chapter 2, in colonial times slaves were limited to informal marriages, meaning in the eyes of religion and the law, their children were technically bastards. And as bastards, slave owners felt no qualms about selling them and separating families. The lives of children born to non-Caucasian, interracial and interfaith partners were undoubtedly harder because of religious and civil laws that punished them for not being legitimate and excluded them for not being white.

The legal disinheritance and discrimination against those born from unmarried parents, which violates a person's natural civil rights, lasted until the 1970s. The U.S. Supreme Court helped redefine marriage and procreation for the better. [XXXIII] In *King v. Smith* (1968) the U.S. Supreme Court ruled that Alabama could not deny public assistance to sexually active, unmarried mothers and their children in order to deter sex and birth outside marriage. Other cases that helped legitimize children born outside of marriage included *Stanley v. Illinois* (1971), which challenged the state's ruling that the children of an unmarried, deceased mother would be better off as orphaned wards of the state instead of with their unmarried father. And *New Jersey Welfare Rights Organization v. Cahill* (1973) was a case where New Jersey argued that it could withhold state benefits and subsidies to unmarried families in order to encourage couples to marry. Its goal was "to preserve and strengthen family life" within heterosexual marriage. Again, the U.S. Supreme Court decided it violated the fourteenth amendment and that, overall, illegitimacy laws should not punish illegitimate children who have no control over the conditions of their birth.

What's insane about these court cases is that for the previous two hundred years, it shows the United States of America would rather harm, exploit, or discriminate against unconventional families, minorities, and other

---

unwed mother and illegitimate child is not? Not to mention, if pops kills the delinquent father before they say "I do," she's still disgraced, so how does the murder solve anything anyway?

citizens in order to endorse the benefits marriage. How good can marriage be if, like benevolent sexism, it's used to punish anyone who doesn't participate in mainstream behavior? I'm not surprised there was an anti-marriage movement in the first and second waves of feminism. Back then, both socially and civilly, marriage was doing a lot of damage, not just to women, but to a whole slew of minorities and children.

Out-of-wedlock births no longer have their once virulent branding. However, sometimes individual cases can reignite unfashionable and obsolete feelings toward pregnancies that society deems "inappropriate" or "irresponsible." Take for instance, John Edwards, who denied an extramarital affair and a resulting daughter, which possibly forfeited his candidacy in the 2008 presidential race. Or there's the infamous "Octomom," Nadya Sulemon, who decided give birth to octuplets via in vitro fertilization (IVF) when she already had six children (bringing the total to fourteen) with no second parent or support source, no job, and no income. Then there's football athlete Travis Henry, who has eleven children with ten different mothers.

Luckily, circumstances have been changing for the better over the last fifty-plus years. If anyone is the child of two unmarried parents today, they can thank Henry Krause and the awesomeness of the fourteenth amendment for their legal right to equal protection. Krause, an Illinois law professor, published papers against illegitimate child legislation that was revolutionary during the 1960s and '70s. Krause believed that illegitimacy legislation was "an ancient prejudice based on religion and moral taboos that properly are losing their taboo status." The Supreme Court ruled that common law disabilities of bastardy breached the Equal Protection Clause of the fourteenth amendment to the United States Constitution.[XXXIV] This new legislature is massively important for all civil rights champions and feminist fiancés out there as it changed the treatment of sex and procreation within the traditional functions of [white, heterosexual] marriage. This created a trickle-down effect, which later benefited same-sex couples who wanted to marry or become parents. This is why the founding fathers knew to separate church and state; religious rules applied to marriage in governmental legislation fundamentally violated many people's human rights.

While in the U.S. this procreation issue is now legally resolved, not everyone in the world is similarly protected. For example, in present day

Monaco, Prince Albert II has two children born outside of marriage. Under Monaco's law, they are not legally entitled to a royal title or his last name, Grimaldi. Due to improvements in child support laws, they do get financial support. Laws discriminating against children based on their parents' marital status made overcoming the station of "bastard" incredibly difficult throughout history, but there were a few historical persons who managed to rise above it such as Leonardo Da Vinci, Argentina's Eva Peron, Marilyn Monroe, and Alexander Hamilton.

Forty years after Krause's wonderful gift to children and their parents, women are starting to rock the baby bump regardless of their marital status. In 2015, 40.3 percent of births[XXXV] were to unmarried women, compared to 28 percent in 1990 (it peaked at 41 percent in 2009).[XXXVI] In 2015, the rate declined for those under thirty, but increased in all age groups above it.[XXXVII] A good reason for this is that more women are getting an education (66 percent of mothers in 2011 had some college education)[XXXVIII] and an increase in older women choosing to raise children without a ring on their finger. Women with more economic means and autonomy are increasingly choosing to become a parent without a spouse or the traditional structure of marriage because the social and civil benefits of marriage are no longer exclusive to it.

In 2004 while on a friend's family vacation, a family member gave us a heads-up on another couple joining us to avoid any awkward questions. They were unmarried, under thirty, successful professionals (the guy had directed Ricky Martin music videos) and with…a child. ¡Qué vida loca! Suavely and politely, he described them as a "very modern couple." In 2004, out-of-wedlock births still carried enough of a stigma that this situation needed addressing. Such modern families help people rethink what it means to be a family and the relevance of marriage. Interestingly enough, pop culture might be the best source of baby bump trailblazers to change the status quo.

Two movies addressed this new demographic trend. *The Back-Up Plan* (2010), starring Jennifer Lopez, and *The Switch* (2010), starring Jennifer Aniston, both dealt with older women deciding to be artificially inseminated. Then there's the presumed Hollywood celebrity trend where leading ladies are buying bassinets in lieu of wedding bands, like Charlize Theron, Meg Ryan, and Sandra Bullock. It's hard not to contemplate the idea that celebrities are influencing a progressive unmarried motherhood trend by breaking new ground and easing a captive audience into less "traditional" ways of life. I'm not even sure these women identify as feminists, but it's safe to argue that their actions are a sign that they are at least benefiting from it. So when reality stars like Kourtney Kardashian, Bethenny Frankel, and Kim Zolciak are pregnant and unmarried on TV, our way of thinking about those topics evolve perhaps toward more accepting attitudes. However, these stars are adults with overwhelming resources to provide financially for their children with or without a partner or social acceptance. Money (and life experience), in this instance, creates an extra safety cushion to break comfortably from religious and social tradition, but not everyone has that luxury.

As *Juno* (2007) hit movie screens, news stories of Jamie Lynn Spears (2007) and Bristol Palin (2008) hit the newsstands. And MTV took teenage pregnancies to new heights and stardom with *16 & Pregnant* and *Teen Mom* (2009). In pop culture and media, teenage sex and pregnancy are widely scrutinized, but these teenagers are held to different, more traditional values than their older contemporaries. Like the young stars who are expected to publicly commit to their virginity (by the way, they never do), young pregnant pubescents are expected to marry the other parent of their unborn child. It is not surprising, then, that Spears and Palin were coerced into an engagement to alleviate the public's disapproval and salvage their family members' careers and political campaigns. Though at what cost does the parents' and child's happiness come if the engagement is done under the duress of family and society to "do what's right?" As of now, neither teenage mom is married to their baby daddies. Four years later, Palin starred in the *Lifetime* reality TV show *Life's a Tripp*, featuring her life as a single mom.

The religious and social pressure to fit into a certain cookie-cutter family image still exists, despite a 2016 National Health Statistics Report that revealed Americans are growing more tolerant to nontraditional families.[XXXIX] *Friends* character Phoebe rents a wedding gown while pregnant from a store called It's Not Too Late, which is certainly a backhanded comment. Some Hollywood couples, who are more traditional, make a beeline for the altar and marry before the baby is born, like Alicia Keys and Swizz Beatz, Jennifer Garner and Ben Affleck, Drew Barrymore and Will

113

Kopelman, and Heidi Klum and Seal, to name just a few. And some couples wait till after the children are born, like Nicole Richie, who married singer Joel Madden after having two children with him. And on the show *Whose Wedding Is It Anyway?* a non-celebrity couple planned to marry after three daughters over the course of six years. A modern perspective is that time and patience is always a healthy attitude. Rushing to the altar used to imply wrongdoing or an ulterior motive. Since a baby out of wedlock no longer means having a bastard as it historically did, some couples find the freedom to wait for a moment that's right for them.

Americans are at a transitional period where almost half of the country's new births are to unwed parents. Marriage no longer means attaining a house, husband, and two kids under certain parameters. Tolerance to different lifestyles and life event chronologies is severely needed now, as we are at a crossroads between old-school advocates and baby bump trailblazers.

Regardless of where you stand on gun control issues, it's time to put down the marital shotgun for the sake of parents and their babies. Sprinting down the aisle is not an easy thing to do, so whatever motivates a couple to do it— or *not* do it—it's important for bystanders to be supportive of them. Concerns over skipping traditional decorum (even if the concerns come from "a good place") still reinforce the bad stereotypes that came with eloping. I imagine my friend would have felt more celebrated in her moment of happiness if I didn't react to it using obsolete elopement criteria. I owed her more respect and support than my initial reaction. If the history of elopements has taught me anything, it's that a tradition isn't special if it would rather punish or reprimand people for acting outside convention then find ways to embrace, support, and love them.

Chapter 11
Altar Endings for the
Wedding Ceremony

Before I get into more unsavory histories of wedding traditions, and before I begin to examine the walk down the aisle with my feminist superpowers, I need to share a personal story about what comes before the wedding ceremony—the wedding rehearsal.

You might recall the debacle that was my second stretch as a bridesmaid, where I became persona non grata, burned my neck, and broke into my house bottomless. Well there's one more story to share. While, I have nothing sexist per se about the rehearsal ceremony that isn't covered in the subsequent wedding ceremony pages, this is a story worth sharing. If there's a moral to this story, let it be to reiterate the insane gauntlet bridesmaids are put through. Enjoy.

By the time the actual wedding came around, I was in survival mode. To say I was a spokeswoman for Murphy's Law is an understatement. I had become the actual Murphy. With the wedding on Sunday, I took off to Vermont on Friday night for another wedding to blow off some steam. With no ceremony rehearsal the day before the wedding (after I asked the bride if there would be one), I scheduled my return on Saturday very precisely: leave at noon, arrive home at 4 p.m., and get to the rehearsal dinner at 8 p.m. Except at noon on Saturday, I received a call from another bridesmaid informing me there was a rehearsal ceremony in two hours, and I was four hours away. With no time to spare, I started driving down Vermont's Route 89 like racecar driver Danica Patrick.

I am now convinced there's a conspiracy against me. I still haven't done anything blatantly wrong, but not showing up to a surprise wedding rehearsal,

I suspect, will be the last straw and the bride will kick me out of the party at the last minute. And while my desperation worsens with every ticking moment and mile on the highway, I'm met with another urgent sensation— the urge to pee.

I can't ignore the call of nature any longer and I pull off the highway and into a gas station. With no time to spare, I find myself facing what must be the grossest gas station bathroom imaginable. To reach the toilet and avoid the suspicious brown puddle at its base, I have to position myself in a Captain Morgan-type stance. Boldly perched atop the bowl, an unfamiliar feeling starts to creep into me, the feeling of confidence. I've cut my commute time in half and by some miracle it looks like I will make the last minute wedding rehearsal. Maybe I'm not a bridesmaid fuck-up after all. I'm feeling a little better so I'm going to reward myself with a much-needed pee. But as they say "pride cometh before the fall" and the moment my bladder relaxed, my shimmied-up dress decided to release itself from my grip, and the unthinkable happens. Yes, I peed all over my dress. Crushed by the powers of the yellow tide, I look at the clock; there's one hour until the rehearsal for me to clean up and dry off. I have no replacement clothes and there's no time to go home and change.

Now, I have a new concern—don't let the wedding party know you peed all over yourself.

Silently swearing and on the brink of tears, I clean up as best I can in the sink, dose myself in perfume, roll up the car windows on this glorious 90-degree day and crank the heat in the hopes of drying myself off. If I managed to show up on time, it means that some higher power took pity on me, but that higher power was not without a unique sense of humor. I arrived at the rehearsal ceremony and luckily no one seems to notice the faint smell of urine at the altar.

I make it home, shower, change clothes, and mosey my way to the rehearsal dinner that (surprisingly) goes off without a hitch (that is, until I lost my house keys afterward, but I digress). While I was saved from further embarrassment at the rehearsal dinner, that tradition is also not safe from obsolete gender rules. As mentioned in Chapter 4, the planning and payment of the rehearsal dinner is traditionally done by the groom's family as a cordial return for the bride's side paying for everything else. It's also a symbolic gesture to show how the groom's side will take care of the bride when she leaves her family home.

Not to sound like a broken record, but of course, fiancés should modernize this tradition because it's based on gendered transactional and planning roles. Maybe both sets of families could work together to create a proper send off for both children before they start their new family. Or maybe the fiancés host it themselves as a sign of unity or thanks to family and friends for all their support leading up to the big day. Isn't that the modern point of it anyway—togetherness and gratitude? Why keep the archaic gender roles that bring the party down?

Now it's time for the wedding ceremony.

Dying to experience the dreaminess of a wedding ceremony, I begged and convinced my parents to sneak me into a "no-kids-allowed" one when I was in elementary school. Perched secretively in the balcony of the church with a bird's eye view, I marveled at how this was just like Ariel about to marry Prince Eric minus the water and fishiness. It was beautiful and romantic, but when the ceremony started in Ukrainian and not in English (knowing that the bride didn't speak a word of Ukrainian) I turned to my parents and asked, "Why is it in Ukrainian if she doesn't speak it?" Now as an adult, what I really meant but couldn't articulate at the time, was, "If this is the most important day in a woman's life, why is it in a language she doesn't understand?" My parents shushed me. Perhaps I delivered the question too loudly and my parents feared their stowaway would be revealed, or maybe my curiosity was ill-timed, but because the groom spoke Ukrainian, I took that to mean the groom's preferences come first and I should not question this. I remember my youthful reaction was an incredulous internal monologue that went something like, "That's crap."

My early feminist radar was not completely wrong. When researching the history of the wedding ceremony to understand how I might structure my own, it became clear women were not calling the shots throughout history. Within ancient Roman and Grecian multi-day weddings, the bride served as more of an object and spectacle than a willing participant. In Rome, the first days were spent praying to the gods. A few days later, the bride would be literally torn from her childhood home and, whether in jest or in reality, it was customary for the bride to kick and scream as she was escorted to her in-laws' home via a parade. The Broadway-like street processional included torches, dancing and the singing of the wedding hymn called (I'm not kidding) the hymen (allegedly, there's no connection to a women's hymen). This history tells me two plausible things: the Romans knew how to throw a damn good party (so long as you weren't the bride and you didn't care about consent); and two, the parade contributed to the tradition where the father escorts the bride down the aisle.

It's very easy to view a father walking his daughter down the aisle as a sweet gesture, but my feminist radar suspected it represented some less than precious symbolism too. Being daddy's little girl in this context extends from ancient to Victorian times when daughters were literally daddy's (or any man's) little property. This idea of owning women is called coverture (sometimes spelled couverture) and it was a profound curse that plagued women and their basic human rights.

Up until the late 19th century, English and American women might as well have tattooed "property of my husband or daddy" onto their derrières because in the eyes of the court, wives belonged to fathers, husbands, or male guardians under the legal doctrine of coverture.[80] In 1603, the Jamestown Colony adopted the British practice of coverture.[XL] The old saying was, "Husband and wife are one person, and that person being the husband." Any property she brought into the marriage through a dowry or inheritance was the sole ownership of her husband and not her own. A wife as *the property* of her husband helped legitimize spousal rape[81] and beatings too. In 1862, a North Carolina court case (*Joyner v. Joyner*) declared, "The law gives the husband power to use such a degree of force as is necessary to make the wife behave herself and know her place." She had no right to vote or sign legal documents. And if a wife did anything illegal, her husband was the one brought to trial, not her. She could work and earn an education, but only with her husband's permission. He was entitled to all her earnings.

In 1848, American suffragists Elizabeth Cady Stanton and Lucretia Mott drew up a bill demanding women's rights reform, called the "Declaration of

---

[80] *Maybe this will give new and more appropriate meaning to brides who wear "Future Mrs. John Smith" or "Mrs." clothing.*
[81] *Spousal rape became more or less illegal in the U.S. during the 1980s (Source: Works Cited 12).*

Sentiments." It influenced thirty-three states between 1869 and 1887 to give women control over their own income and property rights. Stanton wrote to Susan B. Anthony, "It is in vain to look for the elevation of woman, so long as she is degraded in marriage." She recognized that much of women's civil liberty issues sprang from their limited positions within marriage. And I contend that the issue persists today: women's parity outside the house won't change until it is improved inside it.

The parliament of Great Britain passed the Women's Property Bill in 1882. English women could finally retain their original property and income and not hand it over to their husbands. This bill even allowed women extra financial protection if she could prove she was a victim of domestic violence. American coverture laws mostly stuck around until the National Women's Party demanded their removal at their Washington, D.C., convention in 1921, thirty-nine years after their British sisters. However, some American coverture laws lingered into the mid-20th century (some of those will be discussed in Chapters 14 and 15), and socially and symbolically, many remain to this day.

Coverture is represented in wedding traditions through practices such as asking for a daughter's hand in marriage, lifting the veil, the father walking the daughter down the aisle, dowries, purity balls, bridal honor killings, the who-pays-for-a-wedding custom, patronymics, etc. The whole walking down the aisle tradition is a ceremonial gift exchange, which is why the tradition is often called "giving away the bride."

With better rights for women, I can understand how people might think dad walking the bride down the aisle isn't steeped in biased patriarchal practices anymore. Unfortunately, that idea is as misguided as thinking Tupac is dead when he's at home watching *Scandal*. If the tradition were truly modernized, both parents would escort each fiancé.

Also, it's often standard practice for the next male relative to walk the bride down the aisle if dad is unavailable, rather than mom. Why opt for a brother or uncle when mom or Aunt Gertrude might have had an equal, if not bigger, hand in raising the bride? I think a true sign of respect and modernity would be all fiancés incorporating the most important people in their lives regardless of picking two of the opposite sex.

For me, I did not want to feel like a delivered package, so I couldn't in good feminist consciousness only have my father walk me down the aisle. I opted to have both my parents walk me down the aisle, and my fiancé would have done the same if it weren't for some bad knees and hips on his parents' side. No walk, except maybe the one to the electric chair, is as nerve-wracking and pee-inducing as the one to the altar, so it's nice to have balanced support (especially if you don't know how to walk in the high heels you misguidedly bought). In retrospect, though, I regret walking toward my fiancé as he waited for me. Instead of my dad, I now had the whole family and myself help deliver me to his keeping. I wish, instead, we opted for even more parity by walking to the altar hand-in-hand or solo in some type of awesome move like a motorcycle handstand or bareback on a unicorn. As most adults live independently before committing to marriage, walking solo would symbolize our independent decision to commit and marry each other, and I like that sentiment.

For feminist purposes, I also ditched the "who gives away this bride?" language because I am not a raffle prize at a fair; if I didn't, my fiancé's parents would need to be ready to likewise answer, "Who gives away this groom?" which when you say it, highlights its resounding sexism. Instead, we wrote a new part and thanked each set of parents for their contribution to our upbringing and highlighted the importance of their support (not permission) for our union. We also could have asked the same of our entire wedding party to enthusiastically yell, "We do!" Feminist wedding modernization is simple and easy; the upside is a much more positive and inclusive wedding.

When the ancient Roman matrimonial parade reached the groom's family's home, the wedding party shepherded the bride straight to the marital bed. "Doing it" made it official, but only to the extent that she bore him a son. Without a son, she might never be fully accepted into her in-law's family, and her own father could break the marriage contract at will. This inspired bedroom-wedding ceremonies that lasted well into European medieval times.[82] The father or top male household figure presided over the ceremony

---

[82] *The Greeks and Romans laid out the general structure of all ceremonies; but by end of the middle ages Christianity got a better monopoly on marriage and dictated that ceremonies should be performed at the church. Most marriages weren't performed at the altar, though. The few who opted for a marriage sanctified by God and the church held the ceremonies at the church's front door.*

to sanctify the union and bless the bed into the best baby-making machine in all the land. If things weren't awkward enough, this ceremonial bedroom consummation might be witnessed by the bride's father, father-in-law, and by ten or so other men, thus giving new definition to the idea of a small intimate ceremony. So when interacting with the people in the world who tout the importance of traditional marriage and weddings as a way to exclude same-sex couples or any type of civilized progress, feel free to remind them that "traditional" used to mean your father watching you have sex for the first time. That'll put things into perspective for them.

And when they don't know what to say, feel free to use that as an opening to discuss what to say during one's wedding ceremony vows. What's considered some of the most romantic language around is just as unromantic if you know the context behind it. The line "vow to obey your husband" references coverture law. It stuck around for a long time because the dudes in charge had no problem with it staying there, and the ladies who went along with it to avoid reprisal (hostile sexism) had little power to overcome it, so they continued to follow the status quo. It wasn't until those rebel rouser suffragists refused to utter the words in their own ceremonies in the 18th century that things started to turn around. Elizabeth Cady Stanton recalled her own ceremony, saying, "I obstinately refused to obey one with whom I supposed I was entering into an equal relation." Hear, hear, sister!

It's not often the "vow to obey" sentence winds up in a wedding ceremony these days, but it still happens. In Judaism for example, only the groom asserts the ownership vow, "Behold, you are consecrated to me with this ring according to the laws of Moses and Israel." And in 1981, Princess Diana first bumped heads with her former in-laws when she refused to have it included in her own wedding.

Modernizing the vows is insanely easy, even easier if the "vow to obey" line is cut. However, it's possible to miss other chauvinist nuances or cues. It's easy to glaze over the details if everyone else before you decided it was good enough for them and romantic. Feminism equipped me with the right tools to notice phrases that emphasized stereotypically wifely and husbandly duties, procreation responsibilities and references to "whom marriage is for." (I propose such language reinforced anti-marriage-equality sentiments.) I've witnessed too many non-secular ceremonies where the officiant used the altar as a religious soapbox to preach politics while disregarding that the couple in front of them has already violated numerous religious rules, such as having sex before marriage and living together. As a guest, I don't swoon over how romantic this moment is; I cringe at the couple's misrepresentation. And sometimes it's innocent ad lib mistakes; I felt so bad when a priest used the Velveteen Rabbit story as a metaphor to question what real love is, but instead sounded like he doubted the couple was in love. It takes a critical eye and grammar-nerd-like reflexes to catch wordy, sexist moments in such a romantic setting, but it's worth it. For example, I wish I had thought to replace *husband* and *wife* with gender-neutral *spouse*.[83] I did my best to make sure equitable words were spoken to lay the foundation for our marriage, but sometimes my best still fell short.

If feminist fiancés are worried about a sexist slip of the tongue, the safest course of action would be to put that tongue to other uses like kissing. The kiss at the end of the ceremony stems from Roman times too. It was another contractual element to help seal the marriage arrangement. We opted for a sweet and polite (but savory) kiss over the make-your-relatives-blush approach; however, before we locked lips, I was a little conscious of how the ceremonial cue to kiss was linguistically delivered.

Most couples know to kiss when they hear, "I now pronounce you man and wife." This is the romantic apex of the ceremony, but I had to stop and think about this odd demarcation. Why, if we were now married equals, was my fiancé just a man and not a husband or me just a wife and not a woman? It's unfair that in marriage, men always get to be men, but women change their status. These were the wrong words with which to start my marriage. At first, I thought to use "husband and wife," but then it occurred to me that this defines marriage in a heterosexual context, which would be doing the LGBTQ community no favors. Then I considered using the phrase, "you may now kiss the bride" which, if you think about it, is a little boy's club and might perpetuate the idea that men can be physically/romantically assertive/aggressive, but women can't do the same. It also teaches women that their bodies are not their own and that men can have at them as they please. So I had to cross that one off the options list too. (Who knew such a short phrase can hold such big symbolism?)

---

[83] *Chapter 14 will shed light on why these are worth changing.*

I ended up opting for the most basic and obvious turn of phrase that honors the origins of this tradition (in a good way): "You both may now seal your marriage with a kiss." To those romantically egalitarian words, I could definitely swap some spit in front of a hundred-and-fifty of my closest friends and family.

Historically, brides may not have possessed much choice in how their wedding ceremonies went down, but feminism managed to shut down coverture relics and green-lighted brides to marry with more autonomy. My fiancé and I chose to be married outside in a secular ceremony by a friend. And I had the luck of being born with the liberty to make additional improvements toward how I, a woman, was treated within it. All I want is for others to possess the power and vision to marry in an equitable way that best honors them and their relationship. Be that in a feminist ceremony underwater, while skydiving, on roller coasters, or on the Starship Enterprise set in Vegas.

A newlywed couple can't protect a wedding ceremony from all that might go wrong: tears will be shed during the ceremony, makeup will run, and wedding vows will be misspoken. But a couple can control the level of respect that is given to each of them by eradicating the obsolete sexism hidden within so many Western wedding traditions and language. Some might see my fine-tuning as unnecessary because they don't feel oppressed or discriminated against; if that's true, why not perfect the wedding to represent those feelings rather than repeat some stodgy traditions that don't? We wanted to start our marriage on the right foot. Feminism raised the level of respect and representation beyond anything we expected from traditional practices, and we wanted to see more of that positive influence in the wedding reception.

Chapter 12
The Wedding Reception:
Cake in Your Face and
Other Sexual Innuendos

As a party aficionado, I give my best at wedding receptions. While other people find it a good time to check their smart phones, I will watch the newlyweds feed each other food no matter how sexual I find it. I will pass the toilet paper and not judgment when the bride asks me to photograph her taking a dump on the toilet because she thinks it's funny (true story). And I will follow up on my promise to not show the photo to anyone except her. When another guest inexplicably throws some dollar bills on the dance floor, I will run and slide my knees onto them and seamlessly skim across an Amish barn dance floor like I'm Kevin Bacon in *Footloose* without putting a run in my pantyhose and yell, "Let's party!" (another true story).

Giving my all at wedding receptions is not always easy. Sometimes my all gets the best of me. For one wedding ceremony, I found myself marooned atop a Michigan ski mountain after a late summer deluge. There I found myself faced with a moral conundrum, who will drink all this uncorked champagne lest it go bad? After being rescued by not a Saint Bernard with rum but a minivan with more champagne, I somehow managed to make it to the first dance coherent. When Michigan's esteemed music icon Kid Rock started playing, the champagne kicked in, and I careened out of control.

Quarantining myself to a side room, I became a character out of a Masterpiece Theatre movie, like a brooding Mr. Rochester or Heathcliff. There I sat in a leather reading chair and stared languidly into the fire in a desperate attempt to grab hold of myself. Over the next hour or so, friends

KATRINA MAJKUT

would visit with a sympathetic glass of water listening to me incoherently mumble about consuming too much like a regretful Cookie Monster. Driven by this internal greedy and hungry monster, though, I mustered enough balance to saunter over to the grand piano covered in cupcakes. I took one look at them, exclaimed "Nope!" ran outside and promptly puked into the golf club's azaleas. My last ditch attempt to not be the worst person at the wedding reception was to, at least, not be the first to leave. So I sat outside on the curb with my head in my hands waiting for the curbside ex-convict guest (who had just been released from prison) to leave before I did.

I succeeded with a few things that night. One, I out partied a convict who wasn't allowed to party at all due to his ankle bracelet. Two, I ruined some gardener's day. And three, I survived long enough to witness the most important traditions during the wedding so when the newlyweds complained about my conduct I could recall what happened with the same clarity as any other sober schmo.[84] And it's the details of all those reception traditions that I explored with my trusty sidekick, feminism. (If you don't mind, I'm gonna stay sober for this chapter.)

As you can imagine, I'm partial to big entrances (and exits, per the last story). I attribute this to growing up in the prime of *America's Funniest Home Videos* with family-man turned comedic dirty-man, Bob Saget. It taught me wedding entrances are big moments where anything can happen, like when newlyweds become overly confident in their non-existent acrobatic skills and knock over the wedding cake. Then the internet taught me that choreographed dance entrances accompanied by music from a domestic abuser (grrr, Chris Brown) could go viral. There was a lot of pressure to make our wedded introduction perfect. To ensure this, I stopped to consider whether something as simple as the reception's wedding party introductions could possibly be—what's the word I use too infrequently? Oh yeah, sexist. Of course.

At my own wedding, my greatest fear was the Master of Ceremonies

---

[84] *The newlyweds miraculously just wanted to know if I was okay, and now they like to comically bring up the incident during our couples' vacations together.*

(MC)[85] forgetting to introduce us correctly. Since I did not change my last name (and neither did my spouse), I worried the MC would accidentally introduce us as Mr. and Mrs. *His* Last Name since this patrilineal introduction is so common. In such an important moment, being introduced as someone else and not myself as an equal partner in this relationship would have been devastating to me. The fact that the guy gets to dominate the relationship with his name is not fair to any woman or relationship. At one wedding I attended, the officiant accidently inverted the couple's name; introducing them as Mr. and Mrs. *Her* Last Name. It surprised the crowd to hear the bride's surname be used instead of the groom's so much that everyone responded loudly in rebuff and laughter, as if a man taking a woman's name is a hilarious and absurd notion. I thought the hiccup was awesome.

The wedding entrance is the equivalent of the Super Bowl's player introduction; all eyes are on the team members and everyone is cheering in support. In our wedding reception introduction, I wanted us to come out of the gates as equals, so we ditched the "Welcome for the first time ever, Mr. and Mrs. *His* Name!" and we skipped the "...as *husband* and *wife*" part too (you'll understand why in a few chapters). The MC asked everyone to congratulate us but used our full and separate last names. It was the most positive way we could send the message that we were two married folks with different last names. And from there we moseyed our way into our first dance.

I get that some people do not like the newlywed dance or the parent dances and would prefer to hide from the spotlight or take the time to consummate the marriage behind the photo booth. I find these moments endearing. I have the sweetest memories of my father and I at the father/daughter Girl Scout sock hop themed dances.[86] When it came time to hit the dance floor at my own wedding, I was thrilled to revisit those days by dancing to Ben E. King's *Stand By Me* with my father. The dance is a loving

---

[85] *Looking at semiotics, "Master" technically refers to a man, even though women can fill the role too. It's just another example of how divisive and biased gender roles are embedded in language.*
[86] *It's true these dances push heteronormativity, but I didn't get it as a six-year-old. I hope those dances today are much more fluid.*

way for parents to send off their child; it is also an intimate reminder of a family's connection.

That said, there are always just-as-important family members waiting for their dance cards to be filled too. At a friend's reception, a bride chose to dance with her elderly grandfather before her father. Her grandfather recently lost his wife to dementia, and he was dependent on a walker; the compassionate and intimate gesture didn't leave a dry eye in the house. It was proof that sometimes bucking the system can have beautiful rewards, which makes it a great time to point out that there is no rule declaring a newlywed must dance with someone of the opposite sex. It's a crying shame that ballroom-dancing lags behind in gender equality; for example, *Dancing with the Stars* has yet to feature same-sex partners. I say dance with the one you love regardless of what's between their legs.

To modernize this toe-twirling tradition, consider dancing with both parents or whoever has all the right moves. If the bride's (or groom's) mom knows how to Nae Nae, then it's wrong to deny her the dance floor. In retrospect, I should have danced with my mom. She's a damn good dancer and it would have meant a lot to both of us. If the groom wants to do an elaborate choreographed dance, he should take a confident cue from Will Ferrell in *Blades of Glory* and go gorillas with his dad or any dude on the dance floor. And all the dancing is going to build up a good appetite, which makes it a good time for a little slice of herstory and sex.

The wedding cake is one of the most beloved and time-honored desserts; sex is another one. Luckily, the two are often combined in wedding traditions. Those edible undies and body chocolate paint your aunt bought you aren't the only tantalizing wedding desserts. In fact, the wedding cake is chock full of sexual innuendo too. Those towering layers of chocolate and vanilla frosting are all about sex; hot sticky, pour-some-sugar-on-me sex.

The wedding cake dates back to Roman times, though it wasn't the white confectionary tower known today. It was a dry biscuit made from a grain such as spelt. Wheat was one of the period's most prized staples; it represented wealth, health, and plentitude. Newlyweds were blessed with these symbols in in the hopes of growing fortunes and families. The groom would take the biscuit and break it over the bride's head, which literally symbolized the groom breaking the bride's hymen. The falling crumbs would then bless the bride and groom with a fertile future. Procreation was a major focus in Roman weddings, but not necessarily in the because-that's-what-my-religion-dictates way. Children were extra working hands for the peasantry. For the aristocracy, children were the continuation of bloodlines, and heirs were the glue to empires. Children were so important that a husband could also legally dissolve the marriage and return his wife to her family like a used good if the couple remained childless.

After the dry biscuit ritual, guests would rush to collect the crumbs for their own good luck in what I imagine resembled Black Friday shoppers at midnight when store doors opened. It's possible to surmise that this is where the contemporary ritual of sharing the wedding cake comes from. It's one big, I-hope-my-spouse-puts-out-tonight, karmic ritual. So every time modern newlyweds cut and consume the cake, they are adhering to a millennia-old tradition of symbolically breaking the bride's hymen and blessing themselves with good, baby-making sex.

The modern, cake-cutting version of this tradition, prior to the 1960s, was for the new wife to display her domestic prowess to wedding guests and her new husband. She was traditionally the only one to cut the cake and feed it to her husband, thus putting her into a subordinate and domestic position. Vintage photos that show both the bride and groom cutting the cake stem from the rumor that the frosting and cake was too stiff for the bride to cut so she needed the assistance of her strong and strapping husband. His hands were properly placed over hers to act as a guide, because—you know—women shouldn't be handling sharp objects.

In more recent history, the cutting of the cake has evolved into a very symmetrical tradition; it now symbolizes acting as a team. It is one of the few traditions that corrected itself over time. The newlyweds cut slices of cake individually or together, then they mush cake in each other's faces. It's as romantic and fair as a food fight can get. Luckily it lasts a few minutes, so no one will suffer too long, and everyone wins with a little slice of heaven afterwards.

Over the centuries, the wedding cake evolved into two different desserts, although it never dropped its "sexy and moist" symbolic center. On one end, the wedding cake developed into fruitcakes or bride's pie. They included every ingredient related to fertility and sex under the sun. A few of the yummy ingredients in bride's pie are oysters, nuts, lambstone (a.k.a. testicles) and something called cockscombs (a.k.a. waterfowl penis). This pie was most common in Britain and is still practiced today in some British colonized countries. Americans should be very grateful for winning the revolution; otherwise, they might be eating cockscomb at weddings and not buttercream frosting.

The other way it evolved was into sweet rolls. By the 17th century, a fun game was to pile all the rolls up high on a table. The object of the game was for the newlyweds to lean over the pile and kiss without knocking over a roll. Knocking one over meant bad luck for the couple and no one wanted the newlyweds to lose. So the bridesmaids rigged the game by using honey to glue the rolls together. A traveling French chef witnessed the bridesmaids' deceit but also recognized its culinary merits. He took the ritual back to France and evolved it even further into the classic wedding cake. Luckily, Americans can thank the French for the frosted cake enjoyed today and not the British for their pie. Knowing the herstory, I imagine the wedding cake might not taste the same ever again for couples who don't want kids or to feel pressured into parenthood. The feminist question that arises is, can a wedding cake exist without the symbol of fertility?

Unfortunately, my general opinion is no. Wedding traditions exist because something has been given meaning, and from meaning, value is derived. Without these qualities, rituals are arbitrary and meaningless actions. Similar cakes such as retirement or birthday cakes maintain the same symbol of wealth, health, and plentitude but not in the context of children. In the context of procreation, those elements are applied specifically to wedding cakes. I hate to ask or think it, but given all the baby-making superstition, could someone argue that wedding cakes are conservatively pro-life? If that's true, as a feminist, the cake just went from sweet to sour for me. Feminist fiancés must be able to access reproductive choice in all their wedding traditions. What is undeniable, though, is that the wedding cake and the symbol of sex are thoroughly mixed, because a cake can't exist without their symbolically fertile ingredients. Once the batter is made there's no way to separate it.

The 6.9 ounces of sex baked into the wedding cake also cooked up some outrageous cake superstitions. Pre-20th century, people believed a bride baking her own cake would render her infertile. Sort of like other activities like horseback riding, sports, and being on top during sex. (Ladies, please don't overexert yourself next time you whip up frosting—for your lady bits' sakes.) Another one included putting a slice of cake from someone else's wedding under their pillow before going to sleep to increase their chances of pregnancy. (I predict it increased their chances of doing more laundry.) And the one still practiced today is saving the cake top and eating on their first anniversary to ensure a happy, long life together.

It's not just the classic white wedding cake that's chock full of gender roles and sexual innuendos. There's the groom's cake too. It's a second wedding cake presented to the groom by the bride as a surprise. I can't explain why, but this is popular in the American South. The traditional bridal cake is a vanilla cake with white frosting, symbolizing the bride's virginity and purity. The groom's cake is typically chocolate, to oppose the "virginal femininity" of the traditional wedding cake because people accepted men's sexual proclivities.

The cake is also sculpted into the groom's interests, for example, a sculpted masterpiece of Wrigley Field, a beer can, or the Star Wars' Death Star. The groom's cake is problematic because it supports the idea that all cakes, unless decorated in sports team colors with a Playboy bunny hidden inside waiting to pop out, would be considered effeminate. It also implies that anything considered masculine is unsuitable for women. On a day that is supposed to mark the beginning of "us/we," a groom's cake creates a division between the sexes and puts himself above the team. It highlights the character of the groom, but restricts the bride's identity to an aesthetically neutral white cake that's focused on her sexual activity. Isn't that division sexist and therefore distasteful? Not to mention, the groom's cake is costly and totally superfluous. Its excess perpetuates the gross consumerism of the Wedding Industrial Complex anyway. The easiest solution is to skip it, but if a white bridal cake doesn't fit the personality of the couple, opt for something more adventurous and mutual. If a brontosaurus cake accommodates *both* newlyweds' taste, bake it. Sometimes adding some equitable spice can incite wonderful new traditions or mutually meaningful moments.

The best alternative to avoiding all this sexy and sexist symbolism is to change the cake's recipe. When considering all our feminist options, we considered removing all the fertility symbols by serving up a flourless or vegan cake instead. We also explored tossing the cake completely. Ice cream and candy bars are symbolically and politically neutral. Ultimately, we choose to accept the tradition for what it is. A wedding cake doesn't have to promise a baby tomorrow, so we interpreted its superstition as future fertile karma, but we knew we couldn't ignore the symbolism and "have our cake" too. I didn't see the point in practicing a tradition if I was going to ignore its meaning. Understanding the meaning of a tradition shows true respect. However, there is one last option to insert new meaning into this battered issue: turning the superstition on its head by consuming lots of sugary cake in order to increase the couple's ability to copulate around the clock. That's a new, sweet deal if you ask me.

As someone who loves cake a little too much, we gladly accepted the free three-tiered one our rental venue baked. My parents also baked a Ukrainian cake called a *korovai*, which is symbolically obsessed with baby-making, but again, children fit within our future wheelhouse. Ironically, agenda-free desserts like an ice cream bar are healthiest for couples, but the freedom of choice protects the right to choose fertility food. It's hard to imagine that a seemingly innocuous dessert like a wedding cake could symbolize anything more than a saccharine ending to an already sweet day, but the sexy proof is in the pudding.

While everyone is wondering why their wedding cake is making them horny, they may also be watching a similarly erotic tradition play out on the dance floor: the garter toss. In traditional hetero-fashion, the groom disappears under the layers of lace of the bridal gown, searching like Indiana Jones for the Holy Grail between the bride's legs. With a drumroll, he emerges triumphant and smiling, garter in his teeth. The garter symbolizes the unspoken privilege of marriage: sex, sex, and more sex. It's a brazen implication in front of family, coworkers, and maybe a religious official, but I needed to stop and reflect on whether this cunnilingus-innuendo tradition has garter go or garter stay?

The backstory will help you decide. During a European medieval tradition called the bedding ceremony, the bride and groom were escorted by the groomsmen to the newlywed bedchamber. Since any piece of the bride's garment was considered lucky (with the garter as the luckiest), the men would scuffle with the bride to remove the garter. As a result, the bride started preemptively throwing it away. Thus, the garter toss tradition was born based on the good ole medieval tradition of groping and sexual harassment. Sweet ain't it?

During the garter game, I often observe brides demurely laughing and pushing the groom out from her undergarments, but grooms seek the treasured garter with a sexual hubris on par with *Family Guy's* Quagmire. Giggity. I see this as evidence that women (even today) are not completely accepted as—or feel free to be—sexual beings, but men are. What if the bride reacted with her best *When Harry Met Sally* (1989) diner moment as her groom feigned oral sex? I'm pretty sure there'd be at least a few guests awkwardly reacting like Harry in the film. It's a double standard when a man can feign a sexual act but a woman can't respond similarly to it.

Which brings me to the fact that men don't have an equivalent article of clothing to the garter. It seems like a fun, frilly piece of lace meant to be sexy and flirtatious. Other than Victoria Secret models, though, no one wears them anymore for functional reasons like holding up pantyhose and knickers. It promotes the notion that purity and virginity are present, but removable and corruptible. Then, arguably, it's yet another symbol for the bride's hymen, especially since it's her husband who takes it away from her. Since most brides are not virgins, what's the point then?

I discovered more reasons to toss the garter tradition out. At a wedding, my sixteen-year-old friend caught the bouquet and a man twice her age caught the garter. He proceeded to put the garter on my not-legal friend in such a sexual way that it dawned on me that in any other scenario, this guy would be arrested for inappropriate conduct with a minor, but in a public wedding setting, under a socially sanctioned tradition, everyone was laughing and being entertained. Without a bucket of cold water around to throw on him, I yelled out, "She's only sixteen!" but no one heard or seemed to care. This tradition suddenly became a morally dubious sexual situation between a minor and an adult. It also suggested pushing a child into marriage because she was single.

Inappropriate sex stuff aside, creative possibilities exist that can be used to salvage the tradition. Removing the garter can be quite a sensual act, so couples can decide to keep it private for the wedding night. It would definitely be more fun to keep going without an audience waiting to dance the funky chicken.[87] It could be relegated to a Jack and Jill party. Or for the couple who decides to keep the tradition, think about incorporating something equally sexual for the bride, say, removing her spouse's bow tie with her teeth, or for the bold and confident couple, reverse the roles as an evocative feminist message.

No garter toss is complete without the bouquet toss, that wonderful game where women compete to catch the bride's bouquet in order to "win" an express lane to the altar and brand the remaining singles the "losers."[88] As a single woman, I never appreciated this game. I always felt peer-pressured into it or, if I opted out, felt like I was being a party pooper. Participating also felt like I was identifying myself as being on the less desirable team—the singles team—when there's nothing wrong with being single. The superstitious tradition exists to help women be more like the bride, not in love necessarily, but married and at least not single anymore.

Back in the day, marriage was supposed to be all a woman should hope and dream for. By not marrying, a woman was not living up to her biological and social destiny, and these unfortunate women were marked as spinsters and old maids.[89] Participating in the toss often felt like I was announcing that my batting average in relationships was so low that I've resorted to catching a bunch of flowers for good luck in love. The bouquet is just a superstitious promise, reinforcing the negative idea that it's unacceptable for a woman to be unmarried. And that is an asinine assertion.

---

[87] *This would be a great opportunity to dispel any stereotypes that feminists are prudes or sexaholics. On the contrary, feminists love sex. We're just willing to recognize that there are a lot of existing unhealthy attitudes and practices regarding sex and we are ready to mend them.*

[88] *In a wonderful display of a double standard and benevolent sexism at a wedding, men get to throw an erotic garter and women throw innocent flowers. It's possible to argue that the flower bouquet also represents sex and fertility (try to recall a Georgia O'Keefe painting or those environmental science lessons about the reproductive parts of a flower: the stamen and the pistil?) Although, when comparing the sexual symbolism between a garter and flower bouquet, I'd say the latter is rather wilted in comparison.*

[89] *I would like to remove the crazy cat lady from single lady representation. I formally nominate Charlize Theron and Shonda Rhimes as official reps because they are smart, in charge, badass, powerful, single women.*

My favorite feminist bride protest of this game happened on *Sex and the City*. The wedding bouquet fell at all four women's feet, they looked at all it symbolized, and defiantly walked away to show they preferred their empowered single lives. This may not be practical in real life at the risk of offending the bride, but nonetheless, it was a powerful statement and showed that women don't have to feel pressured to play into the status quo. It's no wonder the bouquet toss has fallen out of favor; forget the bouquet, single ladies need to catch a break.

Like the garter, there's room to evolve the game. Newlyweds can make sure it celebrates something that doesn't isolate guests for certain life choices or reinforce repressive ideals of the past. They can modernize it by celebrating being a woman: married, poly, dating, and single. Or by celebrating everyone who is true to themselves: non-binary, cis, queer, a Whitney Houston fan, etc. Couples can choose to celebrate all of the above or none of the above, but I think the game should reinforce the idea that a woman, or whoever, can be strong and independent regardless of their relationship statuses. The modern version of the toss should make these qualities known and something people would be proud to join. If that happens, then I'll be the first to jump out of my seat to participate. If not, I'll beeline it to the bathroom or the bar.

No matter the drama, a wedding day will always be a memorable event. Even if the reception tent or an altar ego's pants fall down, that wedding will be the most talked about and enjoyed wedding after the bruises and prides heal. Even if there's some drunk puking in the bathroom (seen it, done it), the couple won't even notice. Even if the cupid ice sculpture melts into two sloths "doing it," get ready to slowly tell sex jokes. These are the moments, in all their imperfection, I am happy to experience, but I draw the line on sexist or gendered ones. At a wedding, the only sex anyone should be talking about is the sex the couple will have on the honeymoon. Actually, only the couple should be talking about the sex they'll be having—other people should not be discussing other people having sex...that's just weird. But now that I'm inadvertently talking about other people having sex, it's time to talk about the honeymoon.

Chapter 13

The Sweetness and Sourness
of the Honeymoon

With all the sex I've been talking about, you'd think I'd already be on the topic of the honeymoon. I don't blame the couple who treats the honeymoon as a sleep and stress recovery period rather than a saucy sex-fest. Sometimes "getting some" on the honeymoon just means piña coladas, bartender therapy, and sleep on the beaches of Bora Bora. For those looking forward to devouring the edible underwear wedding gift, the honeymoon is still all about dancing the horizontal polka well after the DJ from the wedding reception has gone home.

When my ninth grade social studies teacher returned from his honeymoon at Disney World, my classmates and I grilled him about what rides and parks he visited. To our dismay, he said he didn't see or do anything. Perplexed by anyone who would go to Disney World and not at least meet Mickey, we innocently asked, "Wait, what did you do then?" The teacher gave us a big, mischievous grin to which it finally clicked in our early pubescent minds that our teacher went on lots of rides...private rides. The class erupted; papers were thrown in the air, students smacked their heads on their desks, some tried to high five the teacher but most of us harmoniously protested, "Ew, gross!" We learned that day Disney World is, indeed, the happiest place on earth.

A honeymoon without sex is like Mary Kate without Ashley, the burger without the bun, a Kardashian without attention; one cannot exist without the other. Even the term itself refers in some way to sweet, sticky, finger-licking sex. The honeymoon has several stories of origin and influence. One source stated that the honeymoon started when desperate men raided nearby villages to capture a bride (as we learned where the term *groomsmen* might come from). To avoid her angry relatives, they hid out for around one month's time (or one moon cycle), or to my shock as one source put it, "until the relatives stopped bothering to look for her."[90]

The second story of the honeymoon's origins relates to mead, a wine made from honey. The couple would drink their share of mead to gain liquid courage before the big night; or perhaps to get that kidnapped, reluctant bride to pass out so he could rape her and consummate the marriage. It was also said that the couple drank honey wine for the month in order to superstitiously increase the couple's fertility (back then, a quick pregnancy was equated with high fertility, even though it likely only had to do with increased frequency due to lowered inhibitions thanks to the wine).

Regardless of which story is true, the Victorians turned the honeymoon into a month-long trip. Why a month? It was thought that newlyweds needed to be exposed to Uranus (this isn't just an awesomely appropriate bum pun, it's also true). Uranus was an astrological period thought to introduce the couple to different emotional patterns, ones consistent within the happenings of marriage. Astrological explanation aside, a modern interpretation might be more revealing.

In the Victorian period, it was a thirty-day get-to-know-you trip, both sexually and to see the relatives abroad who couldn't make it to the wedding. The honeymoon functioned as a sort of sexual quarantine, a time to work out the kinks in the bedroom. It was not enough to "do it" behind closed doors. Decent Victorian society needed ample space and time away from that blushing bride. The month was spent getting over the discomfort of new experiences and accepting this new fate, like being removed from her familiar friends and family and traveling with someone she might barely know. To make matters worse, she was required to have sex with this new person too, and she barely knew what sex was.[91]

Without feminism to promote the importance of proper sex education, inexperienced couples needed that honeymoon month to figure out what

---

[90] *This time period might also be to see if she misses her next menstrual cycle (i.e., becomes pregnant).*

[91] *Perhaps this is why people like to ask, "Is the honeymoon over?" It was a crash course in sex.*

goes where. Despite the awkwardness and messiness, people have been worshipping and praising the benefits and importance of being a virgin on the wedding night from the beginning of time. There's the zodiac sign of Virgo, which contrary to popular belief, refers to growth and harvesting and not virginity. Geishas start out as virgin apprentices and participate in a coming-of-age ceremony called the *mizuage*, where a patron finances her and buys the privilege to deflower her. Virgins are the only ones who can survive a murdering rampage in a horror movie.[XLI] In 2009, twenty-two year-old Natalie Dyland legally posted her virginity for sale online, which put people in a rage despite not knowing if her deflowering by the highest bidder actually happened. There's the award winning TV show, *Jane the Virgin* (2014), which features a devout, virgin Catholic who accidentally becomes inseminated after a routine visit to the doctor. Then there's the virgin of all virgins: the Virgin Mary. Everybody loves the idea of virginity, but with 95 percent of the total U.S. population having sex before marriage by the age of 44, statistics prove hardly anyone wants to be one today.[XLII]

The virgin bride is at critical risk for extinction. Today the average sexual encounter for women is 17.3 years old (men are slightly younger at seventeen), but the average age of a woman's first marriage is 27.4 and men's is 29.5 (2016)[XLIII]—a full decade later. However, the average age of a woman's first pregnancy is 26.3 years old (2014).[XLIV] This means that "first comes love, then comes marriage, then comes baby in the baby carriage" is a lovely fictional bedtime story.

Unaware that newlywed virgins still existed or that I knew any, I was totally caught off guard when a religious friend admitted how nervous she was on her wedding night because she and her fiancé were both virgins. It's fine if someone wants to be a virgin, but doing so needs to be based on personal choice and not someone else's pushed ideals (and being one doesn't mean they don't need to know how birth control works, regardless of whether they use it.)

In another kiss-and-tell, he said/she said instance between two friends, it started to become apparent that the woman, who'd promised to save herself until marriage for religious reasons, was lying about her intimate exchanges to appear pure and untouched. Again, virginity is a fine platform (so is being a make out Queen or King), but what good is using religion as a moral high ground if it causes someone to lie about everything that's not sex before marriage out of shame and guilt? The exchange made me thank my lucky stars that I lived in a community that encouraged me, as a woman, to safely and responsibly explore my sexual opportunities (if I wanted to) without subjective confines and pressures. I recognize, though, that not all women or men are that lucky.

Although its mystic qualities are demystified through better sex education and medical understanding, sex is indeed an emotional and spiritual experience. Not being a virgin on your wedding night does not ruin the intimacy or specialness of a wedding night or honeymoon. By increasing women's knowledge of their own bodies and opening up opportunities for women to financially and emotionally support themselves, then sex, pregnancy, and sexual health are no longer fearful or ignorant experiences. They are manageable ones, enjoyable ones, ones that don't have to be put off until marriage, because a woman knows how to take care of herself and *all* her needs. Unfortunately, the reality of how sexually active people are today doesn't stop religion or abstinence education from pushing a totally unrealistic sex/honeymoon agenda onto women.

With a mere 5 percent of virginal newlyweds, this can all seem like a moot point. But religious conservatives are always looking to roll back sex education, prevent access to and coverage of birth control, overthrow *Roe v. Wade* after forty-plus years of life-saving abortions, and increase abstinence education (a.k.a. Sexual Risk Avoidance Education (SRAE)),[92] so a laissez faire attitude toward reproductive health and rights is never the right move. Here's why empowering women to secularly choose their own sexual destiny and not shaming them for those decisions is massively important.

As mentioned way back in Chapter 4, a women's virginity was a tradable, luxury commodity in marriage arrangements. A girl's hymen was the highest-valued asset a girl could bring to a marriage, then her reproductive parts, and then her dowry.[93] While I've already covered how strict sexual mores in

---

[92] *It's important to note that comprehensive sex ed. does not omit the option for people to choose celibacy, but abstinence-only programming, which omits all options outside celibacy, has been proven ineffective in deferring sexual activity until marriage, or preventing unplanned pregnancies or sexually transmitted infections (STIs) (Source: Work Cited 13).*
[93] *Interestingly, and not well known about peasants in medieval Europe, was that it*

developing nations can cause severe human rights violations, the importance of virginity and who is in charge of it is no different in those developing areas than in some U.S. communities. It's an outrageousness notion that in the U.S. anyone other than the woman, herself, would be in charge of her virginity, but it's not always the case. Purity balls treat a young woman's virginity as a tradable and controllable commodity when she is encouraged to pledge it and her hymen to her father until her wedding night.

For all their attempts not to, purity balls prematurely sexualize girls before they understand the "birds and the bees." It sends the message to girls as young as six that their bodies are meant to be sexual, and that their bodies and such sexuality are too burdensome for a woman to manage alone. Furthermore, what good does it do a girl's self-esteem if she's taught her primary value is her purity status? (This preconditioning is even worse because boys aren't similarly policed.) A woman's asset is her brain and compassion, not her untouched vagina.

Purity balls prevent girls and young women from learning how to manage their bodies. If they're taught to pass the buck to men (not even another woman who might understand what a woman goes though), it sets a precedent on all sides that men can dominate and control women's bodies and that women should not have autonomy over their own person. When I was six, I forgot to put on sunscreen at a friend's house and got a terrible sunburn, I'd be horrified today if my parents saw that as a sign that I couldn't handle my own body from there on out rather than seeing an opportunity to educate me about personal care, responsibility, and ultraviolet rays. But I will question the maturity of young girls who pledge their virginity to their fathers before they even understand what sex is. If someone had promised me the entire American Dolls Molly collection in exchange for, say, my beloved cat or sister, I'll be honest, as a six-year-old, I would have given up either without a second thought.

It's troublesome that adult women aren't aware of the pitfalls of this

---

was common for brides to be pregnant by the wedding. In fact, an out-of-wedlock pregnancy was almost encouraged because it proved fertility. If she wasn't pregnant, the engagement could be cancelled and she would be returned to her family. The obscurity of this historical fact goes to show how the culture of higher classes dominates what is considered ubiquitous, acceptable behavior.

practice and are, instead, happily complicit with it. In 2015, Brelyn Bowman did just that and presented a "Virginal Certificate" to her father at her wedding. On Instagram, she posted a photo of herself in her wedding dress handing her father the certificate. Below it she shared, "Dancing with my first love. I was able to present a certificate of purity to him signed by my doctor that my hymen was still intact. Also, the covenant he gave me when I was 13. When you honor God, your life will automatically honor others! I love you, daddy."[1]

After this story went viral, Mrs. Bowman took advantage of the publicity and wrote a book about celibacy titled *No Ring, No Ting*. The Amazon description of the book is (sarcasm alert) very nonjudgmental: "In a world where sexual perversion is so prevalent, it's taboo to be celibate... yet alone a virgin!" So that means if you're not a virgin, you're a pervert? (Also, I had to look up what "ting" means on Urban Dictionary and, FYI, that doesn't sound like the actions of a "pervert" to me.) And in case anyone was looking for a cure to their sex addiction, this book will "give you guidelines to walk you out of sexual promiscuity, including valuing yourself by embracing the purity mindset to catapult your life to the next level." I have no problem if Mrs. Bowman wanted to be a virgin at marriage—more power to her for that. But I do care how she advocates for celibacy because all I hear in that partisan description is someone promoting Madonnas, and judging and punishing those who she thinks are whores.

I think it's great if someone can have a healthy relationship with either of their parents about sex and their love life. But purity balls and certificates cross the line into sexual policing and patriarchal power plays. Allegedly, even Diana Spencer had to medically prove she was a virgin before she could have her fairytale wedding and become a princess. I suppose under different contexts, publicly announcing losing one's virginity could be used as a political action to fight against the stigma of pre-marital sex or knock down the virgin pedestal, similar to the hashtivism campaign of #ShoutYourAbortion and #MeToo. Context is crucial, and this virginity certificate to dad raises too many feminist red flags to be a healthy practice worthy of posting on the fridge next to a report card—or on Instagram.

Besides, contrary to popular belief, the presence of a hymen is not an accurate way to gauge whether someone is a virgin. Too many wedding traditions operate on this idea of breaking the hymen (for example, slicing the wedding cake) or representing purity (the color white) but hymens can be disrupted any ole way beyond sex (ask your doctor how). It can even theoretically survive after sex because each hymen is different and made of pliable tissue.

The idea of virginity lingers in the Unites States because conservatives push abstinence-only programing despite its ineffectiveness and because social customs like wedding traditions promote it despite no one wanting to be one. This disjointedness exemplifies why modernization is imperative. They need to accurately represent people's lifestyles today. Can you imagine how much more rewarding a honeymoon would be if people were pressured to get the Harvard of sex education instead of being pressured to be an abstinent virgin who had no idea what to do on his or her wedding night? No bride or groom would be driving blind under the sheets; each would be equipped with an internal g-spot GPS, expertly driving their own Ferrari to their maximum potential. A honeymoon can be a place where experienced drivers or first-timers can work out the mechanics of the bedroom so long as they arrive at their destination prepared with enough lube to keep the engines running. In this day and age, there's no reason why anyone should drive blind, unless someone wants to role-play racecar driver and cockpit crew in bed…

Anyone who wants to role-play astronaut and alien or magician's assistant that pulls something magical out of a hat during their honeymoon (or any time in the bedroom for that matter) are free to do so. It's just imperative that couples don't fall into stereotypical gender roles too. Anyone can pretend-play president or doctor. While those are fair rules to play by, it was standard practice for the groom to play travel agent and his bride clueless tourist.

In old-fashioned Western wedding culture, the honeymoon tradition outlines that it's the husband's job to plan and pay for the entire honeymoon.[94] It's a ceremonious way for the groom to represent his new role

---

[94] *It's arguable whether this tradition is frequently practiced anymore. If that's the case, this is another example of a ritual self-correcting itself toward more egalitarian practices due to sexism. But for the sake of highlighting obvious unhealthy gendering, I'm going to address it.*

as the bride's primary financial support and family decision-maker. Would the bride prefer something sunny and romantic? Too bad, it's off to a cabin in the woods to hunt and fish or to Comic Con if that's what hubby wants. Granted this is an extreme (and stereotyped) example, but it highlights how within weddings and marriage, money often allocates power and then limits collective choice. Surprise! Another tradition with ties to the wage gap and obsolete gender roles in need of modernization!

The clever aspect of this honeymoon tradition is that this lack of choice, control, and one-sidedness was labeled a romantic and charming surprise (i.e., benevolent sexism). I let a friend plan a trip to surf camp in Costa Rica without asking *any* questions and I will never do it again. Traveling blindly is just poor common sense. It's irresponsible to not have any bearings or understanding of the trip in case there's an emergency. As I learned the hard way, there's nothing fun or romantic about a surprise destination trip when you pick up an intestinal bacterium and didn't come prepared with some desperately needed antibiotic. Feminism aside, a bride should be in the honeymoon planning loop for the simple sake of not getting the shits on such an important vacation.

With so much role-playing and politics already in the bedroom, it seems costumes are unnecessary. Sticking to this patriarchal honeymoon tradition is no good; besides the missionary position with men on top all the time gets boring. It's important to alternate positions and share the reigns because it leads to wonderful new experiences and honeymoon destinations. Couples will then discover the hottest item they can bring to the bedroom is equal power and consideration.

And if the honeymooners are role-playing, I assume there are lingerie-type costumes too. The most traditional honeymoon costume is the classic white negligee that the bride brought with her in her trousseau. If the point of women's lingerie is to excite and promote sex than it must be feminist, right? The issue is not as see-through as a sexy teddy.

The classic honeymoon negligee is white[95] to symbolize the bride's innocence that is about to be taken away (more virginal pressure), and it's long because she's supposed to be modest and shy (good qualities of a virgin). I'll be honest, this constant barrage of virginal rituals and symbols is

---

[95] *I received a black negligee at my rehearsal dinner.*

142

exhausting, and that's not how I wanted to feel as a feminist bride. Only couples on their honeymoon should be this tired, which is why I'm compelled more than ever to modernize wedding traditions. When I surveyed my guy friends about it, the most common response was something like, "It's nice but I just want to see it on the floor." If the traditional white negligee promotes virginity but no one is, and if men are somewhat indifferent to lingerie, who does it really benefit?[96]

It's for women, of course. The positive feminist side to lingerie is that it promotes feeling sexy (a once forbidden fruit to women) and can contribute to a positive, confident body image (remember the part about burlesque). That part is great, but I do understand and agree that the way sexiness is taught, presented, advertised, and exploited could use some underwire reinforcement.

With Victoria Secret as a prominent leader in lingerie sales and famous for its army of skinny, beautiful supermodels, it's hard to ignore the unattainable size 0 and cellulite-free image they promote. But, there is hope for us average to plus-size women. In 2006, Spain banned runway models who were not a healthy BMI,[97] and more fashion outlets are hiring healthier, more realistic models. More positive news includes a market prediction that the plus-size lingerie segment will see huge growth in the future. This means that ladies can get some love in lingerie no matter her size or shape, and hopefully see more diverse models in the clothing too.

Here's another feminist catch. If sexy underwear improved the quality of sex, wouldn't men be going to the same lengths to gloss up their own goods for the honeymoon as women? Why are cotton boxers or tighty-whities enough to improve a man's mojo? If the titillating excitement of a honeymoon is in the presentation of oneself, it seems women alone are culturally conditioned to play dress-up.

At a shower, a friend once gave lingerie to the bride and an outrageous, Borat-type (2006) banana hammock to the groom. It went over great at the party, and it didn't make being sexy a one-way street. Maybe that's a sign stores like Victoria Secret should have a section for lacy ball-huggers too. Lingerie for everybody! However, if feminist newlyweds are opposed to

---

[96] *Lingerie is a $13 billion industry (Source: Works Cited 14).*
[97] *Body mass index (BMI) is a measure of body fat based on height and weight.*

honeymoon lingerie consumerism (oh, that sneaky Wedding Industrial Complex), just opt for naked. That's the point after all.

I don't hear many honeymoon stories or want to share my own. I assume this is because for all the public displays of affection a wedding entails, couples are happy to keep what happens in the bedroom private. And most movies stop the moment the couple gets married and runs off into the sunset, so there are few examples for newlyweds to live up to. My own spouse and I got married on a Sunday then went back to work on a Tuesday.[98] (I don't recommend this, but it's not the end of the world either.) Sunday night is something I'll leave between my spouse and me because I believe in the idea that some things can and should be left private between two consenting adults.

However, I will admit that coming down for breakfast at the wedding venue with my parents and bridesmaids the next morning was awkward as hell. It felt like "what happened on the wedding night" was a huge elephant in the room while we politely discussed the continental breakfast spread. Perhaps it was uncomfortable for me because, for all my willingness within feminism to talk about sex as an important factor that contributes to women's equality, I'm still carrying my own sense of shy propriety courtesy of my own environmental and educational upbringing. There's an unspoken pressure for women to treat sex from a very reserved perspective even though most of them aren't virgins. The details of our wedding night don't need to be shared if that is our wish, but I shouldn't have felt the need to feel or act like a blushing, Victorian bride. No woman should.

Today, honeymoons are vacations where the main goal is to get naked, have sex, order some room service, sleep, and repeat. They are no longer the immediate, lunar cycle, odd sexual quarantine used to get to know your spouse much better (although, if that's the role-playing they want to do and never leave the hotel room, that's the couple's prerogative). However, all the wedding superstitions are still steeped in old-school traditions where the aim is to get the newlyweds' loins wet, their ovaries operating, or their soldiers marching. Newlyweds are so inundated with sexual superstition and

---

[98] *We had a mini-moon the following weekend in Napa Valley, and six months later, we went down under with each other—that is, on a casual two-week backpacking trip through Australia.*

144

symbolism that if someone doesn't get pregnant during the honeymoon, there might be a hysterical pregnancy instead.

After tirelessly working out the sexist kinks in Western wedding culture, I, along with anyone reading this, should be sexperts, or at least sexist sexorcists (people who can get the sexism out of sex) by now. I hope people understand the importance of comprehensive sex education, family planning access, and not worshipping the idea of virginity. Once that happens women will be treated more as equals, and couples can finally enjoy the point of the honeymoon, which is to have mind-blowing, broke-the-bed, I'm-pretty-sure-I-discovered-the-meaning-of-life sex with someone they love.

Breaking the Threshold of Marriage

I had no grand vision of what marriage would be like. Disney movies stopped at the moment the couple married and sailed off into the sunset, and I had long since rejected the idea that marriage would look like a white, picket fence, me at home with the kids while hubby worked to bring home the bacon. Marriage for us was an open book. All we knew was that we wanted to continue honoring and supporting each other as individuals as we had always done and have a fantastic time doing so together. The most common reflection on our situation from people was that nothing would change since we had been cohabitating together for two years prior to our wedding.

My spouse and I disagreed with them, though. We did feel different; we felt married. I was now legally responsible for this person (not in a coverture way; my spouse was still his own person). It's the same as going from just the fun uncle or aunt to now the parent. Shit got real! Before, either of us could leave our relationship with few repercussions, except for maybe sacrificing our DVD set of *The Lord of the Rings* trilogy. Now, if my spouse defaulted on his credit card that would affect my credit score. We felt more connected and more protective of each other because of it.

A month into our marriage, my spouse and I hiked Half Dome in Yosemite National Park, California. I panicked when he began experiencing muscle cramps in the middle of the dangerous cable chains (where multiple people die each year). As his spouse, I vowed to protect him, but as the more experienced hiker, I wrongly put him in danger. I should have executed better judgment and left him at the bottom while I summited. And as I was near tears and thinking these dark, widow thoughts, a fucking marmot scooted up the side of the cliff mocking me because *it* didn't have a care in the world.

Hanging by a small chain and standing on a two-by-four-inch wood plank attached to a mountain's cliffside, scared that I could become a widow at any moment, I made the typical deals with God and vowed to recycle more and not to check my iPhone at dinner if he or she let my spouse survive the mountain. We summited in one piece, but the emotional and physical importance of my spouse hit me. Marriage is serious business, marmots are smug-ass rodents, and it's very easy to get superstitious when you think love is on the line.[99] We took our vows to love in sickness and in health seriously. The hiking debacle taught us that protecting each other meant making good decisions, and with support, we can push through perceived limits. We didn't need superstition to save our marriage. When it came time for my spouse (the groom) to carry me (the bride) over the threshold, we knew we didn't need its superstitious protection.[100]

Superstition is the one of the main reasons why couples practice this tradition. It was thought those bad spirits would make a last ditch effort to spoil the newlywed's future prosperity by climbing into the bride's feet or into the home. So to cut off this spectral connection, grooms starting carrying brides over the threshold and installed a lip at the bottom of it. With such danger lurking for the bride, and with Fabio gracing many romantic book covers, heroically shouldering his love (or sexual conquest), carrying the bride over the threshold became a romantic gesture. What more could a bride want than her strapping groom sweeping her into his arms, rescuing her from the dangerous spirits at their doorstep,[101] and then sweetly carrying her to the marital bed where he will deflower her in the gentlest but most commanding way? Well, if you're a feminist bride like me, a lot more.

---

[99] *I recognize that not everyone feels this way about marriage; there's no reason to think they can't feel as responsible for someone without filing paperwork with the government. For us, at least, marriage was the right choice, and everyone is entitled to their own paths.*

[100] *One reason we didn't do it is because, quite frankly, we forgot, but when we learned of its meaning, we were happy we didn't. The proper time would have been the moment we moved in together, which was before we were marriage.*

[101] *Carrying the bride over the threshold is consistent with Colette Dowling of* The Cinderella Complex *who worries that all women just want to be rescued. Luckily, feminist brides do not need to be rescued.*

The tradition, which dates back to ancient Rome, is another tradition where the groom asserted his strong masculinity over the bride's feeble femininity and odd status as a magnet for bad luck. I'm a badass and strong feminist bride; I don't want or need to be rescued, period. The whole caveman carrying his cavewoman back to the cave just reeked of benevolent sexism,[102] which is not our idea of romantic. If I wanted to reverse the roles and carry him over the threshold instead, the gesture could be interpreted as emasculating and not the same heroic and romantic gesture (hostile sexism/double standard).

Nowadays, it seems this ritual is slowly dying (considering the rise in premarital cohabitation) and lives on primarily through cartoon fairytales. There is no real reason to continue it. For us, the romance is sacrificed because it's so littered with sexism, but if a couple insists on continuing the tradition, all I can recommend is that both partners take turns carrying each other over the threshold.

***

I suppose you think now that the wedding and honeymoon are over, it's time to sail off into the sunset to live happily ever after. Unfortunately, there's a little bit more to uncover, but you're doing great. If you need a little boost, I recommend making another pot of coffee, watching President Trump brag about sexually molesting women and then brushing it off as "locker-room talk," putting on your pussy hat because now you're fired up again, turning on *Unwritten* by Natasha Bedingfield[103] and having a pump-you-up inspirational dance party, and summoning your feminist superpowers. Now you're ready to continue making social traditions respectful toward women and infusing equality in everything. A feminist's work is never done.

---

[102] *If readers take anything away from this book, it's that benevolent sexism is like wedding herpes: it's sometimes hard to detect and cunningly throughout all wedding traditions.*
[103] *The song's lyrics are perfect for this book. It is a great, feminist anthem:*
"I break tradition, sometimes my tries, are outside the lines
We've been conditioned to not make mistakes, but I can't live that way."

Chapter 14
The Language of
Love and Equality

When I reflect on my declarations of love to former boyfriends and for amazing things like avocados, cute animal viral videos, and Tina Fey, I realize I proclaimed my feelings almost to the point of recklessness. "I love you" is a powerful statement, but what felt like love for my romantic suitors paled in comparison to the love for the man I would eventually marry. That, and my affection for smart, funny feminists is not limited to Tina Fey, either (I also have to play my feelings cool when in the clandestine future we do become friends); but cute videos of pandas and baby goats reign supreme.

In the heat of passion, people just want to find the right words to match what they are thinking and feeling. In my married-person, feminist superpower, I-ate-too-much-guacamole maturity, I understand that this is incredibly hard to do. Linguistic hindsight is 20/20 until people have the privilege of experience and time. Maybe then, after getting dumped in the tenth grade, I would not have wasted a week crying profusely, listening nonstop to Celine Dion's *My Heart Will Go On* while playing solitaire locked in the family computer room. Maybe I would have realized my real feelings *for* him did not match my valiant statements of love I made *to* him (and that I needed to learn a lot about coping with rejection).

Navigating the complexities and nuances of language is not always easy. When adults remarked that I threw "like a boy," as a child I accepted it as a point of pride. I didn't understand backhanded compliments that doubted the abilities of my sex. Delivering and deciphering language is as complicated as figuring out if he or she likes you because they complimented your Old Navy cargo pants. As a married adult, tradition encouraged me to scream my new status of *Mrs.* and *wife* from the mountaintops. It felt at odds with the independent identity I spent a lifetime building, and in my relationship, it was super weird and off-putting that I was the only one making these concessions and changes to my moniker. Wary of the brash and passionate proclamations I made in my youth and suspicious of hidden gender inequalities in language, like any good amateur etymologist or Noam Chomsky fan, I set out to uncover what our words of passion and matrimony signified.

My trusty, bullshit-sniffing tool in my wordy adventures was, of course, feminism. It's never tongue-tied when expressing needs and concerns over equality. Plus, it possesses hawk-like eyesight that can spot subtle, hidden, and sexist nuances in language. Not everyone agrees that words like *cunt* or *bitch* are demeaning, and there is still a divide on whether the term *feminist* itself is good (let me settle this—it is). Semantics can seem like a moot point when there are bigger fish to fry. However, big revolutions can't happen without micro-changes. For all the things that keep women as disadvantaged minorities, language might be the most dangerous because everyone uses it everyday, and often too carelessly.

Think about how much easier it might be for women to fill at least 50 percent of Congress and CEO positions if labeling them as *bossy* didn't hold back strong women leaders. Or what if people like Rush Limbaugh didn't call women like Sandra Fluke, who advocated for reproductive freedoms, *sluts*? Would women then demand better access to healthcare? What if people did not say that Emma Sulkowizc was "asking for it" when she was raped on Columbia University's campus? Would more survivors of rape be brave enough to report it? What if women learned not to say *sorry* for every little thing, such as when asking for a raise or promotion they deserve? Would that help close the gender wage gap? What if men learned not to catcall women on the street? Could women then walk at night in safety and comfort? Healthy language is imperative to equality. The best part is everyone has the ability and power to use it toward positive effects.

When it came time for me to swallow whole all the verbal trims and fixings that came with an engagement, wedding, and marriage, I wanted to understand the nature of what I would be consuming. Wedding and marital terms are meant to help me define my new role in my relationship and in the world, like *Mrs.* and *wife*. But I asked myself, why do I need to redefine myself in the first place? I decided the best way to understand this change was to do some more research and soul searching. I needed to make an educated decision and decide if this new wordy baggage benefited women and myself.

Like a true detective, I discovered a mountain of hidden discrimination in wedding and marital language, biased profanities that had been manipulated and painted to look like declarations of love and commitment. Etymologies revealed an insane pecking order of words and names that, based on sex, had stripped minorities of basic civil and social rights for most of human history. If anyone needed their mouths washed out with soap, it was wedding customs' dirty sex politics. As a feminist, a woman in love, and a bride, I wanted whatever sweet words I whispered to be pure and true, not tainted by distasteful tradition. I owed that much to myself, and to whomever I chose to love, whether my spouse or Tina Fey.

The Sordid Semantics of the Words Husband and Wife

The words *husband* and *wife* never sat well with me when it was my time to use them. The concept of having a *husband* and being a *wife* seemed abstract and too conventional for my palate. These are the terms my parents use…my grandparents used; the words felt obsolete, archaic. My own *husband* couldn't wait to call me his *wife* (I think my protests encouraged him). And if Facebook is a place where the truth runs free, it seems like many other fiancés, based on their posts, couldn't wait to use those words too. Figuring I was alone on this island of thought, I decided to explore why the H and W words sent chills down my spine.

I started by examining other sex-oriented relationship labels. Boyfriends and girlfriends are more or less inventions of the last one-hundred years. They're direct in their description: monogamous dating and an indication of the partner's sex. Don't the terms husband and wife imply the same function but elevated in commitment?

Not really.

The husbandry and wifedom club is centuries old, unlike the more sophomoric boy/girlfriend.[104] While I should be excited by this exclusive

---

[104] *Even these terms are becoming more problematic because they exclude gender non-conforming folks. Partner and significant other are gender-neutral substitutes.*

membership, I realized that the terms came with a gross history I'd have to adopt. The word *husband* denotes a man as the primary authority and breadwinner, which is no surprise given that its Old English definition is "master of the house." (Fun fact: the name *hubby* came about in the 1680s.) Similarly, the etymology of *wife* means "mistress of a household," (i.e., *housewife*). A *wife*, in biblical terms, is also known as a helpmeet, meaning her job is just to follow the husband as his helper.

What Webster's fails to communicate is that these terms are balls-deep[105] in divisive sexism. The "master of the house" could be a leading member of the outside community, whereas his "mistress of the house's" leadership was limited, more or less, to just the house. Some may argue that the terms *husband* and *wife* are no longer associated with their boys' club past, but the words just didn't sit right with me. There were vestiges of sexism in those words that I couldn't quite put my finger on.

At a work party, I made my way to the CEO to introduce myself. In my three-champagnes-later state, I had enough courage to say to her, "I just wanted to let you know I think it's pretty awesome you're a woman CEO. Why don't we see more women in your position?" She enthusiastically replied, "I know!" and then we got into a sobering conversation about careers and personal lives. She asked me why, at my fertility peaked-age of thirty, my spouse and I hadn't embarked down the kid path yet. I explained that our priorities were elsewhere. Perhaps we'd jump on the kid bandwagon if one of us was willing to make the sacrifice to cook, clean, and rear the kids more than the other, but that compromise escaped us. She curtly replied, "So what you need to have kids is…a *wife*!" At that moment, every light bulb went off.

My spouse came to understand my distaste for the word *wife* when it became evident that many of the women we knew who identified as a *wife* and practiced patronymics[106] began to fill conventional gender roles. Despite

---

[105] *Some may argue even the term "balls-deep" is just as offensive and sexist and I shouldn't use it, which is a fair point; however, I'm using it as figurative descriptor to describe how literally deep some words are imbedded in the patriarchy, i.e., political pile of male genitalia obstructing equality.*
[106] *Super important term to know:* Patronymics *is a name adopted from the father, grandfather or any male ancestor through birth or marriage ("patro"—father; "nymics"—naming). Just as important terms to know:* Matronymics *is a name adopted from the mother, grandmother, or any female ancestor through birth or*

careers and good educations, they ended up being the ones who quit or cut back on their careers and became the primary caregivers. A Harvard Business School study proved that in the face of life and family changes, women—no matter how educated, feminist, or career-driven—tend to revert to traditional gender roles, even if both the men and women believe in egalitarianism.[XLV] Many friends still claimed to be modern in thought when the reality of their lifestyles tended to not fit their ideals. This paradox is a sign of choice feminism.

Let's use an unbiased coin toss as a fair model. The teams are men versus women; parenting is the prize. The women's team keeps winning the toss. Statistically, the odds should be 50/50 each time; so if women were the undisputed champs, officials would need to investigate whether the coin is weighted or be statistically awestruck at how rare and improbable such a singular result is. It's honorable to become a parent and watch over the kids' upbringing, but there's a greater implication and red flag when it's still women doing the majority of caregiving and household work.[XLVI] If men are consistently getting out of diaper duty, this clearly shouts that the parenting game is still rigged.

Parenting is the default job of women over men because deciding who becomes the primary parent is made within the constraints of a patriarchal playing field. And like any sports team, economics influences a team's performance. Oftentimes, the primary parent is the one who makes less bank. If women earn less professionally, and paternity leave pales in comparison to maternity leave, then it's financially logical to let the mother, or *wife,* stay home over the father/*husband.* These discrepancies indicate the game is rigged. It doesn't matter if a woman declared it was a "choice," outside, biased conditions constricted absolute, free choice. Sure, there are more stay-at-home dads than previous generations, but if Americans existed in a true post-feminist society, dads would be staying home just as much. One team

---

marriage. Neutronymics *includes the mutual adoption of a new name, a reordering* or *combination using the names of the married individuals, or the retention of separate surnames. Neutronymics is meant to be a solution to those who do not want to participate in patronymics or matronymics and want to increase name equality. For the record, I had to invent this term. Change is easier when all options have actual names. And one more, just for fun:* Onomastics *is the study of the history and origin of proper names, i.e., personal names.*

shouldn't be winning that coin toss so frequently.[107]

While the CEO was right that a *wife* would have changed our family planning, in retrospect I should have replied, "Well, if you're concerned, then you could create an equal paternity leave policy for your employees and prove to them, shareholders, and the world that you do truly care about your employee's family welfare and equality. That way, you'd give us more opportunity to grow our families." Despite the efforts of feminism, functionally within marriage as mothers and primary household managers, the lives of modern *wives* still share some similarities to the ones from the past.

I will admit many women identify as a *wife* and maintain a career and family under the "we can have it all" feminist dogma; and I respect their efforts to make sure there is ample parity in their family life. However, studies show that even working moms still tend to fulfill more house, family, and work responsibilities than their male spouses. Even the idea of "having it all" can be unfair as the concept is more often applied to women. Have you ever heard men telling other men that they can also "have it all"? Understanding how much gender politics still play a role in starting a family was the ah-ha moment that sunk the nail in the proverbial coffin on using the term *wife*. Even if other married couples managed to depart from the term's semantics, I can't remove the taste of mothballs from my mouth.

---

[107] *Understanding the true nature of choice can be hard to accept. I know so many women who are smart and take pride in how they conduct their lives, and they should. Before I learned about choice feminism, I'd be offended by anyone who accused me of being illogical or ignorant to the nature of the world around me. But as hard as this may be to believe, identifying the presence of choice feminism in the choices a woman makes is in no way a critique on the ability, willingness, desire or choice to, for example, take care of her own children. Taking care of your children is certainly important; and as a mother now, I empathize with the situation. We are all just trying to do our best with what we've been given. But what if accepting the existence of choice feminism and acknowledging where in our lives this might be true, educating ourselves about the social and civil limitations surrounding us, influencing us, affecting us, and then taking actions to achieve more equality, leads to a much easier, productive, and rewarding life? A life where women are no longer grappling to do the "best with what we've been given." If we did that then, we can access every option imaginable. And when men can choose options once limited to women within the feminine mystique or outside what I call their own masculine mystique, that's real liberty.*

Realizing that I neither fit into the *wife* mold nor wanted to fall into a choice feminism trap, my spouse relented on using *wife*. He understood our need for something more modern and respectful. It's fair to wonder if my resistance to calling myself a *wife* will actually prevent me from playing into patriarchal patterns. It's hard to say. I believe the benefit to resisting the status quo makes me slightly more cognitive of hidden inequalities or of falling into gendered behavior patterns. In the pursuit of equality, I'd rather try and fail than not try at all and maintain the biased status quo.

If you're still not convinced to convert to an alternative term for *wife*, the Dutch have a more cuddly translation for it—*bitch* (Old Dutch). The philosopher Confucius defined a *wife* as "someone who submits to another." And *wife* in Cockney slang is "trouble and strife." Still have that warm and fuzzy feeling for the w-word?

Not willing to settle with a moniker I couldn't digest, I sought other terms. In the past, *fiancé* worked well. The French term sweetly means "a promise, and trust." Historically, it meant "to be betrothed, or affiance," which weren't imbedded in gender inequity. While technically, *fiancée* is for women and *fiancé* is for men, nowadays *fiancé* is used interchangeably. It is an equal opportunity title, but it isn't for married folks.

I decided my marital word, full of equity, would be *spouse*. At first, using it came off formal, and it felt as if my word choice screamed in comparison to using traditional language. It did turn a head or two, prompting more than a few questions. Eventually, the awkwardness of fighting convention wore off, and I realized *spouse* held greater social significance.

Husband and *wife* distinguish roles in marriage by sex and gender.[108] These terms perpetuate the notion that marriage is between a man and a woman, which even under legal same-sex marriage laws subverts social equality. Now, some married same-sex couples will use *husband* or *wife* because that is the dominant practice. When speaking with my married LGBTQ friends, they all individually agreed that using *spouse* made a larger, long-term impact. However, because they were already challenging conventional ideas of marriage by being gay, married, and using *husband* or *wife*, they argued those terms helped challenge the system and acclimate

---

[108] *To be clear, sex relates to biological and physiological characteristics, and gender relates to socially constructive behavior applied to specific sexes.*

people to same-sex marriage too. As a straight woman, I don't have the benefit of that argument. It sounds old-school gendered when I use it. Besides, how impactful can words be if we're all using them to different effects? *Spouse* is a term everyone can use without the muck that comes with *husband* and *wife*.

The beauty of *spouse* is that it also works for those who prefer more gender fluidity. It is a truly intersectional term. As a gender-blind term, deciphering what sex a person is married to is impossible. I get, however, that this lack of distinction makes others (and sometimes themselves) uncomfortable. The challenge of using *spouse* is learning to be comfortable and confident enough to deal with sexual ambiguity. It forces people to deal with and (hopefully) accept more types of dynamic relationships and identities and learn to be more self-assured with their own sexuality regardless of what it actually is. And I think this is critical as the U.S. starts to explore how to treat gay, transgender, queer, and non-binary folks and their relationships better. *Spouse* is simply more inclusive and accepting.

It is true there are larger feminist and discrimination issues in the world of weddings and marriage, and they take more time to change for the better. Dealing with the semantics of *husband* and *wife* is a low priority. It seems almost petty. But failing to act on the smaller issues makes the larger issues harder to amend. Successfully executed baby steps toward a goal are much more palatable than trying (and possibly failing) to make a huge leap. No gesture is too small if it encourages more marriage equality. I decided that using *spouse* is something I can comfortably stomach and easily say.

The best part is that by using it, everyone wins. Word choice when spoken by one person can sometimes be inaudible, but when others join the verbal equality bandwagon, it can create cheering crowds.

What's in a Maiden Name?

A fair maiden conjures fantastical stereotypes of a beautiful woman with flowing locks, a fairytale dress, furry Technicolor friends, and a voluptuous bust, who is helplessly lost on a quest or at the mercy of an evil villain.

In reality, she did not have a lover or husband gallantly riding to rescue her. A maiden is a woman who has never been in a relationship and is a virgin

155

(like a *bridesmaid)* and having a *maiden name* infers that these personal facts are true. And if you're a woman today, this is a hilarious and ludicrous assertion because most people lose their virginity when they're teenagers and marry much later. The purpose of a *maiden name* is to declare a woman's sexual and relationship status.

I try not to be defined by my relationship or sexual status or participate in traditions that slyly and inappropriately reveal these details. Others aren't bothered by or maybe even aware of it. In watching the relationship telenovelas that are my Facebook feed, I have watched countless women change between their original surname (ugh, maiden name) and multiple married names more times than they probably change their IUD. While some are comfortable publicly advertising their life decisions and directions online, there's a precedent for keeping a women's marital status private in order to prevent sexism. For example, in an interview it is illegal for an employer to ask about anyone's marital status (or age or sexuality) because, one, it's nobody's business; and two, it has caused discrimination. Historically and even today, sexist employers have seen married women as a liability (because they might get pregnant and need maternity leave, or quit) or unavailable to cavort with around the copy machine (so why bother hiring her?). (This is one reason why the show *Mad Men* is so curiously captivating and contemptible.) *Maiden names* are not innocent markers for a woman; they mark her identity according to her sexual experience.

It's logical to assume surname change would be equally tracked, but men who change their names are seldom asked to type in their old identities. Professional basketball player Ron Artest changed his name to Metta World Peace (yes, you read that correctly) and footballer Chad Johnson temporarily changed his surname to Ochocinco to match his jersey number. Technically, neither of these men, one of whom wants global harmony and the other to count in Spanish, would fill out the maiden name section of forms despite their radical moniker changes because...they're men. Women who change their *maiden name* are expected to always fill it out. Surprise, another double standard.

Highlighting how men and women's last names are treated comes down to the crux of what a *maiden name* is and how horribly sexist it is. Men traditionally have one surname because in name, men are not expected to change for anyone (their spouse) or anything (marriage). Unlike men, most women are raised to understand they possess a *maiden name* and learn it is considered impermanent, to be changed after marriage. This double standard is a problem. Women who practice patronymics maintain this status quo too. Sure, some see taking his name as a sentimental right of passage into wifedom, but is it such a happy precedent if it treats two people in a relationship so unevenly?

Stopping the linguistic double standards in marital language would be a massive accomplishment for women's rights, so I'm all for booting or modifying names and titles so that my sisters and I can get a little more R-E-S-P-E-C-T. No longer calling a woman's surname a *maiden name* is a great start. It's important to encourage women to view it as permanent and valuable. Calling it a *maiden name* implies that it is ephemeral and therefore less valuable. As far as I'm concerned, the term *maiden name* can join *bridesmaid, wife, and husband* in the pile of gendered words that can be kicked to the curb. It's a simple solution that could have profound effects, and maybe my own surname could get some much-needed love.

Hallowed Be Thy Name and Thyself

I was about eighteen when I received a terrible response to my surname. A sales clerk looked at my credit card, tried to pronounce it, failed and then turned to me, "I bet you can't wait to get married and get rid of that name." In my head, my response would make even a sailor blush, but outside I was just so shocked that someone could be so xenophobic and ethnocentric that I firmly replied, "It's pronounced 'MY-kut,' and I like my last name." Zing, I got him good! I like to think the death stare I gave corrected his ignorance, but he snorted, annoyed I didn't agree with him. If I were a man who was expected to keep his surname, this guy would not tell me he disliked my last name. As a woman, he felt entitled to tell me that not only did he dislike my ethnic surname, but I should change it for his convenience too.

When this took place, I don't think I even called myself a feminist (I always knew I was one, but I was not outward about it). As a kid, I used to dream about falling in love and calling myself by my future lover's last name. I readily accepted changing my name one day without a second thought. But after this ugly exchange, I recognized that my complicated last name was not my problem or one where the right man might put me out of my naming misery as this clerk implied. It's true, I'd spent a lifetime defending my surname and sometimes it was a bit tiring, but instead of giving in, I just realized...this guy's a jerk.

From that moment on, I became a crusader in defending my name. In turn, I developed a newfound pride in it. When my peers and I reached our mid-twenties and started to marry, I realized that my peers did not share my women's name championing. In fact, my unshakable surname passion was often seen as unfashionable, unbecoming, and uncooperative. I felt judged by many of them when their responses reflected the sentiment of, how dare I maintain my own identity while married even though my *spouse* would be doing the same? How dare I not do like everyone else?

I should have anticipated such responses. After all, around 90 percent of brides today take their groom's surname (Holy feminism, Batwoman! After three waves, how could this be?). The number of grooms who take their bride's surname (matronymics) is so statistically insignificant and infrequent that no one has bothered to study or record it. People are more likely to spot a unicorn (let me know if that happens, on both accounts).

Here's where my high school AP statistics class can finally pay off. If, in theory, equality is 50/50, then 90 percent of women taking his name is statistically a massive red flag. When nearly *all* women are bypassing a matriarchal practice and one that honors both people equally and, instead, choosing a patriarchal practice, that is a major indicator of sexist conditioning and practices.

In keeping and defending my surname, I culturally and socially hit a nerve. I wanted to know why my unassuming name-keeping decision should be so controversial and so resentfully received. Surely, such a popular and time-honored practice should not be so threatened by the personal decision of one woman?

In researching name change, I realized that the clerk's response went deeper than personal opinion. It was rooted in how little respect society has historically given women's names in general, and how women have readily accepted such terms. Just look at how publishers explained to Joanne Rowling that *Harry Potter* would be more successful if her female gender was hidden behind her initials. Forget *He* Who Must Not Be Named; it was *her* name that was first forbidden. That salesclerk is not the only one who poorly judges the value of women's names.

As a bride, I felt pressured and expected to change my name. It was so assumed that I would change my name, that people automatically switched it for me without even asking if that was the correct course of action or if *I* even wanted to change it. Setting the record straight was, at times, confrontational, annoying, or wearisome, but always worthwhile.

What became more unsettling were the troves of brides who shared their own name decision-making process. Many proudly declared that they had made an "educated decision" and concluded it was in their own and their relationship's best interest to take his name. When I investigated this "educated decision" by asking what was the name of the tradition they were following, *none* could tell me the actual name of this practice. (It's called patronymics.) I don't know about you, but when it comes to semi-permanent and costly things, like a tattoo, I don't get inked without understanding its language and semiotics first.

And to make sure that their deduction was wholly formed, when I asked how their fiancés responded when asked to take her name (because, of course, a good decision-maker will explore all angles and possibilities) their jaws typically hit the floor. They never considered something so obvious and basic as asking a man to make the same considerations as them. This is the point in the conversation where I drop the mic, triumphantly throw my hands up in the air, turn, and silently exit the room. This exchange does not make me popular, but damn it feels good.

And speaking of being unpopular and bursting readers' champagne bubbles, this is the part when I break it to those 90 percent of brides that, at this point in time, a bride changing her surname to that of her groom's is by far the most sexist and outdated ritual remaining within wedding culture. The truth is hard sometimes (#SorryNotSorry), but we're going to come to terms with this together. If it will help, pour a glass of wine, a dram of whiskey, a shot of tequila, whatever fits your fancy. It's been an eye-opening experience for me too, one through which I learned that no tradition is as solid as it seems, and that it's essential for women to learn that the phrase "to love another, you must first love yourself," includes cherishing their surnames too.

Mrs. vs. Ms. vs. Miss vs. Mr.

Sexism in language does not stop with married monikers. The titles placed before them are worthy of scrutiny too. I've been formally addressed with every female prefix imaginable on wedding invites, table placements, congratulations, thank you cards, etc. Save for your highness or majesty, which I would gladly accept. I started keeping all the mislabeled holiday cards and wedding invites as proof of etiquette gone wild. But you know whose title was always correct and consistent? My spouse's.

I'm not anal-retentive about names (although it might seem that way). I'm not demanding that people "say my name, bitch!" à la American Pie; I'm more like the Childlike Empress from the *Neverending Story* imploring people to say my name correctly so I can thrive and live as myself and not get swept away into the Nothing. And courtesy of feminism and *Downton Abbey*, I'm also not going to apologize for demanding to be addressed appropriately. Names and titles are powerful stuff, people. This is what I've learned from watching too much TV.

Alas, my experiences indicate it seems no one knows what the proper etiquette is when addressing women today, which makes me wonder if they know the social precedent to it too? For this, I'm going to set the verbal record straight with some new age etiquette that won't offend anyone. Even Miss Manners won't be able to argue against it. Actually, she is about to shit a brick because that broad is about respect, and she could have been getting a lot more as a *Ms.* than a *Mrs.* or *Miss*. For today's modern folk, the correct sign of respect is not tied to one's marital status anymore (or even gender). However, to make *Ms.* the only option for women like *Mr.* is for men, understanding the saga and social meaning of *Mrs., Ms.* and *Miss* is imperative.

Mrs., Ms. and *Miss* are all abbreviations for mistress, which is a weird designation because a mistress today is applied to a morally corrupt woman sexually colluding with a separately married person. A mistress or *Mrs.* is historically someone in a position of power and control...over a house or servants, not herself or her spouse, and definitely not over her sex life (thanks,

160

coverture!). Early fifteenth-century English describes a mistress as "the kept woman of a married man" (a wife or an extramarital adulterer).[109] There is no male equivalent term for mistress because men aren't owned by anybody, nor are they blamed or judged for their sexual indiscretions like women are.

Ms. is a combo of *Mrs.* and *Miss.* Reportedly, it first appeared on the tombstone of a Ms. Sarah Spooner in 1767. Writer Nancy Gibbs hypothesizes that it was the result of a "frugal stone carver," or perhaps Ms. Spooner's family just couldn't afford an extra letter.[XLVII] *Ms.* is typically used when the marital status of a woman is ambiguous. In 1901, an editorial from the *Springfield Sunday Republican* offers the first modern literary need for the term *Ms.,* "There is a void in the English language. Every one has been put in an embarrassing position by ignorance of the status of some woman. To call a maiden is only a shade worse than to insult a matron with the inferior title Miss. Yet it is not always easy to know the facts."[XLVIII] In 1972, *Ms.* magazine used this revolutionary title that had just been permitted by the U.S. Government Printing Office as acceptable language in official documents.[XLIX]

Dan Rather of CBS News asked President Richard Nixon about the use of *Ms.,* "Some have taken to not addressing women by Miss or Mrs., but they've gone to the Miss, Ms., why not do that with White House letters?" The President replied, "I guess I am a little old-fashioned, but I rather prefer the "Miss" or "Mrs." But if they want to do it the other way, of course, we accept it."[L] But in the 1972 White House Audiotapes he quipped to Henry Kissinger, "[Dan Rather] asked a silly goddamn question about *Ms.*—you know what I mean?" Kissinger, replied, "Yeah." Then Nixon colorfully shared his true feelings, feelings one could argue reflected a common sentiment toward treating women with more respect, "For shit's sake, how many people really have read Gloria Steinem and give one shit about that?"[LI]

By 1986, they seemed to have relented on the issue and accepted *Ms.* Even today, no one questions the use of *Mr.,* but why the reluctance to using a word that similarly distinguishes a woman and uses the next letter in the alphabet?

---

[109] *And while I found no evidence to support this, maybe* Mrs. *is also the possessive form of* Master/Mr. *It makes sense given that a master owned and controlled a mistress through coverture.*

The three options given to women distinguish their life stages: single, *Miss*; married, *Mrs.*; or neutral, *Ms.* Why is this a problem, you ask? Because men are not characterized or valued by their relationship status in life, but women are.[110]

If I had a dollar for every Facebook post where a woman posted that she can't wait to become the new "Mrs. Casey Smith," I could have financed those life-sized wedding cakes of my spouse and me. I always wondered why people thought becoming a *Mrs.* was a life event worth tweeting or Facebooking about. When I first started dating, I definitely went maniacally running to friends to share that I was dating so-and-so (this was pre-Facebook). I was excited and hoped they'd be happy for me too, but I never went running to them exclaiming that I was excited to call myself *a girlfriend* first or worse, so-and-so's *girlfriend*. To me, it's about the person, not the label.

Facebook relationships status options have changed all that. Suddenly, bedroom buddy relationships are Edward-Snowden-public with people over sharing intimate details that are arguably more appropriate for the private boudoir. I don't have to watch telenovelas for relationship status drama; I just have to troll Facebook profiles. I know it's none of my business, but people are putting it out there; and like a car wreck, I can't look away. So I'm always perplexed by why some women insist on not just updating their profile status, but posting countdowns, "40…30…10 days 'til I am Mrs. Bob Smith!" I also find it super curious why men don't do this too. Did the women who thought highlighting their pending marital status change was so important ever stop to wonder why the men in their lives weren't similarly yelling it from the Interweb's mountaintop?

I worry those contemporary women are just repeating sexist dogma of a bygone era when a woman found her value in her marital status. Becoming a wife was the highest and most respected accomplishment a woman could achieve throughout most of history (aside from wedded mother). A daughter given in marriage created neighboring allies, an extra set of workhands,

---

[110] *A quick side note on the polite use of* Miss/Ma'am *versus* Sir *to address a stranger or a person being serviced: Yet again, men get one title of respect and women get two.* Miss/Ma'am *are based on marital status but they are also rudely based on guessing a woman's age. If people use* Miss, *they see you as someone young and presumably single. If they use* Ma'am, *they see you as old and presumably married.*

lucrative business arrangements, and legitimate heirs. An unmarried one could not. A wife was the currency exchanged for profit and power; that's why being a *Mrs.* is historically considered a sign of prestige. Women were only ever expected to be wives and mothers, nothing else. Men had lives outside their marriage. They didn't need to peacock their marital status to seem important. Sure, someone can be excited for their upcoming nuptials, but *how* it is expressed says a lot.

In today's love-based marital system, this distinction is irrelevant. Today, a woman's character and intellect contributes to the quality of a marriage, not her connections or uterus. But the term *Mrs.* does not celebrate that important individuality. *Ms.*, as the only female prefix that doesn't align with a life stage, is a sign of respect given to a person for who they are regardless of their relationship status.

Using *Mrs.* today implies that a woman's importance is isolated to her husband/marriage, which explains why so many disliked calling Amal Alamuddin "Mrs. George Clooney." As an accomplished and respected international human rights lawyer, many thought her professional life outshined Clooney's Hollywood one. To prove the point, many started referring to the couple as "*Mr.* Amal Alamuddin and her husband." Checkmate.

Consider that men or *misters* don't similarly brag about their marital status via a prefix. George Clooney, despite having a less noble career, didn't go so far as to change his prefix after attaching himself to such an impressive woman. That's because a man's value is found in who he is as a person, not who he is in a relationship. Guy culture celebrates the individual leader, the lone wolf; gal culture…not so much. What's alarming as well is that too few women and men catch the one-sided discrepancy. To my feminist grooms out there, you can help correct this imbalance by asking yourself and all your guy friends to either consider changing their married prefix (maybe *Msr.* is the right equivalent) or encouraging the women in your life to honor themselves as a *Ms.*

Don't get me wrong, relationships provide a great sense of community and strength, but I believe their health is contingent on the level of each member's self-confidence. There's an important difference between saying, "I can't wait to marry Casey" and "I can't wait to <u>become</u> *Mrs.* Casey Smith." The first shows a real excitement for spending a lifetime with Casey; the latter hints at the hope that marriage will improve one's worth. It shows more interest in the idea of marriage over Casey, the individual. How fun and fuzzy can *Mrs.* truly be if I am the only one in my relationship changing my marital identity? Isn't marriage supposed to be a unified front? I distinctly remember my high school health class explaining that a sign of a bad relationship is when one person changes for the other.

For women who want to get some unadulterated professional and personal respect, use *Ms.* as a prefix.[111] First, because it promotes equality and is the most equivalent to the prefix used by men; and second, it provides a sign of respect that is based on individuality, accomplishment, intelligence, or quality of character. It does not judge one's value based on bedside manners. When filling out a form, a letter, or card, always opt to use *Ms.* (In fact, if you are in charge of those forms at work, just take off *Miss* and *Mrs.* Altogether and treat yo'self for your bold and progressive thinking.)

I love the person I married. I love the sense of a team we've created together and that should be celebrated. But I also understand that our team would not be what it is if we didn't respect what we each bring to it as individuals. My marriage means more to me because we encourage each other to maintain that separate sense of self. Defining ourselves within the confines of marital naming convention would circumvent everything that makes us stronger and more united. We also learned that we don't need to prove we are happy and united through this type of formal etiquette.

Mrs., Miss, Ms. and *Mr.* still define a person by their gender, though, and that doesn't work for everyone. Society needs an honorific prefix that everyone can use. *Mx.*[112] is an upcoming term that is more prominent in England but appeared as early as 1977 in the American magazine *Single Parent.*[LII] *Mx.* is wonderfully gender-blind and suitable for those who don't fit or don't want to fit into a gender binary. And in case readers encounter anti-P.C. people: the politically correct nature of this suffix has nothing to do with restricting anyone's freedom or pursuit of happiness. In fact, it grants more linguistic freedom and personal happiness to those who might be oppressed by traditional, restrictive gender roles. And I think that is beautifully American.

---

[111] *Or* Dr., *if you are one. Insisting on professionally using* Ms. *or* Dr. *while married does not devalue a private relationship either.*
[112] *Pronounced like mix or mux.*

Chapter 15
Uncovering the History and
Practice of Patronymics

As a child, I was both a prolific doodler and a hardcore romantic. When I had friends over, we played "date" with imaginary boyfriends and went on imaginary double dates. I had many imaginary first kisses. My Lisa Frank binders were public diaries of lost loves, current crushes and potential future suitors. I fervently scribbled my first name and the last name of my crush into it. And since I had a lot of crushes, I was a repeat patronymics offender. Sacrificing my name proved I loved him; him giving me his name proved he loved me; having the same name proved you would live happily ever after. That was my childhood logic.

Then I grew up. I met that jerk of a sales clerk. I signed paintings with my name and sold them. I got promotions at work as Ms. Katrina Majkut. I rediscovered my heritage by participating in a short but intensive Ukrainian cultural/language program. And I started to become pretty proud of my accomplishments made under my birth name.

But I fell in love too. If I was going to live the fantasies inscribed on my old LA Gear folder and usurp my birth name endeavors, I wanted to know why this tradition existed and to see if there was any good evidence as to why I should change my name.

I discovered that there are three reasons why the name change tradition exists today. The first reason is religion: "...whatever Sarah says to you, do as she tells you, for through Isaac shall your offspring be named." (Genesis 21:12). When God embraced Abram as the "father of many nations" and renamed him Abraham in his image, the tradition of patronymics began. Name change signified the joining to a covenant and using the single name of the father, the established male lineage, and patriarchy.

Furthermore, in biblical times, surnames were not widely used, which meant that women upon marriage became "the wife of so-and-so." When surnames became a set practice in the ninth century, they were still fashioned after the men or their professions.[LIII] "Johnson" means "the son of John." "Bob Goldsmith" means Bob was, surprise, a goldsmith. And married women followed suit as it showed to whom she legally belonged. Throughout the centuries, the Pope and Catholic Church made name change more or less a necessary practice in Europe, which influenced name practices in America.

Today, whether a woman takes the name of her husband based on religious reasons depends on her relationship with the Big Guy (or Big Gal if you're Alanis Morissette in *Dogma* (1999)). However, if we're all God's children, why is it that one is honored more than the other by being able to pass their name down the generations? Like the purpose of the bridal veil and religious headgear, it was because man was made in the image of God and woman in the image of man. Using religion to defend the choice of patronymics is, again, choice feminism and not a decision made within an equitable system. As a spiritual person but not an organized religion sort of gal, this reason for name change didn't hold any holy water for me.

The second historical reason why wives adopt their husband's name is to prove their children's legitimacy, or as I abrasively call it, "bastard prevention and protection." Back before those fancy-pants DNA paternity blood tests that Jerry Springer and Maury Povich like to use so much, paternity was proven through properly inherited namesakes. A legitimate child must be born to married parents and share the name of the father; therefore, the wife, through civil or religious channels, needed the name of her husband in order to transfer it. (This is evidence of how women serve as relationship bridges.) A family sharing one name became a tradition when King Henry VIII passed an act to create a parish registry system for families.[LIV]

As discussed in Chapter 10, children born outside of marriage were deemed illegitimate and a huge no-no. The policy, created mostly by England and other European monarchies (and influenced by the Catholic Church), dictated that illegitimate children were not legally entitled to a father's surname and thus his title, money, land, or assets. And because inheritance and coverture laws stated that all estate assets could only be transferred to a male heir bearing the name of his father, patronymics practices were an absolute must. This is yet another explanation why daughters were historically undervalued.

With this history, it's no wonder men are still taught to honor and carry on their names. They get titles of privilege like "junior" (e.g., JFK Jr.) and other generational suffixes, like Thurston Howell III (a Gilligan's Island reference for the baby boomers) or Usher Raymond IV (for the hip generation X/Millennials).[113] Unless they are royalty (e.g., Queen Elizabeth II, Queen Mary II), daughters rarely receive titles of distinction or lineage and even today are not encouraged to pass on their names to future generations in the same way men are.

With the help of Henry Krause fighting illegitimacy laws in the 1960s and '70s and Sir Alec Jeffreys's invention of DNA blood testing in 1985, children born out of wedlock eventually enjoyed more protection through new legitimacy laws. With this new baby-daddy-proving technology gaining popularity and inheritance laws and bastard stigmas disappearing, the need for sons and daughters to bear the same name as their fathers became unnecessary. Which makes the need for the mother to bear her husband's name also pointless.

Regardless of whether I am a mother, I see no technical reason or need to change it. The function it once served just no longer exists. Besides, I wouldn't want to give it any credence on the small chance my friends who become parents in or outside marriage would face an ounce of discrimination like the parents before them had over a name.

The last reason women historically took a man's name was to protect mothers and widows. Prior to the 19th century, if a wife survived her husband, it was unlikely she could inherit the estate. It passed over her and landed in the arms of her (legally named) son or the next male kin to her husband. However, it was expected the son would support his mother, as she had little to no money or means for supporting herself. Hopefully her son did not have any mommy issues or she'd be out in the cold. These rules are consistent with the plot in Masterpiece Theatre's *Downton Abbey*, where a male heir could inherit the estate but not a female one. Since the Crawley family had all daughters and didn't want the estate to leave the family, they pressured Mary into marrying cousin Matthew in order to keep it *literally* all in the family. Eventually, laws relaxed a bit and required that one-third of an estate be bequeathed to a widow in order for her to support herself.

---

[113] *That's the full name of singer, Usher, in case you're not hip.*

Jumping forward into the late 19th century, a widowed wife could now inherit her husband's estate, but to prove she was in fact the deceased's wife, she had to have his last name. Sharing his last name meant the couple had gone through the appropriate legal, civil, and religious channels and procedures. Legally wed? Bearing your husband's name? Here's your inheritance. Today, Western inheritance laws aren't contingent on a namesake, which makes reason number three also irrelevant now.

What I learned about the origins of patronymics is that they were originally meant to protect women in a benevolent sexist way. The men in power withheld certain rights from women (and children) if they didn't follow the rules dictated to them; if they followed the rules, they were praised and received those benefits. The rules were meant to protect the propriety of women and punish those who did not demonstrate "proper decorum." I believe in law and order, but I also believe in not having my sense of value and civil rights dictated by arbitrary codes of conduct that are enforced through punitive schemes. As a kid, I may not have understood what my romantic scribbles meant, but I sure as hell understood that whatever random reason the cool kids at school used to deem me uncool and unworthy to sit at their lunch table was bullshit.

Patronymics' deep misogynistic history gave me no reason why I would want to keep this tradition going. While I'm still blown away at the sheer number of women who want to practice it regardless, I was thrilled to discover I was not alone in my anti-patronymics sentiment. While we were born 164 years apart, I found a kindred spirit in Lucy Stone. Yes, everyone, I am the best type of stoner there is...a Lucy Stoner to be exact. [114]

The Herstory of Lucy Stone and Modern Name Change

"A wife should no more take her husband's name than he should hers. My name is my identity and must not be lost." —Lucy Stone

If I could create my own female-centric Mount Rushmore, I would add Lucy Stone between the carved cutout of Susan B. Anthony and Harriet Tubman. That is how amazing I think she is.

---

[114] *A "Lucy Stoner" is a real title. It was applied to members of the Lucy Stone League, a group that lobbied for name equality protection. While much needed today, it is an inactive group now.*

When I was looking for case studies about patronymics, I discovered the love story of Lucy Stone. She was an active abolitionist and suffragist and her story is not often told. It is a powerful testament to how cultural traditions often impede women's civil rights, and how what can seem like a sign of love and commitment can be manipulated into a misogynistic tool of control. It also shows how such injustices can linger into the present day without people knowing it.

Born on August 13, 1818, Lucy Stone grew up in West Brookfield, Massachusetts, with a father who believed women were the property of men (i.e., coverture). She watched her mother suffer under the weight of nine children. Her father would not relinquish the funds to feed and clothe the children unless her mother begged. Stone realized that it was women's lack of education that created their short sticks in life. In a vow to change her future (and women's), she became the first woman in Massachusetts's history to earn a college degree (badass). She also swore to herself that she would "call no man master."

As a famous orator on women's civil rights, her passion and vigor caught the eye of Henry Blackwell, who proposed marriage to Stone one hour into meeting her. She refused. Blackwell knew the way to her heart was to convince her that they would be complete equals, an unheard of assertion in marriage at the time. After a four-year friendship/courtship (#ItsComplicated), Stone accepted Blackwell's proposal to marry on the condition that their marriage reject the conventions of state and church, which submitted women as property into the hands of their husbands.

On May 1, 1855, the two wed in a fashion they *both* saw fit. Together they drafted the "Marriage Protest" and disseminated it to guests. In front of friends and family, with the omission of the "vow to obey" line, they exchanged vows and read the protest aloud, "We protest especially against the laws which give to the husband: one, the custody of the wife's person; two, the exclusive control and guardianship of their children..."

After her wedding,[115] Stone continued to speak around the country on women's rights. But people, without her permission or approval, began referring to her as Lucy Stone Blackwell, or even more screeching to her ears, *Mrs. Henry Blackwell*. It took her awhile to officially denounce her married

---

[115] *Lucy's marriage lasted 38 years.*

name and insist on keeping her birth name upon marriage. This maverick became the first woman to *ever do so* in the history of America (double badass).

Amazingly enough, in 1879 when Lucy Stone informed the Massachusetts courts that there was, in fact, no law requiring women to change their names to their husbands', they defiantly responded by drafting one. Unfortunately, this set off almost a century of legal last name discrimination toward U.S. women. Other U.S. states followed suit and created laws forbidding women from registering to vote or getting a driver's license unless they shared their husband's name. Believe it or not, many of these lasted until the mid-1970s.

It's insane public policy when the men in power thought, "What's the most logical punishment for the crime of not taking your husband's name? Not being able to drive a car, definitely." Or, "Can you imagine the anarchy if we allowed women to vote under their birth name? Next they'll be wanting to ride bicycles and wear pants." The disproportionate punitive reactions by the courts proves that a woman recognizing her right to self-titling and an independent identity would give women unprecedented power and personal authority. This is why I think it's so important for women to realize their brand value.

Names are powerful. It's a person's trademark. There is absolutely no rhyme or reason why a woman keeping her surname should be connected to any of her civil rights like driving, of all things. Lucy Stone knew that the cultural tradition that withheld basic civil rights was a bad one; the question now is, do most people feel the same today?

For the last one-hundred years, Japan's constitution has required families to share one surname. "While the law does not stipulate which name married couples should adopt, in practice women take their husband's name in 96 percent of cases—a reflection, critics say, of Japan's male-dominated society." [LV] Despite being one of the most advanced nations in the world, Japan's marital surname law is a real lingering hold-up to equality. Japanese women tried suing their government, believing this rule violated their civil rights, but lost the case in 2015.

Not all U.S. women are as enlightened about our constitutional rights as these Japanese women are. A 2009 survey by researchers at Indiana University showed that 71 percent of respondents believed a woman should change her name, and half of those respondents went so far as to say the practice should be legally required.[LVI] If America's Declaration of Independence says "all men are created equal,"[116] passing a law forcing women alone to change their surnames upon marriage would be illegal discrimination based on sex and, therefore, a violation of the fourteenth amendment and of the founding principles of the United States of America. That 71 percent is breaking my heart and potentially my rights—and the rights of all of our daughters. For the love of Lucy Stone, why?

Amazingly enough, even the U.S. Supreme Court took a while to understand the discrimination it was placing on women. In the case of *Forbush v. Wallace* (1972), the U.S. Supreme Court upheld a previous Alabama ruling declaring a woman *must* use her husband's name on her license. Now this part is very important: the social norm of a woman adopting her husband's name upon marriage was so strong that even the highest court in the land assumed this was common law. No such law (common or written) ever existed except in Hawaii and Massachusetts. The district attorney, bored by the proceedings, quipped that the case was about nothing more than a disgruntled housewife in an unhappy marriage.[LVII] This unfortunate verdict is nothing more than a vestige of coverture.[LVIII]

It wasn't until the case of *In Re Petition of Kruzel* (1975), in the Wisconsin Supreme Court, that a woman's right to her birth name was set as the precedent, recognizing that not all societal traditions result in common law practices.[LIX]

Women may be able to vote and get a driver's license now without having her husband's name, but husbands are also sorely discriminated against by the patronymics tradition.

Lucy Stone and Henry Blackwell decided to keep their original names, but what if Blackwell wanted to prove a real point about sexism and asked the courts to change his name to Stone? I think the courts would have locked him in the stocks and thrown away the key. While the patriarchy may have historically encouraged (forced) women to change their names, it also set up barriers preventing men from doing the same. On the off chance a groom wants to take his bride's name (matronymics), a man will likely experience more legal barriers. In fact, modern men face more name change

---

[116] *I wish this were changed to "all humans are created equal."*

discrimination than women.

In most states, a man will have to do some combination of the following: pay a fee (one that is often higher than what women pay); fill out paperwork at a courthouse (filed at a different time than his marriage license); wait for an official letter of intent. The man must then present the letter to his local newspaper, which can now officially run his personal advertisement announcing his name change to the public (to alert any debt collectors, bounty hunters, the law, etc. in case he's up to any funny business). Afterwards, the man must appear before a judge, who then makes the name change official. Then, like women, he gets to tack on all the other identification change procedures and fees for changes to his passport, license, social security, etc.[LX] A woman sometimes only has to pay a nominal fee and hand in paperwork alongside her marriage license. Sometimes a woman can just pay a name-changing service to do everything for her.

Outraged at this blatant reversed sexism and violation of the equal protection law, Michael Buday teamed up with the ACLU in 2007 to sue the California Department of Health.[LXI] Buday wished to take the name of his fiancé, Diana Bijon, since her father had become his surrogate. Buday, now Mr. Bijon, won his case.

California is only one of nine U.S. states to adopt laws making men's surname change on par with women's name change procedures. As of 2015, a man who wants name change fairness for himself will have to travel to California, Georgia, Louisiana, Oregon, Hawaii, Iowa, Massachusetts, New York, or North Dakota.[117]

As for figuring out whether name change is for me, I can't overlook my distrust given its complicated civil history, but that's only half the story. I had to consider if it offered something I could get on board with socially and emotionally.

Peer Pressure and Following Your Heart

"And he said: 'Son, this world is rough
And if a man's gonna make it, he's gotta be tough

---

[117] *If you are a man living in the U.S. but outside one of these nine states and want to change your surname, please contact your local ACLU office.*

And I knew I wouldn't be there to help ya along.
So I give ya that name and I said goodbye
I knew you'd have to get tough or die
And it's the name that helped to make you strong."'
—*A Boy Named Sue,* sung by Johnny Cash[118]

If man culture praised bucking the mainstream and didn't see women's names as sissy, Sue wouldn't have specialized in bar fights. It seems guys can do anything they want, though that might be limited to the unspoken rules that govern man-land. There is lot of boys' club bullying regarding stepping outside the tradition of patronymics (and women can reinforce the masculine mystique). For example, choosing to take a woman's surname might get him endless wedgies, or (arguably) friendly ribbing about being "pussy-whipped," or pestering that he has a "mangina" or "tucks it." My own spouse's reaction when first considering the idea of me not sharing his name was, "What would my friends think?"

The masculine mystique is the other problem that has no name. It's a culture controlled by the subjective judgment and treatment by male peers, where men are boxed into their own gender stereotypes as women are. Hanging out with a friend, he lamented the restricting expectation that men must be breadwinners. He felt little freedom to be a stay-at-home dad or have a job he loved even if it wasn't lucrative without being judged for it. Emma Watson gave a famous speech at the United Nations for the launch of the HeForShe campaign and touched on this idea of the masculine mystique. "I've seen young men suffering from mental illness unable to ask for help for fear it would make them look less 'macho.' In fact, in the U.K., suicide is the biggest killer of men between twenty and forty-nine years of age, eclipsing road accidents, cancer, and coronary heart disease. ... I've seen men made fragile and insecure by a distorted sense of what constitutes male success."[LXII]

Heterosexual men (generally speaking: Caucasian and cis ones) have every liberty in the world, but the company they keep and the culture they adhere to influences their lives just as it does a woman's. Breaking away from the pack is not always appreciated. That lone wolf is now the hunted. Even in the movie *Hot Tub Time Machine* (2010), Craig Robinson's character is teased

---

[118] *Fun Fact: Shel Silverstein wrote the song.*

for taking his spouse's name. There's the mentality of *if you're not with us, you're against us*, which can explain why name culture never equalized among the sexes. If names are that powerful and men continue to retain their names (and that power), it's easy to understand why so many are motivated to preserve the status quo. Stubbornness to change or reluctance to go against the grain should not come at the expense of women or men who want to consider all possibilities. For the men who say, "No thanks, I'm a traditional guy," remember not all traditions are good ones, and learning to adjust with positive, equitable change can have powerful effects.

When I first approached my spouse about keeping my name, he gave the idea (and me) a snarl. Like many others, he was ready to go with the traditional marital flow and didn't appreciate me throwing a wrench into it. Of course he felt that way. Existing tradition is easiest and benefits him the most. From generations of culture placing false value on a man passing his name down the line, patronymics was so ingrained in his head as a basic milestone that it took him years to understand my personal and professional needs and how the name change tradition hindered gender equality. As a traditional, sometimes conservative guy, he wasn't necessarily open to the idea overnight. It took time for this new concept to resonate and germinate for him. In the end, I think he realized name change unfairly demoted me but propped him up. That, and he realized his friends' opinions were irrelevant. I was searching for the same respect, recognition and honor toward my lineage the tradition afforded him, and he couldn't argue against that.

I think it would be amazing if both men and women were presented the luxury to make decisions in a safe space, without the confines of social convention. Talk about real freedom. What if name change were an equal opportunity event, one where men considered it just as frequently as women? While this is not necessarily the reality today, there is no reason it can't be. That's why feminism is just as important for men and why it's necessary to explore and be vocal about how name change affects them too. When a woman entertains changing her name, a man must do the same. He also needs to recognize that a woman's name has just as much reason to stay as his. Name change isn't just on women's shoulders; it's a shared weight.

A person of real character feels no qualms about being their own self and living life according to how they see fit, not according to another's vision. The smart ones recognize that bullies are the inherently insecure ones. Sue's father purposely gave his son a name that went against the masculine mystique and made him an instant outsider. Changing his name and giving into convention would easily remedy the situation, but Sue stuck to his guns. Aside from the daddy issues he developed, I think his resoluteness to stand out from the pack is pretty awesome.

Like Mr. Bijon and Sue, I faced a fair amount of backlash from folks when I shared that I wasn't changing my name. Most of it was passive aggressive, some snarky, and one person lovingly told me to "take my feminism and shove it." Most people shook their heads, irritated that I couldn't play nice like everyone else. Some people questioned my decision-making intelligence. Others pretended I changed it and refused to use my actual name. Some shamed me for not putting family first, and others asked why I was bothering to marry at all.

In my quest to thoroughly understand patronymics, I had to understand all the social and emotional motivations others used to rationalize practicing it. Maybe despite its sordid history, there were emotional reasons I hadn't considered? Here are the major reasons women personally rationalize practicing patronymics and why none convinced me to take his name...

It's romantic. I used to believe it was, trust me. Well into college I would secretly sound out how my name fit with the object of my affection's. Make no mistake, I was not singing the romantic tunes of Babyface or Mariah Carey about a boy if you overheard me. I was listening for auditory harmony between my name and a real boy's to figure out whom I was destined to marry. However, to understand why it's considered romantic, I had to turn off Boys II Men and put on my pragmatic, feminist anthropologist hat.

Here's the thing about this argument: I challenge anyone to say that my spouse and I love each other any less because we have different surnames. I think it's more romantic for us to continue to love each other with our given names—who we originally fell in love with.

Besides, sharing a family name is an arbitrary measure of commitment and love. This became obvious to me as I watched friends, who once swooned over becoming *Mrs. His Name* begin to divorce. Name change doesn't cement a relationship or love. Not to mention how unromantic it will be when the woman returns to the dating game and her new partner yells out her full name in the heat of passion—the name she adopted from her previous marriage. Birth names will prove to be the one solid foundation people can always rely on, because nobody, except themselves, can give it meaning or take it away.

It unites a family. This rationalization also irked me. It felt like others were implying that because my new family doesn't share the same name, we are somehow less committed to each other. I'm not sure how anyone could accurately make that assumption. After all, since most brides take the groom's surname and the chance of divorce is 40 to 50 percent, one could play devil's advocate and argue that it, in fact, doesn't help a relationship survive longer.[LXIII] I've also observed extended families with shared names that fall further and further out of touch, but I've also seen non-nuclear families grow incredibly close and share no name. Modern families come in all shapes, sizes, colors, and sexes now. A lot of them come with different backgrounds and names. This pro-name-change argument implies that multi-dimensional families are less special or united because they don't share a single name. I learned that a name does not unite a family—the people within it do.

It's tradition. I love tradition (it's why I've spent so much time studying it), but I'm willing to accept that not all traditions are healthy ones worth repeating. There's hardcore evidence that patronymics is super sexist under current patriarchal conditions. No tradition should be practiced for tradition's sake if it comes at the cost of treating someone unfairly. Maybe if there's ever a time when the name change tradition can be done in a post-feminist world, where both men and women consider the tradition evenly, I might understand this argument. However, that day hasn't arrived yet. It is possible to respect tradition so long as users have the ability to modernize it and remove any lingering bias. Tradition is always changing. For me though, I think keeping my name has a more substantial and positive impact on equality, my relationship, and me.

It's what my husband wants. What about what the wife wants? My spouse wants me to stop trying to get him to like salads, and I want a cure to the common hangover, but not everyone gets what they want in this world. It's possible to argue that this justification is a function of simple domineering patriarchal patterns, where in the household the man singlehandedly calls the shots and the woman goes along with it. This train of thought reflects the qualities of a one-sided relationship. Who can guarantee such one-sidedness won't be repeated for issues like kids, career, money, etc.? I'm always conscious of these patterns. Between my spouse and I, being able to communicate our individual needs and arrive at mutually beneficial decisions has forged a stronger and happier union between us, so I'm hard-pressed to believe that name change should be made under such one-sided conditions.

I don't like my own name/prefer his name/want to identify with his family. I can understand not liking a name when someone wants to forget and disassociate themselves from their family for whatever reason. (Think about how many people are removing their Bill Cosby tattoos right now.) Name change alone won't necessarily open a family's arms. Instead, character and social skills will forge real reconnections. I wonder about the women who are ambivalent about their surnames. I get that not everyone's last name is exciting (but if it is, that's exhilarating), but could that ambivalence originate from how women are taught to not get too attached to a *maiden name* because it's ephemeral, not valuable, or because they're not a man?

It's convenient. One name is easier to manage, but that does not necessarily make it better. My teacher friend is pro-patronymics on the grounds that, as a teacher, it was super annoying and inconvenient to have to learn *all* the parents' and students' different surnames and remember who was connected to whom. That is just professionally lazy. Having worked in an office, I know I would be spending a lot of time in HR talking about professional respect if I told Alex in accounting or Taylor in marketing that I was too inconvenienced to learn their last names. Sure, people these days are obsessed with life hacks and shortcuts, but if something is personal, there's no such thing as a burden. Sometimes things are just worth the extra effort. If you're not convinced, you know what's convenient (and cheaper)? Not changing your name when you get married, and not changing your name back if/when you get divorced. That's real convenience.

I am not professionally established yet. Lean in, ladies. Lean in no matter where you think you are on the professional totem pole. There's always a promotion around the corner if you want it. It disappoints me when women are willing to change their names because they haven't established themselves significantly yet. They believe nothing of great importance bears their maiden name, so they may as well change it. Why do some women assume they will never accomplish anything great later in life? I'm over thirty, and even if it takes me until I'm sixty to do something significant, I want it to bear my name because *I* earned it. And you know who didn't earn it? *Mrs. His Name.* No one should sell themselves short just because "it" hasn't happened yet. Changing one's surname to another's won't increase your odds, either. Besides, who's to say *he* has already made it or has accomplished more?

What's the point if I'm just keeping my father's name? Great point, but that argument is just a check, not a checkmate. It's true surname retention and even a matronymic name, at some point, originated from dad. One could then argue it's still patriarchal no matter how you spin name change equality. Seems like futile feminism to some. It's a good point worth addressing. Let's consider that every first action meant to correct an imbalance would bear some residual evidence of the original biased system. It's just a growing pain toward equality. It does not mean that any effort for positive change is worthless. Practicing matronymics or neutronymics over time eradicates the patriarchal imprint that was once there. Think of it as buying a used house: the original inhabitants disappear and over time the new owner claims full authority over the homestead.

What will we call the kids? This is the most common pro-patronymics argument I hear. First for me, it's better to not worry about what hasn't happened yet (i.e., kids and the zombie apocalypse), so my philosophy is to just truck ahead (i.e., store up for the zombie apocalypse and future college tuition) and be as true and honest to yourself as possible (i.e., don't become a zombie). Second, when and if they do show up (kids, not zombies), whatever they are called, they will be healthy and happy (as long as the apocalypse hasn't come). I'm willing to bet that whatever name they receive, be it a hyphenated name, a new invented name, or just one iconic name, like Madonna or Prince, will still result in a smart and well-adjusted child. Well...I can't promise the kid won't turn into an egomaniac with the one iconic name, but I can guarantee they will know how to rock (or slay zombies).

If parents wonder what to name the kids there's always...oh I don't know, the women's surname. Moms all over the world sacrifice their bodies for nine-plus months to nurture a baby inside their bellies, endure painful labor, then continue to sacrifice their bodies a little more after the kid's birth, and they are likely to rear them the most, too, regardless of their employment status. If that's not enough of a woman's blood, sweat, time, and waistline to justify giving her surname to the kid, I don't know what is. I've worked far less hard on projects and still demanded top billing. Parents can also use neutronymics in order for each parent to be fairly represented.

When women approach me about the kid concern, I level with them. Kids are smart. If they grow up with a different name than mom or dad, it will not matter so long as they know mom and dad love them. Just like how a kid can be adopted but know the love their parents give them is still absolute even if they aren't biologically connected. The emotional connection is what makes you a parent—and a family—not a name.

In the case of emergencies, some also fear any difficulty in being legally identified as their child's guardian. It's a legitimate concern. Having more than one surname is not the problem; the problem is the legal systems that don't take into account the multi-dimensional families I was referring to earlier.

Speaking About Name Change: Whodunit?

After diving into the deep subjective and objective reasons women practice or forego patronymics, I was curious about who these women were. Are they, like me, caught between their love of tradition and personal independence? Do they eat too much artisanal cheese as well? Or are they nothing like me because they haven't yet discovered the podcast *Stuff Mom Never Told You*, boxed wine, and their own feminist superpower? Would studying the demographics of the pro-patronymics majority versus the I'll-keep-my-name-thanks minority create a juicy exposé on women's equality, women themselves, and their choices?

The awesome cohort of women from the 1960s and '70s who declared they were entitled to their own identity inside marriage (i.e., who practiced neutronymics), consisted of less than 5 percent of the female population. There weren't many of them, but that was enough to turn heads and put a lot of people in a tizzy. Neutronymics-practicing women peaked at just below 25 percent in the 1980s. The practice hovered a little above 20 percent in the 1990s, dropped below it in the 2000s, and most studies claim the current rate is around 10 percent. However, "around" is the key word here; most name change studies are dubious.[119] The most reliable study concluded the rate is a measly 6.4 percent, but it excluded middle name substitution, which is an option within neutronymics. Other studies included middle name substitution but also included women-only hyphenation, which isn't neutronymics, and those studies claimed around 10 percent.[LXIV] So for the purposes of this writing, we'll say it's somewhere between 6.4 and 10 percent—damn low, regardless. My sadness over the life curve of name equality is totally validated because if you line chart its development over the decades, it literally plots an unhappy frown.

This means over 90 percent of women in the United States take their husband's surname after marriage.[120] Ninety fucking percent. If I were given a 90 percent chance of winning the lottery, I'd donate my life-savings to *Planned Parenthood*, save a few bucks to treat myself to a massage, and then I'd buy a lottery ticket. It is more probable that a woman will take a man's surname than a condom will prevent pregnancy.[121] Part of me says it's not even worth examining who is in this 90 percent, considering 90 percent basically includes all women.

Well, not everyone. I'm not included. When it comes to name change politics, it feels as if I'm alone on a neutronymics island. Wait, no, I'm not alone. Beyoncé is on this island with me. I am alone on an island with Beyoncé! Who's cool now? It's true. When Beyoncé married Jay-Z, she became Beyoncé Knowles-Carter, and he became Shawn Knowles-Carter. That means Jay-Z is on the island too...shit, I went from being cool to being a third wheel. Great.

If you're still struggling to understand that the big deal is about

---

[119] *It's important to recognize that there are barely any adequate or comprehensive studies that extensively tracked patronymics across different races, sexualities, or classes within Western culture. The studies' sample sizes are often small and demographically limited, and are, arguably, blindingly white sample groups too. And there are none dedicated to men on this topic (at least I couldn't find one). There's massive room for improvement. I've done my best to highlight missing or questionable data, but the 6.4 percent is real. What is reliable is the generalization that name equality is abysmal in the Unites States.*

[120] *10 percent and 90 percent are rounded to account for discrepancies between sources.*

[121] *WebMD reports condoms, as birth control, are 82 percent effective.*

patronymics versus neutronymics, feminism versus choice feminism, who is on what side, and why I won't shut up about what a big fucking deal this is, here is my best analogy for you. In *Star Wars* speak, the patriarchy is the Evil Empire and patronymics is the Death Star that is so massively big it's capable of destroying anything that's not on its side or doesn't support the status quo (i.e., patronymics). Neutronymics is the tiny faction of rebels trying to neutralize the Empire, and feminism is The Force that gives power to the rebels. Choice feminism is how the Dark Side manipulates The Force to serve its own wicked game, and those who accept patronymics and choice feminism are Stormtroopers. They're just regular people who have been taught from birth that the Empire's way is the only way, and so they are fiercely loyal to it and will defend it to the death. But as we saw in *The Force Awakens* (2015), it is indeed possible for a Stormtrooper to switch to the Light Side of The Force.

Sheesh, I can feel my coolness fading. It wasn't meant to last anyway because I'm about to start sounding a lot like Bernie Sanders by dropping a massive amount of statistics. And I'm just as passionate about these statistics as he is to stats. Back to understanding who that 6.4 percent of neutronymics-practicing women are.

Of that small percentage, 4.9 percent of women have a completely different name from their husbands and 1.3 percent of women hyphenate or uses two surnames. (This study excluded middle name substitution, people who swap their birth name as their new middle name.)

Race and ethnicity also play an important role. Fourteen percent of married interracial couples have different last names. Hispanic women are more likely to maintain their surnames (15 percent) than non-Hispanic women (5.9 percent). American Indian and Asian women are more likely to do the same than black and white women. The percentages above reflect native-born American women exclusively, but it's impossible to ignore outside cultural and ethnic influences. While most global cultures practice patronymics, there are a few matronymic ones that offer insight into these findings, such as naming practices in Latin America or certain Asian countries like China.[LXV] And it's not just where a woman's heritage comes from that affects her surname choice. Where she lives in the United States also matters. Women from the West or Northeast are more likely to practice neutronymics.

While most name study results vary wildly, they all agree that women who practice neutronymics are most likely to have advanced college degrees, hold more prestigious careers, and marry older than other others. Is it no coincidence that Lucy Stone, who was born and raised in Massachusetts, was the first woman to attend college in the U.S. and was the first to keep her surname in the Unites States? If you're going to bet on whether a woman will practice neutronymics, a bachelor degree makes her 1.7 times more likely; a master's degree, 2.8 times; a professional degree, 5.0 times; and a doctorate, 9.8 times more likely. One reason women are pro-neutronymics is that they want the recognition and accolades that come with advanced degrees and high-profile careers to be associated with their own surname.

Even with such a low neutronymics percentage and probability, there are, in fact, plenty of women with advanced degrees who choose *not* to be on an island alone with Beyoncé (fine, and Jay-Z too). Basically, it doesn't matter who you are, the power of patronymics is so strong that it manages to get nearly everyone on its side (i.e., the equivalent of the villainous Empire and Death Star). If you believe everything you've read so far about patronymics—the history, the discriminatory laws, its effect on wedding traditions—then you might be wondering how this could even be happening.

One of the most famous name change studies is by a Harvard professor and a student.[LXVI] They speculated that surname retention increased when more women attended college, began to marry later, use birth control, and deposit money into that 401k. I assumed it's because education and its associated professional and economic advantages should be increasing a woman's sense of equality and understanding of feminist issues. Despite women making up a slight majority of college students today, the study found that patronymics' popularity has instead *increased*.

The Harvard study suggested this new generation of college-educated women view women's equality as almost resolved and, therefore, they believe the need to mark one's parity through gestures like neutronymics is unnecessary. My friend's mother fought to be one of the few women to attend college in the '70s, and she kept her surname after marriage. She made a gesture of independence in the face of prejudice that sought to exclude her. However, for her daughter, there were no collegiate barriers to entry, and she took her husband's surname. Perhaps she never perceived the same sexist resistance her mother did. Is this a failure of American education to teach both men and women how to identify and correct inequalities?

I hypothesize that it has a lot to do with being white and in college. That Millennial friend, a white, middle-class woman, had all the freedom in the world to go college, and keeping one's name simply wasn't part of the cultural conversation of her generation. I often read that those with privilege tend to be blind to it in the first place. There might be some truth to that, but no one lives in a post-feminist world, so it might be more accurate to say that the closer one gets to equality, the harder it is to observe lingering disadvantages.

Most name change studies rely on college students for sample group data, but colleges still have a very high percentage of students who identify as white.[122] [LXVII] This means that the name change statistics are going to be more representative of habits in white cultures. But looking at this through an intersectional feminism lens, the way white women perceive the world is not how most minorities experience it. White privilege is one way to explain the contradictory name change-to-education trends from the Harvard study, and others.

In my personal interviews and observations, I found that most pro-patronymics women perceived themselves to be their partner's equal, and believed their decision to change their name was rooted in feminism and freedom of choice. Yet their actions didn't match those perceptions of equality: they took his name but he didn't change his, quit or cut back on work, and were the primary caretakers of the home and kids.[123] Digging back into the research, one 1993 study (which, granted, had a small sample size from a Midwestern college) supported my observations. It revealed that 92 percent of women agreed it is acceptable for a woman to keep her name after marriage, but regardless of those beliefs, 82 percent intended to take their husbands' names.[LXVIII] It reminded me of when I spoke to my friends about proposing. All of them agreed women should do it, but none of them actually wanted to. Beliefs about equality don't always match observed reality, and

---

[122] *Of 2.9 million post-baccalaureate students enrolled in fall 2015, some 1.6 million were white, 364,000 were black, 243,000 were Hispanic, 200,000 were Asian/Pacific Islander, and 14,000 were American Indian/Alaska Native (Source: Works Cited 15).*
[123] *If around 90 percent of men chose to take their wives' names, I'd be lobbying for the name equality of men.*

addressing the disparity is a minefield to navigate because those choices are rooted in emotion and deeply held beliefs. I can't explain why there is such a difference between ideals and actions. I can only guess that it is the evil Emperor using his choice feminism to Jedi-mind-trick his subjects.

Most of my surveyed brides cited the importance of making "educated decisions" or "being free to chose" when it came to taking their husband's surname. Most claimed the "freedom to chose" as their right to take his name, but few had heard of choice feminism or understood how the two were different. (In their defense, the concept of choice feminism is not common knowledge, even among advanced degrees.) And even fewer brides had heard of patronymics despite practicing it. Despite invoking feminism's "freedom of choice," there also seemed to be no moral qualm about benefiting from or using the advances of feminism and then disclaiming any association with it. I frequently heard, "I'm not a feminist, but..."

Some women shared with me how they legally changed to their husband's surname but use their maiden name professionally. It's a striking divide. In this case, a woman cares enough about her identity to assert her independence and equality in the public sphere by using her surname but doesn't want to do the same at home. There are good intentions here, but I think there's value in showing that same sense of pride and strength at home too. This is a reminder that women's equality will never be achieved if she doesn't expect it or practice it in the home.

I also wonder whether this 90 percent majority can be explained by people believing that their private actions have no impact on the outside world, or that their private decisions are independent of outside influences. When one person litters, it has little to no effect on them or the world. When 90 percent of everyone litters, it becomes mass pollution and starts adversely affecting everybody. That means it's almost impossible to act irrespectively of the world around you—you have to think about collective impact. And frankly, evidence shows that pro-patronymics people are not thinking of that collective impact.

I understand that most of my choice feminist friends thought they were doing what was best for them and for their new family, but the damage is done. The Force was strong and they chose to turn to the patriarchal side. I seldom hear of a friend reverting to her birth name even after a divorce (and if she does, it's often temporary). This is why, as a feminist bride, I am the small yet feisty Yoda of neutronymics trying to teach my wisdom of, "Honor yourself, you must."

And in trying to honor ourselves, my spouse and I explored all neutronymics options we could imagine. And there are a lot of options everyone can use.

Equal hyphenation was the first option we looked at. This is becoming more common, which hopefully means modern women and men are beginning to recognize the value of honoring both partners' surname origins. As mentioned, superstar couple Beyoncé Knowles-Carter and Shawn (Jay-Z) Knowles-Carter are neutronymics supporters. It is extremely rare to see a man practice neutronymics, which is why this gesture is so powerful. Had Beyoncé only hyphenated her name, she would have only supported one-sided hyphenation and not full neutronymics. This is an important distinction.

Among my choice feminist friends, there were those who chose one-sided hyphenation and felt totally feminist empowered in their decision. Which, yeah, okay, great—but, humor me one second. Grab a pen and paper. Draw a straight, horizontal line and write "patronymics" and "matronymics" on opposite ends. Those two ends represent the two extremes of name change. Now place a dot smack-dab in the middle and write "neutronymics" above it. This spot represents name equality along the name change spectrum. Place another dot halfway between patronymics and neutronymics; this is where one-sided hyphenation sits. It is not completely biased, but it ain't quite equality either.

While Queen B may be touted as a great feminist role model, I wasn't ready to announce her as queen of our neutronymics island because of what she called her 2013 world tour—*The Mrs. Carter Show*.[124] What type of message does it send when this powerful, independent, pop-icon and role model romanticizes patronymics professionally and publicly? Why wasn't it *The Ms. Knowles Show*, or at least accurately, *The Ms. Knowles-Carter Show*? The couple's hyphenation is a great example of team parity, but it stopped at the professional level. To highlight how disparate the power couple treated their new hyphenation gesture professionally, Jay-Z's tour was called the

---

[124] *And she was using* Mrs.*!*

Magna Carter World Tour, not the *Mr. Beyoncé Show* or the *Magna Knowles-Carter World Tour*.

Clearly, it's easy to be Jedi-mind-tricked into thinking one hyphen is enough in the crusade for equality. One person hyphenating in a marriage is like building one side of a bridge. There's no real unity in it when it's done by only half of a marriage. I suppose the consolation is that it's a step in the right direction. The politics of the hyphen are often difficult to navigate, but my spouse and I discovered plenty more neutronymics options.

The Million Mile Moniker turned out to be a unique tongue-twisting option (also a popular option in Latin culture). This approach just tacks on a second name to the Western three-name structure. Some dislike this option because they fear a full name can get too unwieldy and clunky (also an argument used against giving a child both parents' names). But don't feel self-conscious about having a long name, by any means. The longest name award goes to a German immigrant born in 1904 named, Hubert Blaine Wolfeschlegelsteinhausenbergerdorff, Sr. ...for short. His first name is twenty-six words, and each word starts with the letter of the alphabet. His surname itself has 590 letters, for a total of 746 overall. This guy was a name-defending diehard and insisted on people using it. "When somebody calls my name, I don't have any trouble finding out whom they mean. I don't like being part of the common herd."[LXIX] If people treat long names as normal, like Mr. Wolfe +585 did, it won't be inconvenient or abnormal.

My spouse and I also considered the option of saying sayonara to our middle names by replacing them with either our original surnames or our spouse's. For example, if Casey Rory Jones marries Taylor Ryan Smith, Casey would become "Casey Jones Smith" or "Casey Smith Jones" and Taylor would likewise change. Swapping middle names for a spouse's surname is a great gesture of unity and a way to maintain original branding.

We also considered the Scramble Name Game, an option for the brave name trailblazers. The Scramble Name Game inspires a couple to create a new surname altogether. For example, Smith and Jones might choose to become "Jonsmith" or give themselves an entirely new name. The options are limitless. If my spouse and I combined our surnames, our family name would translate to "Left-handed orange-Saxon kilt," which makes no sense, but it was hilarious enough to consider.

The easiest and cheapest neutronymics option was to just retain our surnames, which is what we did, and we didn't have to lift a finger, except to tell people I didn't change my name. (There was no need to tell people my spouse didn't change his name because no one assumed he would. Baby steps, I guess.) This option is great because our time and energy is limited and precious. Life is too short to file unnecessary paperwork when we could be spending it as a newlywed in the boudoir or re-watching *Broad City*. Priorities, people. In case, you're wondering why my spouse and I went with surname retention. Being a man, my spouse kept his name for all the traditional reasons men typically do. As I'm a woman, I needed to reflect on the culture that pressured me to change mine and find the intellectual and emotional ammo to counter it. After some soul searching, I realized I am a Majkut, now and forever.

My last name is pronounced "MY-kut," and I've heard some pronunciation doozies over the years. People get tongue-tied and end up adding in z's, q's, and r's. If you get close to pronouncing it right, I will high five you.

Very few people can guess its origins either. A person once inappropriately asked me if I was Eskimo. They were dead serious. When I tell people it's Ukrainian, they nod in understanding. "Ah yes, I should have guessed Russian." This mix-up is a bad cultural faux pas. Ukraine barely retained its own identity for thousands of years. When it gained autonomy from Russian rule in 1991, Ukrainians celebrated being their own people, in their own land. Ukrainians could finally be Ukrainians. However, in 2014, Russia annexed Crimea, and with Russia waging war on Ukraine's eastern side, their hard-won autonomy is being threatened once again. I was brought up to take great pride in my heritage, to defend it against people who just want to brush it off as the ethnicity of its ruling neighbor. My surname is Ukrainian. And I am Ukrainian.

I married a man with a French last name, who couldn't be more American and disinterested in his ancestral origins. He's hardly French anyway. Heritage and history are important to me, and since I don't identify with being French, nor does my spouse, keeping my Ukrainian roots by name was a natural decision. I will never be the ethnicity of the person I marry: genetically, theoretically, or emotionally. No one can Rachel Dolezal themselves to fit their new surname. A person could come to understand it, empathize with it, but their inclusion in it will be limited to honorary.

My ethnicity was not my only reason. As an artist, I have many pieces of artwork out in the world with my birth name on them. My name is my brand and I have no intention of tracking down pieces just so I can change my name in the corner. Once it's on canvas, it's permanent. My work is unique. There's one artist who can create a Katrina Majkut masterpiece, and that's me. Keeping my surname was a beyond-easy decision. It honored who I am and all that I've accomplished.

When it was time to approach what would happen to our last names as a married couple, I had to plant the seed early. Way before there was even an engagement ring, I laid out all the facts as I did above. Then the final conversation went something like this.

"I want to keep my last name. Are you willing to hyphenate, create a new name, or take on mine fully or partially?"

His response, "No."

"Well I don't think I should have to take yours on if you're not willing to take on mine, especially since I want to keep mine. So...I guess it sounds like we will just keep our separate names as a married couple?"

His response, "Okay." He is a man of few words. Stern but fair.

I'd like to think that the innovating couples choosing neutronymics would win *The Amazing Race* or *Cupcake Wars*. Those who can navigate neutronymics are, to me, exhibiting excellent examples of teamwork, selflessness, consideration, and communication. I get it, though; neutronymics is still a relatively new and uncommon concept. It didn't even have a proper name before this book. It still faces a certain level of social scrutiny from those who are reluctant to change and prefer the old ways. My advice: smile and buy them a beer, then calmly and confidently explain that your spouse is so proud of their heritage or the accomplishments they've made under their name, how could you ask them to change it? Maybe you're saying all those things about yourself. Showing that you're the bigger person versus following the status quo shows a lot of confidence, security, and care.

So now, young feminist grasshoppers, I've exhausted all my discoveries and ideas about name change politics. If you haven't figured out that naming politics is more twisted and deceitful than Francis Underwood in *House of*

Cards, then I have failed you as your onomastics sensei. I'll just take my drink, sit in the corner, and be alone for a spell. But maybe, just maybe, I've planted that seed of awareness that the name change game goes both ways. And when you are listening to a girlfriend talk about changing her name, a little red light will go off in your head, and I will appear in miniature form on your shoulder asking in an emphatic '90s dialect, "Wuzzup wit' that?" And you will then discover your feminist superpower and courage to at least ask her, "What did your fiancé say when you asked him to change his name?" Then you will be that sexy provocateur who set off a red light in *her* head about how she's approaching name change. And if you can do that, that means the student has become the teacher. That's some powerful and amazing stuff.

Chapter 16
The State of the Union:
A House Divided and in Disrepair

As newlyweds, my spouse and I didn't want to know of any unhappy drama that went on at our wedding. We wanted to look forward to a lifetime of love and happiness together. We didn't want to know if someone dropped the wedding cake or if the champagne prematurely popped. We wanted other people to deal with it and leave us in our blissfully ignorant bubble that our wedding was flawless. Western wedding culture and the Wedding Industrial Complex cajoled us into this fear of acknowledging anything that might be less than perfect lest it ruin the big day, but feminism coaxed us out of that hedonistic and selfish perspective. If we wanted to be responsible citizens and empathetic newlyweds who cared for more than our union, the state of the union we needed to be most concerned about was the condition of Western wedding and marriage traditions.

To understand the state of the union, I think of Western marriage as a house. Ancient Rome built its foundation, the Victorian era set the framework, and individuals, consumer culture, and businesses furnished it. Religion was squatting in it for a while and put it in a gated community, but then government claimed it in eminent domain. Now it sits in disrepair without modern appliances, waiting for someone to fix it up. That is the state of marriage today. As neighbors, potential buyers, or frequent visitors to this house, everyone has ideas on what's best for it and how to improve it. How people come to think of themselves as experts on the matter is typically through cultural hearsay. Traditions, general wedding structure and the meaning of marriage are learned from family, friends, or religion, but the greatest influencers of the last hundred years have been media, pop culture, business, and consumerism. And what is handed down to everyone is typically taken at face value. Face value is the Western idea of honoring and respecting the institute and its customs. Tradition for tradition's sake. As newlyweds who just became part owners of this house, we needed to consciously repair it so that it became a healthy structure that supported and sheltered everyone, not just ourselves.

My spouse and I learned that wedding and marriage contained structural problems of sexual discrimination, punishment, and ostracism. We realized that strong gender roles currently linger in marriage's rituals and traditions, and this limits Westerners' march toward more egalitarian lifestyles. Though this knowledge was difficult for us to process, it couldn't dismantle the love we had for each other. Its imperfections burst our bubble that everything was copacetic, and we felt compelled to try to improve and repair this ramshackle house.

Some aren't hopeful romantics like us through. Others argue tearing down the house of marriage altogether is the only way to right all the wrongs of its past and present. I think such an extreme is unrealistic at this point in time. People still want, and sometimes need, the mental and physical commitment of marriage. Progress is done with baby steps. The lesson of "for better or for worse" taught us to responsibly accept the good parts of marriage but to work on improving the bad parts as well.

As cis heterosexuals, my spouse and I needed to wake up to the money (and social) pit that was the current, dilapidated house of marriage. As part of the group (cis, heterosexuals) that has been in possession of the house the longest and dominates the Wedding Industrial Complex, the most impactful change starts with us. We are not the only contractors who can repair it, though. With legal same-sex marriage in all fifty states, same-sex couples are using heterosexual traditions as a framework for their own weddings. They are, in turn, making them gender-neutral and modernizing them, which is a wonderful, powerful, and massively important influence for everyone. If people care about the future strength of marriage, everyone needs to pick up a hammer and nails and work together.

Positive change can set off a chain reaction. That's the great element of intersectionality: people have different experiences and needs but resolution for one group can have positive effects on another. Any good marriage is built on empathy, communication, and teamwork. The same metrics need to be applied to modernizing these wedding and marriage traditions. Together, we need to make them accessible to and inclusive of all people, and that means updating language, symbols, and consumerist practices.

Legalizing same-sex marriage across the U.S. was a huge start, but everyone needs to be socially and civilly on board too. It is still too easy for people and businesses to discriminate against same-sex couples or LGBTQ individuals. As of 2015, thirty-one states do not have "clear, fully-inclusive LGBTQ non-discrimination laws," meaning, for example, a same-sex couple can get married, but an employer can legally fire them if the individual or company argues that same-sex marriage violates their faith.[125] Even wedding services are being denied to couples, as in the case with Jack Phillips of Masterpiece Cakeshop in Colorado, who refused to make a cake for Charlie Craig and David Mullins' wedding on the argument it violated his first amendment (Phillips lost in court). And there's Kentucky county clerk Kim Davis who refused to issue marriage licenses on the basis of her religion. Davis violated an order by the U.S. Supreme Court to do so, but somehow still managed to wriggle out of signing them *and* kept her government job where there is a defined separation of church and state. The reality is that everyone lives in this proverbial marriage house; roommates can't arbitrarily lock others out.

It's that separation and individual sense of ownership that has created a house divided. Historically, marriage has been treated as an exclusive membership. Not everyone has been or is a welcomed guest or roommate. This is problematic because, culturally, it's been established that by participating in marriage, people can measure one's capacity for intimacy, friendship, and sociability. A wedding acts as a right of passage and an opportunity for public community acceptance. When such measures for success are created, standards for failure are too ("failures" being defined as anyone who doesn't get married or can't legally marry, all of whom become

---

[125] *Some legislatures are trying to improve this inequality. "The Equality Act would provide consistent and explicit non-discrimination protections for LGBTQ people across key areas of life, including employment, housing, credit, education, public spaces and services, federally funded programs, and jury service," (Source: Works Cited 16).*

social outcasts). These social outcasts once included interracial, interfaith, different classed, lifetime singles, and LGBTQ couples, regardless of whether they in fact found intimacy and a partnership with someone. This "you're not welcome" doormat helped create this house in disrepair. It built fences and kept out people who would otherwise help build, maintain, and improve it.

It is not enough to argue in favor of this exclusive community because it is time-honored and "traditional" either. There is no such thing as traditional marriage or a wedding. Both have been evolving for centuries. Defenders of "traditional" marriage today are benefiting from years of its evolution too. For example, marrying for love became mainstream in the 20th century. It gave marriage emotional meaning and helped to change a culture that instituted the mistreatment of minorities. The U.S. Supreme Court case *Obergefell v. Hodges* (2015) magnified this positive change.[126] By legalizing same-sex marriage, love became marriage's prevailing cultural element. And because everyone is capable of love, it proved that government couldn't regulate marriage as an exclusive privilege. Before the mid-20th century, love was not the basis for how the U.S. government controlled and managed legal marriage—heterosexual procreation and ownership of women was. This led to discriminatory laws that treated citizens unfairly, such as DOMA, Prop 8, and most other historical marital laws. Absolutely everyone (at some point in time) benefited from civil marital progress. If people want that positive development to continue, updating wedding and marriage culture is essential.

Some are concerned that modernization means downsizing and downsizing is viewed as bad for the institution of marriage and the family unit. Marriage participation decreased 5 percent between 2009 and 2010, but increased by 113,000 marriages in 2012. A big reason for the decline was that many couldn't afford a big wedding, during the economic downturn of those years. If traditionalists want to improve marriage's participation rate, they need to send their kids to college. Of the new 2012 marriages, 87 percent were by those with a college degree because they could afford it more than those without a degree.[LXX] Unlike in previous generations, people with an

---

126 *This landmark civil rights case legalized same-sex marriage. On June 26, 2015, the court decided in a five to four decision that same-sex marriage was protected by both the Due Process Clause and the Equal Protection Clause of the fourteenth Amendment to the United States Constitution.*

undergraduate college degree are more likely to marry before those with a high school degree or some college. College even raises the chances of a marriage succeeding long-term. 78 percent of marriages with a college degree are expected to last at least twenty years compared to 40 percent for those with a high school diploma.[LXXI]

Academic advances, women's improved financial independence, and better civil rights are not gradually eradicating the institution of marriage, but they are steadily pushing back the overall age of first marriages.[127] This change is good change though. It benefits women the most because they do not need their husbands' support to put a roof over their heads, get a loan, or buy a house.[128] And without laws that discriminate against unwed mothers, they don't need husbands to raise a family or be treated ethically.[LXXII] And with less restrictive social customs that punish women for having sex outside of marriage, women can lead the life they want outside it.

And just because people are moving into the house later in life does not mean they aren't interested in it. A 2013 Gallup Poll revealed a mere 5 percent of Americans never want to marry.[LXXIII] In 2012, half of Americans were married. That means despite all its shortcomings as the most racist, homophobic, classist, and misogynistic institution in the world, people still want to try it out, sometimes more than once.[129] This means people have hope in what marriage *can* be.

The syllabus from the *Obergefell v. Hodges* court case puts marriage into beautiful perspective. It says, "The history of marriage is one of both continuity and change. Changes, such as the decline of arranged marriages and the abandonment of the law of coverture, have worked deep transformations in the structure of marriage, affecting aspects of marriage once viewed as essential. These new insights have strengthened, not weakened, the institution. Changed understandings of marriage are characteristic of a Nation where new dimensions of freedom become

---

[127] *Less financial security (women were still starting from a disadvantaged point and still experience income inequality) and cohabitation are contributing too.*
[128] *The U.S. government passed the Housing and Community Development Act of 1974, which made it illegal to deny housing financial consideration and support based on sex (Source: Works Cited 17).*
[129] *It's important to note that most of these statistics exclude same-sex marriage statistics.*

apparent to new generations."

The point of tradition is to give something meaning and value, offer individuals a sense of belonging and community and provide guidelines for inclusive and appropriate behavior. If wedding and marriage traditions continue to be imbued with instructions sanctioning acting with discrimination, then they aren't that wholesome, romantic, or beneficial in the first place.

Americans spend an average of $35,329 on a wedding.[LXXIV] It's time people committed themselves not to the idea of marriage, but to maximizing that expensive investment by learning exactly what they're buying into. No one buys a house without due diligence and multiple home inspections. That is why the future health of marriage is contingent on understanding wedding traditions and having the ability to modernize them. Until people align their cultures with modern lifestyles and an open door policy, the future of marriage will remain, as it is—a house in disrepair.

The House of the Future

Feminism is the visionary architect that will update this dilapidated house. Its impact is already felt. For example, if America's suffragist mothers, like Stone or Cather, hadn't had marriages based on respect and equality, I'm not sure the women's first civil rights movement would have happened at the turn of the 19th century. And without the women's civil rights movement in the mid-20th century, I might be secretly writing this book from the confines of my kitchen while the kids napped and before hubby came home with the bacon. And without intersectional feminism, I would not have known to engage my own spouse and my diverse friends who had different and equally important perspectives and needs to share.[130] While married, feminism has allowed me to put education and career first. It provided me the freedom to challenge the status quo of marriage while simultaneously building the integrity of my relationship. And for that, I am forever grateful. After studying wedding and marriage's history so much, I've been able to see how it has already influenced the past, and I hope it continues to influence its future.

---

[130] *It also alerted me to how choice feminism and white feminism can hurt the long-term marriage reforms, as it can inadvertently support only the patriarchy.*

In the future, despite feminism, I foresee wedding and marriage evolution to be a complicated one. I predict more scandalous celebrity marriages and divorces that will push the limits of conventional marriages (I'm looking at you, Kardashians). I foresee with same-sex marriage even more people becoming susceptible to the Wedding Industrial Complex. I foreshadow more diversity in the couples those wedding TV shows exploit. I envisage rom-coms will continue to define a woman's value by the relationship she gets before final credits. And I prophesize I won't recognize most of my female friends on Facebook because they will change their surname when they get married, and I predict I'll be able to still identify all my male friends because they won't. I anticipate ruffling some people's feathers with my ideas and revelations.

But in the spirit of weddings and marriage celebrations, here are some positive predictions and outlooks.

I hope to empower even more people—women and men—to become feminist fiancés and find their feminist superpowers. I predict, like interracial marriage, same-sex marriage will be commonplace worldwide in the next fifty years and our children (born inside or outside of marriage) will read about this civil rights movement in their history books. I anticipate that sexuality will be on a broader spectrum than it is today, and gender roles based in tradition will become a thing of the past. Dating and marriage options will be more diverse than monogamous twosomes too.

In the near future, I anticipate people will come to better understand that mass cultural institutions cannot take precedence over a person's private rights protected under the fourteenth amendment. I believe same-sex marriage will help eradicate sexist gender roles in wedding and marriage traditions, and we will be better off for it. I predict every person, regardless of their race, age, gender, and sexual orientation will eventually access the same rights, the same benefits, and the same protections provided by marriage, not because they fell in love with someone and got married, but because society came to respect and love humanity above the exclusive privileges marriage currently retains for itself. Most of all, I hope the terms same-sex and gay marriage disappear and are characterized as just marriage.

I predict the next big issue in marriage will be among lifestyle singles. With 95 percent of people trying marriage at least once in a lifetime, the next minority to feel excluded from the remaining special provisions marriage retains for itself will be individual singles, single families, and non-immediate families. This means that fixing the cracks and dents in our existing family law will be the next relationship reform issue. And it's a major one. We seldom realize that America's existing family law discriminates against almost everyone, regardless of demographics. I foreshadow that in the current effort to eradicate singlism, the next great debate will not be "what is marriage," but "what constitutes family."

I foresee that the quality of marriage will be contingent upon everybody's access to a good education (and the positive embrace of feminism). If people are provided access to higher education, great sex education, and a supportive environment, I expect marriages will be more likely to succeed. It's also possible that education will increase a person's tolerance and ability to adapt to change, which will help modernize time-honored traditions with acceptance and not hostility. If couples invest in their future outside the relationship and home, I predict a healthy future for marriage at home.

And I hope one day when I'm old and gray, some fresh feminist blood will come on the scene and denounce this book as obsolete as well. I won't take it well, but I'll come around. I hope that fiery feminist breaks through people's inherent need to define their relationships in order to give them value. Hopefully, society will progress to a point where we will not be limited to the labels we apply to ourselves and to others. Only then will our psychological needs and demand for family and intimacy transcend our habit of labeling.

Some might worry this would mean a loss of "good family values," but this does not mean the idea or spirit that marriage bestows on a couple or family will disappear. If the Grinch descended down from his mountain and depleted humanity of white wedding gowns and sparkly engagement rings, made it illegal to call someone a spouse, ripped up wedding albums, and burned marriage certificates, it would never change how humans felt or how committed they are to their partner or family. No one (and no Grinch) can change those sentiments except for the individual. After all, the labels of *marriage*, *husband*, and *wife* have been sources of discontent, discrimination, abuse, and other atrocities since the words originated. They've prevented many from accessing basic human rights and economic and health benefits.

People's ability to trust in their relationships without consumer items, ceremonies, elaborate parties, and labels will show true enlightenment of the human race.

After finishing this book, I hope how you perceive, define, and act within your relationships will change. I hope you'll be more aware that your personal, intimate relationship has a profound impact on you and the people around you. I hope you feel empowered to make tough and sometimes unpopular decisions, and at least know that if you do, that you've got good company out there.

I've often been a wedding pariah because I'm outspoken about this sacred institution, but I believe the weird looks, the confrontations, and the disastrous wedding mishaps in my underwear are totally worth it. I think my convictions have made me more tenacious because I choose to think for myself. This prevents convention or peer pressure to control my actions and decisions. I think my marriage is stronger, because for every page you read, I sat for hours and hours with my spouse poring over these ideas and brainstorming them together. That collaboration and communication put us on the same page, redefined our expectations of each other and of ourselves rather than accepting preconceived ideas about the role of a *wife* and *husband*.

Chapter 17
Final Words of Love from
a Feminist Bride

Before I got married, both feminists and non-feminists asked me all the time, "If you're a feminist, why bother getting married?" The comment reminded me of a scene in the movie *Father of the Bride* where a similar exchange takes place. The daughter, Annie, breaks the news to her father (Steve Martin) that she is engaged. He's confused: "Aren't you a feminist that believes marriage turns women into subservient housewives?" Annie rolls her eyes and explains, "Dad, don't you get it? I fell in love."

Both of these exchanges imply that because I am a feminist, I am incapable of falling in love. It implies that because of my political convictions, I shouldn't commit myself to another. But feminists fall in love just as easily as non-feminists, conservatives, and Pepé Le Pew. Feminists are human. Contrary to hateful stereotypes, feminists might have the biggest hearts around because they will go to great lengths to do what's right for people out of compassion and empathy, regardless of who they are, where they come from, or what they believe. It is only natural for some of us to want to share that big heart with another. However, when feminists commit, they simply ask that their commitment be done under the utmost integrity and equality, just like Lucy Stone and Henry Blackwell. Feminism lets people balance between preserving and honoring the self while being committed and teamed with another. Teamwork is a core principal of intersectional feminism, after all.

And to those who implied that marriage and feminism are incompatible, well, I disagree. Feminism has always made marriage better by encouraging both partners to enjoy sex, control the size of their family, contribute to a joint household, and expect mutual respect. Even feminism's demand that women receive an education helps provide a couple with better conflict resolution, financial security, and interpersonal skills, which are proven components of a long and successful marriage. If it weren't for feminism, marriage would be controlled by coverture and not influenced by love.

My naysayers viewed marriage as a distinctly feminine tradition, so why would a feminist like me want to be associated with such frilliness? While the stereotype survives that all feminists are hard, butch castrators of men and beheaders of Barbie dolls, there's no truth to it. We come in all shapes and sizes, genders or no gender, races and ethnicities, sexualities. Feminists kick just as hard in stilettos as we do in work boots. Third-wave feminism was great because it established that strong feminist women could be feminine. A fiancé can be feminine, so long as feminine does not imply powerlessness.

The question also implied that feminists shouldn't participate in their own culture. This absurd exclusion is what created the need for feminism in the first place. Feminism simply demands a respected presence and role for people in their community and culture. And that's all I ever wanted. There's value in marriage, but I'm realistic in understanding and recognizing that there are issues within the system that need fixing. There is this mentality that pointing out weaknesses is a sign of disrespect. I disagree completely. If mistakes, shortcomings, or problems go on unrecognized, society can never progress. And progress is still sorely needed. Feminism means understanding history, how it affects the present day, and being able to set sights on a better tomorrow. How am I, a feminist, disrespecting tradition by choosing to learn about it, recognizing there are issues, and working to improve the problems? When did ignorance become an acceptable form of respect, and when did educating oneself about your culture become disrespect? Feminism sees the potential in something and gives the tools and power to reach that potential. Feminism only wants the best for everyone.

I also disliked the question from people because it reiterated this false idea that weddings are only the bride's "big day." Intersectional feminism taught me that weddings are a community event and newlyweds are the hosts of it. Fiancés should not only be concerned with just themselves and their happiness, but also about how this cultural event affects others. If you ask me, I would rather define my wedding by intersectionalism's altruism, kindness and respect than the selfishness of "it's my day." And when it comes to intersectionalism in this book, I tried to do my best. Obviously, given my demographics and perspective, my understanding of what additional discrimination other women might face is limited. I wanted to hit on what I saw as Western wedding culture's most pervasive sexist tradition culprits. When studying and reflecting on sexism in Western wedding traditions, it became apparent that the most long-lasting and detrimental traditions that affect any minority person or couple were sexist heterosexual traditions. These wedding traditions are the basis on which people discriminate against basically anyone who isn't a white, cis, and hetero man. It's for this reason that I genuinely saw hetero wedding traditions as the most urgent to address and correct—for everybody's sake, not just my own.

It wasn't just in my personal life that people resisted the idea of me being a feminist and a bride. My research revealed a lot of other writers asking the same question. I tend to ignore the articles because the obvious answer is—fuck yes, you can. I do admit that this may not have always been the case. The condition of marriage brides enjoy today was not the same climate in previous decades and centuries, as we've discussed at length in this book. Even the feminist of all feminists, Gloria Steinem, refused to participate in the institution initially, having said, "You become a semi-non-person when you get married."[LXXV] Although, when marriage became a more equal system, Steinem joined the club for the first time in 2000 at the age of 66 with David Bale (who happens to be the father of actor Christian Bale). Sadly, the marriage was short-lived; Bale died of cancer three years later. In an interview with Barbara Walters, Steinem revealed that marriage was an appropriate avenue over living together because she and Bale "both felt that we wanted to be responsible for each other."

Steinem's comment touches on the final point my naysayers were wrong about—that my feminism was *my* problem, that I was alone in my discoveries and adventures. But I tell *them* "nay!" I had my fiancé with me at every step, and I had my altar egos with me, and as it turns out, during this journey I met many other feminist fiancés who wanted to share their concerns and find solutions to these sexist problems too. *Many* felt a responsibility to makes things better within wedding and marriage culture—not only for their own weddings, but also for the next generation of feminist brides. That gives me hope for our future. It gives me hope for the future of marriage.

So ask me again if it's possible to be both a feminist and a bride, and I'll tell you with pure confidence and faith: I can't imagine doing it any other way.

Works Cited

1. J. Courtney Sullivan, "How Diamonds Became Forever," *New York Times*, May 3, 2013.
2. Gardner, Martha N., and Allan M. Brandt, "'The Doctors' Choice Is America's Choice': The Physician in US Cigarette Advertisements, 1930–1953," *American Journal of Public Health*, (2006): 222–232.
3. S.84 - Paycheck Fairness Act, 113th Congress (U.S. Senate 2013-2014), https://www.congress.gov/bill/113th-congress/senate-bill/84.
4. C.J. Thompson, "Caring Consumers: Gendered Consumption Meanings and the Juggling Lifestyle," *Journal of Consumer Research*, 22, (March 1996): 388–407.
5. Judith A. Howard, *Social Psychology of Identities,* Annual Review Sociology (New York: Columbia University), 2000.
6. Associated Press, "Why don't women propose to men?" *CBS News*, May 5, 2014, https://www.cbsnews.com/news/why-dont-women-propose-to-men/.
7. David McClendon and Alexsandra Sandstrom, "Child marriage is rare in the U.S., though this varies by state," *Pew Research Center*, November 1, 2016, http://www.pewresearch.org/fact-tank/2016/11/01/child-marriage-is-rare-in-the-u-s-though-this-varies-by-state/.
8. Judd Everhart, "Bill would ban rice at weddings," *Associated Press News Archive*, February 12, 1985, http://www.apnewsarchive.com/1985/Bill-Would-Ban-Rice-At-Weddings/id-cc18db6b4a708e277bbedc8e75a53c5d.
9. "Here Comes Wedding Season: How Consumers Will Pay for Others' Big Day in 2016," *American Express Spending & Saving Tracker*, April 26, 2016, http://about.americanexpress.com/news/pr/2016/how-consumers-pay-for-others-wedding.aspx.
10. "What is the female equivalent of a misogynist?" *Oxford Dictionary*, YouTube video, 2:15, Posted: November 20, 2015, https://en.oxforddictionaries.com/explore/what-is-the-female-equivalent-of-a-misogynist.
11. H105, American History I, "Virginia laws of servitude and slavery (1643-1691)," *Indiana University at Bloomington,* http://www.indiana.edu/~kdhist/H105-documents-web/week03/VAlaws1643.html.
12. Lily Rothman, "When Spousal Rape First Became a Crime in the U.S.," *Time Magazine*, July 28, 2015.
13. John Santelli, "Abstinence-only education doesn't work. We're still funding it," *Washington Post*, August 21, 2017, https://www.washingtonpost.com/news/posteverything/wp/2017/08/21/abstinence-only-education-doesnt-work-were-still-funding-it/?utm_term=.1c2f3a08ed64.
14. Trefis Team, "Amazon Might Be Looking To Venture Into The Intimate Apparel Segment," *Forbes Magazine*, February 16, 2017, https://www.forbes.com/sites/greatspeculations/2017/02/16/amazon-might-be-looking-to-

venture-into-the-intimate-apparel-segment/#12f838a771bf).

15. "The Condition of Education: Postbaccalaureate Enrollment," *National Center for Education Statistics*, May 2017, https://nces.ed.gov/programs/coe/indicator_chb.asp.

16. "The Equality Act (H.R.2282; S.1006)," *Human Rights Campaign*, November 6, 2017, https://www.hrc.org/resources/the-equality-act.

17. Gerald R. Ford: "Statement on the Housing and Community Development Act of 1974," Online by Gerhard Peters and John T. Woolley, *The American Presidency Project*, August 22, 1974, http://www.presidency.ucsb.edu/ws/?pid=4632.

18. Marilyn Yalom, *History of the Wife* (New York: Harpers Collins, 2001).

19. Stephanie Coontz, *Marriage, a History* (New York: Penguin Group, 2005).

20. Carol McD. Wallace, *All Dressed in White: The Irresistible Rise of the American Wedding* (New York: Penguin Group, 2004).

21. Vicki Howard, *Brides, Inc.: American Weddings and the Business of Tradition* (Philadelphia: University of Pennsylvania Press, 2006).

22. Anne Kingston, *The Meaning of Wife: A provocative look at women and marriage in the twenty-first century* (New York: Picador, 2006).

23. Cele C. Otnes and Elizabeth H. Pleck, *Cinderella Dreams: The allure of the lavish wedding* (Berkeley, California: University of California Press, 2003).

24. Jaclyn Geller, *Here Comes the Bride: Women, Weddings and the Marriage Mystique* (New York: Four Walls Eight Windows, 2001).

25. Karen K. Hersch, *The Roman Wedding: Ritual and Meaning in Antiquity* (New York: Cambridge University Press, 2010).

26. Ariel Meadow Stallings, *Offbeat Bride: Creative Alternatives for Independent Brides* (Berkeley, California: Seal Press, 2010).

27. Jessica Valenti, *The Purity Myth: How America's Obsession with Virginity is Hurting Young Women* (Berkeley, California: Seal Press, 2010).

28. Bertram H. Raven, *The Bases of Social Power*, (Los Angeles: University of California), 1959.

29. Christina Simmons, *Making Marriage Modern: Women's Sexuality from the Progressive Era to World War II* (New York: Oxford University Press, 2009).

30. Nancy D. Polikoff, *Beyond (Straight and Gay) Marriage: Valuing All Families under the Law* (Boston: Beacon Press, 2008).

31. Andrew J. Cherlin, *The Marriage Go-Round: The State of Marriage and the Family in America Today* (New York: Vintage Books, 2009).

32. Judith Martin, *Miss Manners: Guide to Excruciatingly Correct Behavior* (New York: Warner Books, 1979).

33. Betty Friedan, *The Feminine Mystique* (New York: W.W. Norton & Company, 1997).

34. Molly Dolan Blayney, *Wedded Bliss, A Victorian Bride's Handbook* (New York: Abbeville Press, 1992).

35. Azziz Ansari, *Modern Romance* (New York: Penguin Press, 2015).

36. Ernest L. Abel and Michael Kruger, "Taking Thy Husband's Name: The Role of Religious Affiliation," *Names: A Journal of Onomastics*, Volume 59, Issue 1 (2011).

37. Tara Parker-Pope, "Is Marriage Good for Your Health?" *The New York Times*, April 12, 2010.

38. Broadsheet Staff, "A Feminist! In the Vows section!" *Salon.com*, October 21, 2009.

39. Tracy Clark-Flory, "Attack of the feminist bridezilla!" *Salon.com*, March 13, 2009.

40. Royal Wedding Mania! *OK Magazine*, December 6, 2010, 36-41.

41. Belinda Luscombe, Marriage: Making Divorce Pay, *Time Magazine*, September 13, 2010.

42. Aryn Baker, "Maria Bashir: Fighting for the legal rights of women in Afghanistan," *Time Magazine*, April 21, 2011.

43. Ben Zimmer, "Ms.," *New York Times*, October 23, 2009, http://www.nytimes.com/2009/10/25/magazine/25FOB-onlanguage-t.html.

44. Alexandra Silver, "Brief History: First Family Weddings," *Time Magazine*, August 9, 2010.

45. Megan Friedman, "How Do I Love Thee? Let Me Tweet The Ways," *Time Magazine*, March 28, 2011.

46. Aryn Baker, "Afghan Women And the Return of The Taliban," *Time Magazine*, August 9, 2010, 20-27.

47. Feifei Sun, "The New Shape of Retail," *Time Magazine*, September 10, 2012.

48. Rana Foroohar, "The 100% Solution: Women still earn less than men. But equal pay will make us all richer," *Time Magazine*, May 23, 2011, 22.

49. Belinda Luscombe, "The Rise of the Sheconomy," *Time Magazine*, November 22, 2010, 57-60.

50. Belinda Luscombe, "Marriage: What's It Good for?" *Time Magazine*, November 29, 2010, 46-50.

51. David von Drehle, "How Gay Marriage Won," *Time Magazine*, April 8, 2013, 16-24.

52. Simon Charsley, *Wedding Cakes and Cultural History* (New York: Routledge, 1992), Chapter 3.

53. Linda Hirschman, *Homeward Bound,* The American Prospect, November 2005, http://prospect.org/article/homeward-bound-0.

54. Gayle Tzemach Lemmon, "Too Young to *Marry,*" *Ms. Magazine*, Winter 2015, 24-27.

55. Belinda Luscombe, "Behavior: Between The Sheets," *Time Magazine*, October 18, 2010, 69.

56. Belinda Luscombe, "Family: The Myth of The Slippery Bachelor," *Time Magazine*, February 14, 2011, 51-52.

57. "Feminism Still Relevant?" *Elle Magazine*, 412.

58. Andrew Francis-Tan and Hugo M. Mialon, ""A Diamond is Forever" and Other Fairy Tales: The Relationship Between Wedding Expense and Marriage Duration," *Economic Inquiry*, Vol. 53, No. 4, October 2015, 1919–1930.

59. Sophie Coulombeau, "I'm getting married: should I change my surname?" *The Guardian*, December 12, 2014.

60. Stephanie Coontz, "Why Gender Equality Stalled," *New York Times*, February 16, 2013, http://www.nytimes.com/2013/02/17/opinion/sunday/why-gender-equality-stalled.html?_r=0.

61. Stone, Pamela and Meg Lovejoy, "Fast Track Women and the 'Choice' to Stay Home," *Annals* 596, November, 62-83, 2004.

62. Karen Z. Kramer, Erin L. Kelly and Jan B. McCulloch, "Stay-at-Home Fathers: Definition and Characteristics Based on 34 Years of CPS Data," *Journal of Family Issues*, Vol. 36(12) (2015) 1651–1673.

63. Chávez, Karma R. and Cindy L. Griffin, *Introduction: Standing in the Intersection: Feminist Voices, Feminist Practices in Communication Studies, Intersectional Theory*, SUNY Press, 4-25, 2012-2013

64. "The Simple Truth about the Gender Pay Gap," *AAUW*, 2015.

65. Glick, P. and Fiske, S.T., "An ambivalent alliance: Hostile and benevolent sexism as complementary justifications for gender inequality," *American Psychologist* (2001) 56, 109-118.

66. Fiske, S. T., "Controlling other people: The impact of power on stereotyping," *American Psychologist* (1993) 48, 621-628.

67. Kurzban, R. & Leary, M.R., "Evolutionary origins of stigmatized: The functions of social

exclusion," *Psychological Bulletin* (2000) 127(2), 187-208.

68. Eagly, A. H., & Steffen, V. J., "Gender stereotypes stem from the distribution of women and men into social roles," *Journal of Personality and Social Psychology* (1984) 46, 735-754.

69. Darley and Gross, "A Hypothesis Confirmation Bias in Labeling Effects," *Journal of Personality and Social Psychology*, Princeton University (1983) Vol. 44, No. I, 20-33.

70. Carl O. Word, Mark P. Zanna, and Joel Cooper, "The Nonverbal Mediation of Self-fulfilling Prophecies in Interracial Interaction," *Journal of Experimental Social Psychology*, Princeton University (1974) 10, 109-120.

71. Crocker, J., & Major, B, "Social stigma and self-esteem: The self-protective properties of stigma," *Psychological Review* (1989) 96, 608-630.

72. Dominik Lasok, "Virginia Bastardy Laws: A Burdensome Heritage," *William & Mary Law Review*, Volume 9, Issue 2, (1967), http://scholarship.law.wm.edu/cgi/viewcontent.cgi?article=2966&context=wmlr.

73. Robin Lakoff, *Language and Woman's Place* (New York: Harper & Row 1975).

Notes

[I] Sex and the City, Season 4, Episode 12, "Just Say Yes" (2001).

[II] "Highlights of women's earnings in 2015," U.S. Bureau of Labor Statistics, Report 1064, November 2016, https://www.bls.gov/opub/reports/womens-earnings/2015/pdf/ home.pdf.

[III] Judith A. Howard and Jocelyn A. Hollander, Gendered Situations, Gendered Selves: A Gender Lens on Social Psychology (Washington, D.C.: Rowman & Littlefield Publishers, 1997).

[IV] D'Vera Cohn, "Marriage Rate Declines and Marriage Age Rises," Pew Research Center, December 14, 2011, http://www.pewsocialtrends.org/2011/12/14/marriage-rates-declines-and-marriage-age-rises/.

[V] Dr. Nicholas Alipui, "Adolescent girls: the girls left behind? Addressing discrimination and promoting their well being," UNICEF, April 8, 2009, https://www.unicef.org/infobycountry/files/Nicholas_Alipui_Speech_at_IPU_Panel_on_Adolescent_Girls.pdf.

[VI] Andrew J. Cherlin, The Marriage Go-Round: The State of Marriage and the Family in America Today (New York: Vintage Books, 2009).

[VII] Kim Parker and Renne Stepler, "Americans see men as the financial providers, even as women's contributions grow," Pew Research Center, September 20, 2017, http://www.pewresearch.org/fact-tank/2017/09/20/americans-see-men-as-the-financial-providers-even-as-womens-contributions-grow/.

[VIII] Robnett, "Girls Don't Propose! Ew," Journal of Adolescent Research, January 15, 2013, https://news.ucsc.edy/2013/01/marriage-traditions.html.

[IX] Shelton J. Nicole and Rebecca E. Stewart, "Confronting Perpetrators of Prejudice: The Inhibitory Effects of Social Costs," Psychology of Women Quarterly (2004) Volume 28, Issue 3, 215–223.

[X] Molly Dolan Blayney, Wedded Bliss, A Victorian Bride's Handbook (New York: Abbeville Press, 1992).

[XI] "The One with The Proposal," Friends, Season 6, Episode 25, 2000.

[XII] Michael J. Silverstein and Kate Sayre, "The Female Economy," Harvard Business Review, September 200ssue, https://hbr.org/2009/09/the-female-economy.

[XIII] Jennifer Gilhool, "The Power Of Just One Woman," Forbes Magazine, August 26, 2013, https://www.forbes.com/sites/85broads/2013/08/26/the-power-of-just-one-woman/#6e760c4b1a05.

[XIV] "Wedding Services in the US: Market Research Report," IBIS World, August 2017, https://www.ibisworld.com/industry-trends/market-research-reports/other-services-except-public-administration/repair-maintenance/wedding-services.html.

[XV] Gus Lubin, "The 12 Most Expensive Weddings In History," Business Insider, April 20, 2011, http://www.businessinsider.com/most-expensive-weddings-2010-7?op=1.

[XVI] "The biggest royal wedding since Charles and Diana: How Kate and Wills will bring the world to a standstill," Daily Mail UK, November 16, 2010, http://www.dailymail.co.uk/news/article-1330183/Prince-William-Kate-Middletons-royal-wedding-biggest-Charles-Diana.html#ixzz1Cflejcjk.

[XVII] Fay Schlesinger, Daniel Martin, and Charlotte Gill, "Charles to Pick Up William and Kate's Lavish Wedding Bill: But the Taxpayers Could Still Have to Find £20M the Security," Daily Mail UK, November 17, 2010, http://www.dailymail.co.uk/news/article-1330695/Kate-Middleton-Prince-Williams-wedding-picked-Charles.html.

[XVIII] "Cost of U.S. Weddings Reaches New High as Couples Spend More Per Guest to Create an Unforgettable Experience, According to The Knot 2016 Real Weddings Study," The Knot & XO

Group, New York, NY, February 2, 2017, http://xogroupinc.com/press-releases/theknot2016realweddings_costofweddingsus/?__hstc=131446032.505c93334411fce5ec
0134079d734cde.1498770921862.1498770921862.1498770921862.1&__hssc=131446032.1.1498
770921863&__hsfp=3093675016.

[XIX] "Good practices in legislation on "harmful practices" against women," United Nations Division for the Advancement of Women, May 2009,
http://www.un.org/womenwatch/daw/egm/vaw_legislation_2009/Report%20EGM%20harmful
%20practices.pdf.

[XX] "An information sheet: child marriage around the world," Girls Not Brides, November 23, 2016,
https://www.girlsnotbrides.org/wp-content/uploads/2017/01/Child-marriage-around-the-world-Nov-2016.pdf.

[XXI] "Good practices in legislation on "harmful practices" against women," United Nations Division for the Advancement of Women, May 2009,
http://www.un.org/womenwatch/daw/egm/vaw_legislation_2009/Report%20EGM%20harmful
%20practices.pdf.

[XXII] Burwell v. Hobby Lobby, 573 US _ (2014).

[XXIII] Lois Smith Brady, "Royal Exes: Royal Excess or the New Social Norm?" New York Times, March 11, 2011,
http://www.nytimes.com/2011/03/13/fashion/weddings/13field.html?pagewanted=1.

[XXIV] Gretchen Livingston and D'Vera Cohn, "Childlessness Up Among All Women; Down Among Women with Advanced Degrees," Pew Research Center, June 25, 2010,
http://www.pewsocialtrends.org/2010/06/25/childlessness-up-among-all-women-down-among-women-with-advanced-degrees/.

[XXV] "As Marriage and Parenthood Drift Apart, Public Is Concerned about Social Impact," Pew Research Center, July 1, 2007, http://www.pewsocialtrends.org/2007/07/01/as-marriage-and-parenthood-drift-apart-public-is-concerned-about-social-impact/.

[XXVI] A Wink and a Smile: The Art of Burlesque, Film, Directed by Deirdre Allen Timmons, First Run Features, 2008.

[XXVII] Deborah A. Christel & Susan C. Dunn, "Average American women's clothing size: comparing National Health and Nutritional Examination Surveys (1988–2010) to ASTM International Misses & Women's Plus Size clothing," International Journal of Fashion Design, Technology and Education Vol. 10, Issue 2, 2017, August 5, 2016,
http://www.tandfonline.com/doi/abs/10.1080/17543266.2016.1214291?journalCode=tfdt20&.

[XXVIII] Lawrence B. Finer, "Trends in Premarital Sex in the United States, 1954–2003," Public Health Reports, 2007 122.1: 73–78, https://www.ncbi.nlm.nih.gov/pmc/articles/PMC1802108/.

[XXIX] Maggie Seaver, "The National Average Cost of a Wedding Hits $35,329," 2016 Real Weddings Study. The Knot, February 2, 2017, https://www.theknot.com/content/average-wedding-cost-2016.

[XXX] "Marriage and Divorce. National Marriage and Divorce Rate Trends," U.S. Centers for Disease Control and Prevention, National Vital Statistics System, 2014,
https://www.cdc.gov/nchs/nvss/marriage_divorce_tables.htm.

[XXXI] "Wedding Services in the U.S.: Market Research Report," IBIS World, August 2017,
https://www.ibisworld.com/industry-trends/market-research-reports/other-services-except-public-administration/repair-maintenance/wedding-services.html.

[XXXII] "Loving Decision: 40 Years of Legal Interracial Unions" All Things Considered, National Public Radio, June 11, 2007, http://www.npr.org/templates/story/story.php?storyId=10889047.

[XXXIII] King v. Smith, 392 U.S. 309 (1968).
Stanley v. Illinois, 405 U.S. 645 (1972).
New Jersey Welfare Rights Organization v. Cahill, 411 U.S. 619 (1973).

[XXXIV] Herschel E. Richard Jr., "Constitutional Law - Wrongful Death - Illegitimate Children -

Equal Protection," Louisiana Law Review, Volume 29, Number 2, February 1969, http://digitalcommons.law.lsu.edu/cgi/viewcontent.cgi?article=3599&context=lalrev.

[XXXV] Joyce A. Martin, M.P.H.; Brady E. Hamilton, Ph.D.; Michelle J.K. Osterman, M.H.S.; Anne K. Driscoll, Ph.D.; and T.J. Mathews, M.S., "Births: Final Data for 2015," National Vital Statistics Reports, Division of Vital Statistics, Volume 66, Number 1, January 5, 2017, https://www.cdc.gov/nchs/data/nvsr/nvsr66/nvsr66_01.pdf.

[XXXVI] Gretchen Livingston and D'Vera Cohn, "The New Demography of American Motherhood," Pew Research Center, May 6, 2010, http://www.pewsocialtrends.org/2010/05/06/the-new-demography-of-american-motherhood/.

[XXXVII] Joyce A. Martin, M.P.H.; Brady E. Hamilton, Ph.D.; Michelle J.K. Osterman, M.H.S.; Anne K. Driscoll, Ph.D.; and T.J. Mathews, M.S., "Births: Final Data for 2015," National Vital Statistics Reports, Division of Vital Statistics, Volume 66, Number 1, January 5, 2017, https://www.cdc.gov/nchs/data/nvsr/nvsr66/nvsr66_01.pdf.

[XXXVIII] Gretchen Livingston and D'Vera Cohn, "Record Share of New Mothers are College Educated," Pew Research Center, May 10, 2013, http://www.pewsocialtrends.org/2013/05/10/record-share-of-new-mothers-are-college-educated/.

[XXXIX] Jill Daugherty, Ph.D., and Casey Copen, Ph.D., "Trends in Attitudes About Marriage, Childbearing, and Sexual Behavior: United States, 2002, 2006–2010, and 2011–2013," National Health Statistics Reports, Number 92 (, March 17, 2016, https://www.cdc.gov/nchs/data/nhsr/nhsr092.pdf.

[XL] Wilbur Miller, The Social History of Crime and Punishment in America: An Encyclopedia, (Los Angeles, SAGE Publications, 2012), Volume 5.

[XLI] Scream, Directed by Wes Craven, film, Dimension Films, 1996.

[XLII] Lawrence B. Finer, "Trends in Premarital Sex in the United States, 1954–2003," Public Health Reports, 2007 122.1: 73–78, https://www.ncbi.nlm.nih.gov/pmc/articles/PMC1802108/.

[XLIII] "Historical Marital Status Tables: Table MS-2. Estimated Median Age at First Marriage, by Sex: 1890 to the Present," U.S. Census Bureau, November 2016, https://www.census.gov/data/tables/time-series/demo/families/marital.html.

[XLIV] T.J. Mathews, M.S., and Brady E. Hamilton, Ph.D., "Mean Age of Mothers is on the Rise: United States, 2000–2014," NCHS Data Brief, No. 232, January 2016, https://www.cdc.gov/nchs/data/databriefs/db232.pdf.

[XLV] Robin J. Ely, Pamela Stone, Colleen Ammerman, "Rethink What You 'Know' About High-Achieving Women," Harvard Business Review, December 2014, https://hbr.org/2014/12/rethink-what-you-know-about-high-achieving-women.

[XLVI] Kim Parker and Wendy Wang, "Modern Parenthood: Roles of Moms and Dads Converge as They Balance Work and Family," Pew Research Center, March 14, 2013, http://www.pewsocialtrends.org/2013/03/14/modern-parenthood-roles-of-moms-and-dads-converge-as-they-balance-work-and-family/.

[XLVII] Nancy Gibbs, "Mrs., Ms. or Miss: Addressing Modern Women," Time Magazine, October 26, 2009.

[XLVIII] Larry McDermott, Word sleuth finds Ms. origin in Springfield, Mass Live (The Republican), November 1, 2009, http://www.masslive.com/opinion/index.ssf/2009/11/word_sleuth_finds_ms_origin_in.html.

[XLIX] Marlee Richards, America in the 1970s, The Decades of Twentieth-Century America, (Twenty-First Century Books, 2010), 64.

[L] Abigail Pogrebin, "How Do You Spell Ms.," New York Magazine, October 30, 2011, http://nymag.com/news/features/ms-magazine-2011-11/.

[LI] Gerhard Peters and John T. Woolley, "Richard Nixon: A Conversation With the President," Interview by Dan Rather, Columbia Broadcasting System, January 2, 1972, http://www.presidency.ucsb.edu/ws/?pid=3351.

[LII] "A Gender-Neutral Honorific, Mx: Words We're Watching," Merriam-Webster.com, Accessed on September 7, 2017, https://www.merriam-webster.com/words-at-play/mx-gender-neutral-title.

[LIII] Patricia J. Gorence, "Women's Name Rights," Marquette Law Review, Volume 59, Issue 4, 1976, http://scholarship.law.marquette.edu/cgi/viewcontent.cgi?article=2239&context=mulr.

[LIV] Patricia J. Gorence, "Women's Name Rights," Marquette Law Review, Volume 59, Issue 4, 1976, http://scholarship.law.marquette.edu/cgi/viewcontent.cgi?article=22.

[LV] Justin McCurry, "Japan upholds rule that married couples must have same surname," The Guardian, December 16, 2015, https://www.theguardian.com/world/2015/dec/16/japanese-court-rules-married-women-cannot-keep-their-surnames.

[LVI] Brian Powell and Laura Hamilton, "Survey: Most Americans say wife should change her name: IU research at the American Sociological Association annual meeting," Indiana University, August 11, 2009, http://newsinfo.iu.edu/tips/page/normal/11558.html#7.

[LVII] Forbush v. Wallace (405 U.S. 970).

[LVIII] Wilbur Miller, The Social History of Crime and Punishment in America: An Encyclopedia, (Los Angeles, SAGE Publications, 2012), Volume 5.

[LIX] Patricia J. Gorence, "Women's Name Rights," Marquette Law Review, Volume 59, Issue 4, 1976, http://scholarship.law.marquette.edu/cgi/viewcontent.cgi?article=2239&context=mulr.

[LX] James Kosur, "When I decided to take my wife's last name, I was shocked by how different the process is for men," Business Insider, December 19, 2015, http://www.businessinsider.com/i-took-my-wifes-last-name-and-was-shocked-by-how-different-the-process-is-for-men-2015-12.

[LXI] Jennifer Steinhauer, "He Does Take This Woman. Now, About Her Last Name," New York Times, December 16, 2006, http://query.nytimes.com/gst/fullpage.html?res=9C0DEED71231F935A25751C1A9609C8B63.

[LXII] Speech by UN Goodwill Ambassador Emma Watson, HeForShe Campaign, United Nations Headquarters, New York, September 20, 2014, http://www.unwomen.org/en/news/stories/2014/9/emma-watson-gender-equality-is-your-issue-too.

[LXIII] Casey E. Copen, Ph.D.; Kimberly Daniels, Ph.D.; Jonathan Vespa, Ph.D.; and William D. Mosher, Ph.D., "First Marriages in the United States: Data From the 2006–2010," National Survey of Family Growth, National Health Statistics Report, Center for Disease and Control, Number 49, March 22, 2012, https://www.cdc.gov/nchs/data/nhsr/nhsr049.pdf.

[LXIV] Gretchen E. Gooding and Rose M. Kreider, "Women's Marital Naming Choices in Nationally Representative Sample," Journal of Family Issues, 2010, 31:681, September 8, 2009, http://jfi.sagepub.com/.

[LXV] Didi Kirsten Tatlow, "For Chinese Women, A Surname is Her Name," New York Times, November 11, 2016, https://www.nytimes.com/2016/11/12/world/asia/china-women-surnames.html.

[LXVI] Claudia Goldin and Mara Shim, "Making a name: Women's surnames at marriage and beyond," Journal of Economic Perspectives, 18 (2004).

[LXVII] "The Condition of Education: Postbaccalaureate Enrollment," National Center for Education Statistics, May 2017, https://nces.ed.gov/programs/coe/indicator_chb.asp.

[LXVIII] L. Scheuble and D.R. Johnson, "Marital name change: Plans and attitudes of college students," Journal of Marriage and the Family, 55 (1993): 747-754.

[LXIX] Norman Goldstein, "What's in A Name? 666 Letters," The Free-Lance Star, June 25, 1964.

[LXX] Richard Fry, "New census data show more Americans are tying the knot, but mostly it's the college-educated," Pew Research Center, February 6, 2014, http://www.pewresearch.org/fact-tank/2014/02/06/new-census-data-show-more-americans-are-tying-the-knot-but-mostly-its-the-college-educated/.

[LXXI] Wendy Wang, "The link between a college education and a lasting marriage," Pew Research Center, December 4, 2015, http://www.pewresearch.org/fact-tank/2015/12/04/education-and-marriage/.

[LXXII] Gretchen Livingston and Andrea Caumont, "5 facts on love and marriage in America," Pew Research Center, February 13, 2017, http://www.pewresearch.org/fact-tank/2017/02/13/5-facts-about-love-and-marriage/.

[LXXIII] Frank Newport and Joy Wilke, "Most in U.S. Want Marriage, but Its Importance Has Dropped," Gallup.com, August 2, 2013, http://www.gallup.com/poll/163802/marriage-importance-dropped.aspx.

[LXXIV] Maggie Seaver, "The National Average Cost of a Wedding Hits $35,329," 2016 Real Weddings Study. The Knot, February 2, 2017, https://www.theknot.com/content/average-wedding-cost-2016.

[LXXV] Gloria Steinem, "Walters Interviews Gloria Steinem, ABC News," Interview by Barbara Walters, ABC News, April 18, 2001, http://abcnews.go.com/2020/story?id=124030.

About the Author

Photo Credit: Village Cat Productions

Katrina Majkut, a visual artist and writer, is dedicated to exploring how social practices affect civil rights. Her writing has appeared in Bust, Bitch and Bustle. Majkut exhibits her artwork nationally. Mic Media listed her as an artist starting a new chapter in feminist art. Her art catalogues are in several library collections including the National Museum of Women in the Arts, D.C. A proud Bostonian, Majkut currently lives in New York City.

www.KatrinaMajkut.com

View other Black Rose Writing titles at <u>www.blackrosewriting.com/books</u> and use promo code **PRINT** to receive a **20% discount** when purchasing.

BLACK❀ROSE
writing™

CPSIA information can be obtained
at www.ICGtesting.com
Printed in the USA
FFOW01n2323290318
46082254-47039FF